D0906927

FORENSIC VOICE IDENTIFICATION

FORENSIC VOICE IDENTIFICATION

Harry Hollien

San Diego San Francisco New York Boston
London Sydney Tokyo

VILLA JULIE COLLEGE LIBRARY
STEVENSON, MD 21153

This book is printed on acid-free paper.

Copyright © 2002 by ACADEMIC PRESS

All Rights Reserved
No part of this publication may be reproduced or transmitted in any form or by any means, electronic or mechanical, including photocopying, recording, or any information storage and retrieval system, without permission in writing from the publisher.

ACADEMIC PRESS
A Harcourt Science and Technology Company
Harcourt Place, 32 Jamestown Road, London NW1 7BY, UK
http://www.academicpress.com

ACADEMIC PRESS
A Harcourt Science and Technology Company
525 B Street, Suite 1900, San Diego, California 92101-4495, USA
http://www.academicpress.com

ISBN 0-12-352621-3

Library of Congress Control Number 2001090395
A catalogue record for this book is available from the British Library

Typeset by Kenneth Burnley, Wirral, Cheshire
Printed in Great Britain by CPI Bookcraft
01 02 03 04 05 06 BC 9 8 7 6 5 4 3 2 1

CONTENTS

Dedication

again to Patti

and to

my family and students

PREFACE

There are several reasons for writing this book. First, I wish to expand and update my three-chapter presentation on speaker identification found in another of my books (*Acoustics of Crime*, Plenum Press, 1990). Second, much has happened since the late 1980s and, naturally, I wish to review these developments and add my personal perspective to it all. However, it is the third reason that is the really serious one: I wish to respond to an unfortunate situation in this field, one which I believe to be counter-productive to good progress. The two major groups – phoneticians and engineers – who are responsible for solving the riddle of speaker recognition have not seen fit to cooperate to any great extent in either their research or practice. This tendency is most unfortunate since it has clearly impeded progress. So, what is the problem? Well, it appears that the engineers think that phoneticians do not know enough about mathematics and equipment to be effective catalysts, whereas the phoneticians complain that the engineers do not know enough about human behavior or experimentation to do an adequate job. The irony is that they both are correct and, as it turns out, it is doubtful whether either can come up with a solution without the other. Accordingly, one of the goals of this book will be to provide a little common ground for them; perhaps it will aid each in better understanding the other. If reasonably good relations can be achieved, effective cooperation and coordination should result. In any event, I will address this issue (in various ways) in several of the chapters to follow plus structure all of the last chapter as an illustration of how effective good collaboration can be. If you find my efforts in this regard a little redundant, so be it. It is my judgement that such repetition may lead to progress and, if it does, it will be well worth it. Anyway, if you already are convinced that I am right, you can skip over those sections.

The fourth reason that this book was written was to effectively describe speaker identification, and do so in a manner that can be easily understood by those different types of people who are interested in the area. Nearly all of these groups are professionals, of course. The problem is that, taken as a whole, they come from wildly divergent backgrounds. Thus, the challenge – how does one reach them?

First, let us consider jurists and attorneys. Their backgrounds allow them to understand more about the courts and the criminal justice system than I ever will. Yet I must attempt to communicate directly to them about the nature of speaker identification, how it is carried out, why we do it the way we do it and how it fits into their world. Hopefully, I can explain what they can expect (and not expect) when they must deal with these processes. In turn, we will want to learn how we 'fit' into their systems. Second, while law enforcement personnel know more about forensics and criminal investigations than I do (or ever will learn), we forensic phoneticians have something in common with them. We both 'investigate' – we both seek answers to questions and to problems. Third, I already have touched on the problems phoneticians have in interfacing with members of the engineering community. They will want to know what we think about a particular algorithm; we will want to tell them about memory, the hearing mechanism and how these systems can play tricks on an 'auditor,' be it human or machine. We also can predict (sometimes anyway) how shifts in human behavior actually can affect machine processing. Conversely, we will want to learn from them why certain physical processes can predict human behavior. All in all, phoneticians and engineers can contribute materially to each others efforts. Perhaps my efforts here will contribute to this dialog.

Of course, other phoneticians and forensic phoneticians will be easy to reach; all I have to do is use the appropriate systems and jargon. Correct? Don't hold your breath here. All that will be necessary for me to do is inadvertently tread on some phonetician's revered dogma and it will be 'Look out, Charlie!' Add in all the other types of 'communication' professionals (linguists, speech pathologists, physicians, communication specialists and so on) who sometimes have a bonafide interest in the area and World War III just might erupt under my teepee. In any case, I will try to reach most of these groups too. A daunting task? Definitely. Will I also attempt to reach the lay public (journalists, private detectives and the like) in any material way? No, to try to do so simply would be asking too much of my tired old cortex.

So, these are the target audiences. How can such diverse groups be reached? Perhaps a straightforward writing style will help. It is a technique I have worked at during my entire (and long) career. Permit me to tell you a little story about why I have adopted this style of writing. If you are not interested in where it came from, just skip this section. But for those of you who wonder a little as to why this old fellow writes the way he does, perhaps the following will provide a perspective. Moreover, it *could* make reading this book a bit more pleasant. The story. When I was a fairly young graduate student at the University of Iowa (back before we had electricity), I had the good fortune of getting to know a professor by the name of Wendall Johnson. He was in the Speech Pathology section of a loosely organized 'communications' group or department there; one which ranged all the way from theater to experimental phonetics (my area). His specialty was stuttering and he was quite well known in that area; he also was one of the originators of general semantics. Johnson wrote a large number of books as well as many articles. Included among them were tomes on stuttering (of course) plus several aimed at helping people cope with their everyday problems. A couple of the latter were 'People in Quandries' and 'Your Most Enchanted Listener.' At first, I did not take Johnson very seriously. For one thing, he was not a phonetician, for another, he was into clinical stuff. Moreover, he was pretty busy and had little time for students other than those that he directly supervised. However, we had some contact (a little of it confrontational in nature, I must confess) and, over the next few years, I grew to respect him both personally and for the principles he stood for. In turn, he seemed to develop an interest in me. He said that he thought that I probably would have a career in the sciences and that, in any event, I would have to spend much of my time communicating my observations, findings, opinions or some such to others. After I graduated, he paid me the compliment of spending a little of his time mentoring my professional development. One of the things he did was to provide me with insight about some of the ways he thought I could effectively upgrade my writing. I am not sure just how well I learned all that he had to teach but I must confess that I have experienced a modicum of success over the past 40–50 years with many thousands of written projects (i.e. books, articles, grant proposals, reports, critiques and reviews).

But what is the point here? It concerns one of Wendall Johnson's most fundamental precepts. He said: 'When you write, you must try very hard to communicate with an audience which is broader than that found within the limited boundaries of your discipline. You should do so even when presenting scientific or technical material.' 'Think of your audience,' he said, 'as consisting of reasonably intelligent people who have, at least, a basic education. You do not have to assume that they will know a lot about your field – just that they are bright enough, schooled enough and, of course, motivated enough to read what you have written. You will find that they can understand what you present *if* you spin a decent yarn. So avoid jargon like the plague, carefully explain what you are doing and, especially, what it all means. If you do so, you will reach many, many more people than if you confined yourself to your own narrow specialty. Better yet, some of the individuals you will reach actually will need to know what you have to tell them. And, just as important to you personally, sometimes they will be the very people who will be making critical decisions about you and your work.'

'Make no bones about it,' saith Johnson, 'Some of your colleagues will take offense at your writing style if you do not restrict it to their little world. A few scientists will want you to "tighten down." They even may say that they cannot understand what you are writing. But . . . do not let them put you off. If you write clearly and broadly, your contributions to both society and your field will be substantially greater than if you crouch down in your own little corner of the world.'

Well, I found Johnson's approach a most attractive one and, for better or for worse, adopted it. I do not know if I have succeeded. After all, talent plays a big role in endeavors such as these. However, since most of the people who will read this book are *not* phonetic scientists, I will try to write in such a way that they also can master the materials to follow. Anyway, this book is as much for policemen, judges, lawyers, law enforcement agents and other forensic scientists as it is for people like me. The challenge, of course, is to see if I can make what I have to say *both* interesting and understandable.

From another perspective, this book is not intended to be some sort of exposé. Some of the people who know me will remember that I tend to be a hard task master (especially of myself). Moreover, I plead guilty of having said harsh things about the charlatans who try to invade our field(s). I also have condemned the use of 'psychological stress evaluators' (PSE) and have been pretty severe in my judgment of 'voiceprints'. Of course, several of these issues have little relevance to speaker identification and, hence, will find no place in this book. There will be a chapter on 'voiceprints,' however. It will be more of a history (than a condemnation) partly because nearly everyone (except a few private detectives and the like) have relegated this approach to the dustbin. Indeed, I doubt that the 'method' has been seriously used in years. On the other hand, I have to concede that there was a positive side to the 'voiceprint' controversy. Its threat or challenge resulted in an increase in the number of scientists carrying out research on SPID (SPID will be our codeword for speaker identification). Hence, 'voiceprints' will be described and I will try to keep them in perspective.

I am not going to attempt any kind of 'exposure' of the American criminal justice system or even of those few 'experts' who prostitute themselves for monetary gain. In the first instance, I do not believe that our criminal justice system is 'broken'. Of course, some abuses have taken place but they usually were carried out by people who would try to abuse virtually any system. Moreover, those of you in the scientific community must remember that attorneys and law enforcement personnel are *advocates*. Their behavior (especially that of the lawyers) sometimes is extreme but, in my observation, it is a very rare case where they actually violate ethics or engage in misconduct. If you encounter them, what you will usually experience will result from their enthusiasms or their conviction that they are 'correct' (law enforcement) or 'in the right' (the attorneys). However, I do not feel as kindly about certain of the 'experts.' While most are unbiased and ethical, I must confess that I have been appalled at the behavior exhibited by a few. I simply cannot condone, or even understand, why there are professionals who will testify to whatever the attorneys ask them to just to earn a little money. I realize that attorneys are advocates and that it can be a little difficult to 'disappoint' them if your testimony does not, or would not, support their position. Worse yet, the pressure on you can be severe, especially if you (as a citizen) intellectually and/or emotionally support the position or people for whom you have been retained. I concede that you can be torn; however, when this happens, it is mandatory that you maintain a strong ethical position. Let me illustrate this problem by describing a case which I refer to as 'Waco for Everyone.'

First, let me provide a little perspective as to why I have a strong personal bias about this case. Like a lot of people in the United States, I have recently become concerned that our federal government seems to be moving away from the structure (and freedoms) that has made us a society which is unique in all of human history. What used to be a 'well meaning' liberal concern appears now to be an effort designed to protect us from ourselves – and everybody else but them. Thus, a government which appears to be more afraid of its own citizenry than it is of any potential foreign threat seems consistent with what we call 'Waco.' What happened there was that a tiny band of religious extremists settled in a big field just outside of Waco, Texas. They then proceeded to build themselves a compound to live in – one, incidently, that they hoped would 'protect' them from the evil outside world. Though hardly attractive, and sometimes annoying, they tended to keep to themselves. A few years ago, they attracted the attention of the US Bureau of Alcohol, Tobacco and Firearms (BATF). They did so, apparently, because they were pretty paranoid and, hence, stockpiled firearms (legally, however) that they thought they would need to defend themselves. So, instead of contacting the Brazos County Sheriff (who knew their leader – a David Koresh – and reputedly sometimes drank beer with him), they (the BATF) carried out a large-scale SWAT team type raid on the compound. Even though BATF knew the Branch Davidians had been forewarned, they went ahead with the raid and, hence, several people on both sides were wounded and killed. Thereupon BATF, the FBI and several other US Government agencies laid siege the Branch Davidian compound and the horrors to which they subjected these poor people have been well documented. After about 8 weeks of a stand off, they sent in tanks and most of the Davidians (including a number of children) were killed.

My role in this tragedy involved a number of issues, all of which concerned tape recordings. They included: (1) speaker identification (this problem was quickly resolved); (2) tape authentication (the issue here became moot because all of the tape recordings were edited and admittedly so); and (3) gunfire. In short, my ultimate involvement was limited to work in the third area of contention, in particular to a video taken from one of two (or more) government helicopters that flew over and around the compound. The attorneys for the Branch Davidians thought they could hear gunfire when they listened to the audio track but were told (variously) that it was not or, if it was, it came from the ground. Naturally, what 'might have' occurred was of great import to their case; hence, I was asked to analyze these sounds. Indeed, they appeared to be gunfire and possibly came from the helicopter directly in front of the one where the video was made. If this proved to be true, the information would be particularly valuable to the surviving Davidians and their attorneys as they were suing the government for 'wrongful death.'

So, what was my problem? As a private citizen, I was outraged with, and a little apprehensive about, what went on at Waco. Hence, I confess to a personal desire to help the attorneys with their suit. I might also be able to provide our society with a better perspective about those federal agencies which might have overstepped their prerogatives. To be able to testify would be desirable, however, a problem existed here. I could not conclusively show that the recorded impact noises on the tape actually were gunfire. They met only half of the necessary criteria (see Hollien and Hollien, 1995, *Journal of the Association of Tool Mark and Firearms Examiners*). Moreover, I could not conclusively demonstrate that these 'shots' came from the lead helicopter. I probably could have testified if I had been permitted to conduct simulations of what had happened, but to accurately decode the sounds on the tape I would have had to reconstruct the entire event at an appropriate site with, at least, two helicopters, several shooters, appropriate guns and parallel recording equipment. The people involved could not afford such an expensive demonstration. Hence, I could not conduct the necessary tests and had to refuse to testify. I could not testify because, although I was pretty sure what had happened, I did not have the data.

Do you see my point? No matter what an expert witness thinks, wants or feels, they cannot, and must not, be an advocate. If they are, they can only damage both the criminal justice system and themselves. In this regard, please be assured that, just like everybody else, I have my biases and they will sometimes be found in what I write. But also be assured, that I will identify them and try to avoid letting them unfairly distort any of the data presented. On the other hand, I am not under oath here am I?

Finally, I would like to recognize the assistance I have received from both a number of sponsoring agencies and a lot of people. Indeed, many of my contributions have resulted from the support received from these organizations; they also are the result of the things I have learned from these people. Of course, I cannot recognize them all as they number in the hundreds. Still, a few of them are particularly relevant to speaker identification and this book. Those are the ones I would like to thank. The agencies which supported most of my research in this area were the National Institutes of Health, the National Institute of

Justice, the Army Research Office and the Dreyfus Foundation. Secondary (but critical) support came from the Office of Naval Research, the Fulbright Commission, the University of Florida, the National Science Foundation, the Veteran's Administration, the US State Department, the IREX Board, the Gould Foundation and the Voice Foundation. In addition, I thank the more than a dozen people who have had a direct impact on my work in speaker identification (and, hence, this book): they include (alphabetically) Drs Gea DeJong, E. Thomas Doherty, Marylou Pauswang Gelfer, James W. Hicks Jr, Ruth Huntley-Bahr, Ming Jiang, and Wojciech Majewski; also helpful were Drs W. S. Brown Jr, James F. Curtis. Jens-Peter Köster, Hermann Künzel, Lester Oliver and Reva Schwartz; as were several other individuals who are no longer with us (Drs Robert E. McGlone, Gordon Peterson, Thomas Shipp, Gilbert Tolhurst and Ronald W. Wendahl). Of my children (Brian, Christine, Karen, Keith, Kevin, Stephanie and Steven), Kevin served admirably as my assistant and Brian also helped out. This manuscript could not have been completed without the aid of Ann Partin and Abby Sia; thanks also go to my editor Nick Fallon. And then there is Patti. Without all that my wife, Patricia Ann Hollien, ScD has done, and at all levels, there would have been no books at all.

CHAPTER 1

INTRODUCTION

INTRODUCTION

First, let us consider the case of 'Women Can Be Stupid Too.' That is a pretty bold statement for a man to make, I know. It is especially so because, currently, many women do not think that men are blessed with very much in the way of intellectual capacity. Perhaps so, but not all women operate at superlative levels either. The following case should serve as an example.

There is a circuit court judge from a city near mine who has admitted my testimony on speaker identification (may we shorten this term to 'SPID'?) on several occasions (twice for the prosecution and once for the defense). Apparently, he believes that I am competent in this area. One day, this jurist received a telephone call. On the other end of the line was a woman who gave him her name and then asked if he remembered her. 'No' he replied 'I don't believe I have had the pleasure of meeting you.' This answer apparently frustrated the woman so she gave him her telephone number and address – still no recognition. The woman then described her testimony on behalf of her sister who had been on trial for some infraction of the laws designed to protect the peace and tranquility of the great state of Florida. 'Oh yes' he said, 'I remember you now. What can I do for you?' Her response was to make a death threat. What she actually said was 'I am going to kill your ass!' A surprised and concerned jurist immediately called local law enforcement and, since all telephone calls to the courthouse were routinely tape-recorded, he had them make a copy of this evidence tape and then obtain an exemplar of what was presumed to be her voice. What they did was go to the address she provided, arrest her and *then* obtain the exemplar. The judge subsequently instructed the agents to bring me the two recordings so I could carry out an analysis.

Can you imagine my disbelief at what appeared to have happened? Is anyone in this wide, wide world so 'mentally challenged' that they would carefully identify themselves just before committing a felony? Obviously, this had to be some sort of a joke or, perhaps, a conspiracy to make trouble for the poor woman. She just could not have made that call. Well, as you might expect, the case aroused my interest and I went to work to determine if she actually was the culprit. You, dear reader, will have to wait until later in this book to learn what I did, how I did it and what I found out.

A PERSPECTIVE

Speaker identification! What is it all about? Well, almost anyone who has normal hearing and who has lived long enough, will tell you that they have had the experience of recognizing some unseen person – usually someone familiar to them – solely from listening to his or her voice. It was probably from this common, everyday experience that some of the concepts – and indeed, some of the myths – about speaker identification were conceived. However, the many references to this phenomenon found in the movies, in novels, in the comic strips and especially on television, have resulted in the dissemination of as much misinformation as accurate intelligence. For example, many people believe things such as: (1) the speaker identification process is an infallible one, or nearly so; (2) people at laboratories can *easily* carry out voice identifications; (3) 'voiceprints' are the direct equivalent of fingerprints, and so on. Pretty heady stuff, but are these statements true or are they just fantasy? These questions are difficult to answer, hence, I must respond 'yes and no' to both of them. As you will discover, the process is a complex one and a neat, simple answer simply does not exist.

However, you also will find out that some useful relationships can be (and have been) established between people and their voices. The seemingly 'funny ideas' listed in the paragraph above are based (at least in part) upon these interactions. Indeed, you will find that a surprising amount of speaker identification is already possible and an understanding about yet more of the relationships fundamental to this process is taking place. If you think that my statement here is an exaggeration, consider the following interchange. The telephone rings, you pick it up and hear a voice saying 'How goes it?' (or even simply 'Hi'). Almost instantly you realize that the person calling is your mother, or your spouse, or your best friend or whomever. Another example, have you ever heard, but not seen, someone talking on your television and known right away who that actor or announcer was? Of course you have. Naturally, it sometimes is the language being used that tips you off; certain people tend to use certain words in a specific order, others use idiosyncratic phrases. In still other instances, it might be the time of day that alerts you and cues of this type can be quite subtle. Alternatively, you simply may be responding to your 'analysis' of the talker's speech and voice. In any event, you do it and you do it often.

An even better perspective needed? Let me provide you with an example drawn from one of my research programs. You are aware, I am sure, that many people think that a mother can tell what her baby is crying about just from hearing its howl. Is this true? Perhaps it is. Anyway, several of my students and I decided to investigate this notion way back in the 1970s. Basically, we asked a group of mothers to participate in several controlled experiments. First, we recorded their babies crying (one at a time, of course) when we snapped their (the infant's) bare foot with an elastic while they were playing (*pain*). As you would expect, the strength of this 'impulse' was controlled. Later, we *startled* the children with a loud clapping noise and in a third session we had the mothers deny food to their hungry offspring immediately after starting their overdue feeding (*hunger*). These tapes then became the basis for several experiments. The individual samples were pooled, randomized and then played back to the moms. In the first study, we asked them if they could tell what their child was crying about; i.e., from *hunger, pain* or *startle* (1). They were unable to do so with any accuracy. A surprise, but we soon realized that, in their normal environment, mothers make these decisions only after processing all sorts of cues (time of day, feeding schedule, infants' health and so on). It is those elements (plus the cry, of course) which allow them to make reasonably good judgments about their child's needs. Thus, while the discovery that the mothers often could not tell what their child was crying about was unexpected, the relationship was, in retrospect, an understandable one.

In our second study we asked yet another pertinent question. It was one that was more to the point if you are considering speaker identification. In this instance, we asked the mothers to *identify* their child from its cries when all of the samples were mixed into a kind of a 'cry lineup.' The answer here was both different and positive (2) as the mothers demonstrated rather good aural–perceptual speaker identification. Curiously, another relationship also emerged from this second project; it was that 'sound alikes' existed among the babies when they vocalized. When two babies sounded similar, their mothers not only correctly identified their own child but also identified the other one as theirs. The above are but a couple of illustrations, and there are many more examples of people being able to identify familiar speakers from their voice just by hearing a brief sample of it. Indeed, there are so many that they alone would fill a book, but it would probably be a pretty dull one.

Finally, how does speaker identification fit into forensic phonetics? My explanation will be more meaningful if you consider Figure 1.1 (3). As you can see, it is a chart which is structured much as are many others. First, we have identified our areas of interest; they can be seen in the top portion of the figure. Also important are the operations found at the bottom. This book best fits into the lower left-hand box but it also describes what goes on in the other two. Note also the five 'areas'at the top; they all are basic functions but ones which have been specifically adapted for the forensic model. The one which forms the basis for this book is, of course, speaker identification. It is an area unique in itself but it does enjoy a functional interface with the other four.

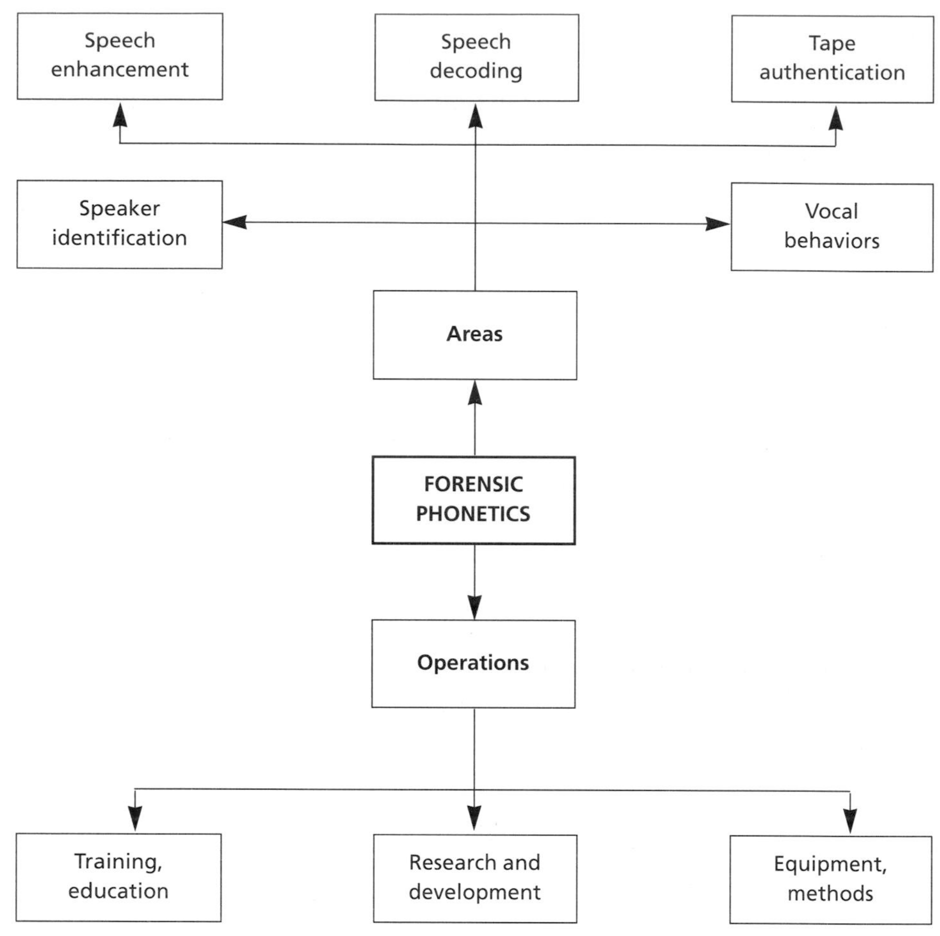

Figure 1.1
The structure of forensic phonetics. The five content areas most basic to this speciality are seen at the top of the figure, and its three major activities at the bottom.

FACTORS OF NOTE

There are several relationships in the SPID domain which should be considered at this juncture. First, you should be aware that we now know rather a great deal about the area both from the research that has been reported and from common experience. This should be kept in mind as it is quite important. Second, there are a number of 'truisms' that should be filed away in your cortical computer. For one, you probably realize already that some people are better at SPID than are others; that voices with which you are really familiar are much easier to place than ones which are less familiar to you. You also have worked out, I am sure, that some voices are distinctive and others are not, and that sometimes external conditions (of various types) can make it difficult for you to make an identification. If you already are aware of these relationships, we are on our way, as they are seminal to what I have to impart. They certainly will be discussed in this book, and so will others – ones that are not quite so obvious.

In addition, I will attempt to keep them all in perspective by not just focusing on what they are, but also on why they occur and how they can be dealt with.

DEFINITIONS

As you must have noticed, several specialized terms (or jargon) already have been used in this chapter; perhaps some of them are new to you, perhaps not, but let me define a couple of those that are critical. Of the many terms used, three are particularly important; they are speaker recognition (SR), speaker verification (SV) and speaker identification (SPID). You may even have run into parallel terms for them; ones where the word 'voice' was substituted for 'speaker,' 'authentication' for 'verification' and so on, but these other terms are simply synonyms. So, let us confine the initial definitions to the three cited. Speaker recognition (or voice recognition) is a general concept which subsumes the other two. Basically, it identifies the overall process of recognizing a person from their speech and/or voice and doing so by assessment of these factors alone. That is, in speaker recognition, you do not make the identification by analyzing the language used, by remembering what the speaker looks like or by any other means. This term is sometimes used when a person is not quite sure whether the process is that of verification or identification. In any case, it is generic and subsumes the other two; in turn, they are at once similar to each other and different. They are similar in that both involve the task of identifying a person from their speech. They differ as to the hows and whys.

SPEAKER VERIFICATION

The problem of speaker verification (SV) is generally on a par with that of *speech* recognition. However, in this case, it is not necessary to determine what is being said but rather who is talking. Moreover, in the basic verification paradigm, the speaker actually wants to be recognized. As you might guess, the potential uses for a working system of this type are virtually endless; they surely would be lucrative. Access by a person to secure areas 'by voice command' is one example; the verification of the identity of an officer giving instructions over a radio, 'walkie-talkie' or any channel where they cannot be identified by sight, is another. It also can be important to verify the identity of individuals who are speaking from airplanes, space capsules, hyperbaric chambers/habitats, armored vehicles (tanks) or from some other remote station or location. Banking by telephone is yet another example. In any event, substantial research has been, and is being, carried out in the area; it is going on at a number of laboratories. Taken as a whole, the scientific effort on speaker verification is extensive and literally hundreds of excellent experiments have been completed and published. If you are interested in the area, you would do well to read some of the reports available; a few are listed for your convenience as Further Reading for this chapter (see Speaker Verification References). They should provide you with a healthy introduction to the SV area and to some of the more important approaches utilized by the relevant investigators and practitioners.

As indicated, the verification task, while formidable, is relatively straightforward. The individual talker usually is cooperative (that is, unless they are an imposter), the equipment used ordinarily is powerful and of very high quality, and the speech samples employed are under the operator's strict control. Then too, extensive 'reference' speech sets can be developed and redeveloped for each talker. Finally, one aspect of SV very much favors it over SPID. That is, the SV trials always are 'closed' (i.e., the speaker is a member of the group). Nevertheless, rather substantial problems remain yet to be solved and, even today, there do not appear to be any on-line systems that will permit the universal verification of large numbers of individuals solely from analysis of their voices. Remember, however, that this book is about speaker identification, not verification; hence, only casual reference will be made to SV.

SPEAKER IDENTIFICATION

The more difficult of the two problems subsumed under SR is that of identifying an unknown speaker by voice analysis, especially when they are talking in an environment which distorts or masks their utterances (channel distortions) or when they are excited or stressed (speech distortions). That is, the unknown speaker on an evidence tape may be talking in a noisy environment or where the transmission link limits the acoustic transfer of his voice (for example, over a telephone), or the distortion may result from his fear or excitement when committing the crime, or he may attempt voice disguise. The suspect's exemplar tape recording may also exhibit some of these very same problems. Incidently, did you pick up on the terms 'evidence tape' and 'exemplar'? They will be used often in this book. An evidence tape is defined as the source of the *unknown* speaker's voice. It is he or she who must be identified. An exemplar is a recording (usually taped) of any person who might be the 'unknown'; hence, it contains the voice of a *known* talker. At the risk of being redundant, please remember that neither the evidence or the exemplar tapes will be of studio quality or contain the voices of cooperative subjects (as in SV). Rather, any of a number of degradations may be present and their presence can seriously complicate the task of the SPID practitioner. Finally, one of the most severe problems here is that any evaluation that may be carried out will involve 'open' sets of trials. Specifically, the unknown must be detected from within a large to very, very large population of 'possibilities.'

You have deduced, I am sure, that there are many uses for a system that can effectively determine which talker, from among many possible talkers, is actually the 'unknown' speaker. Permit me to illustrate; it might be necessary to decide: (1) which of the several pilots or astronauts was the one who actually uttered the distress call; (2) if the individual on the telephone is the kidnapped child; (3) which of a number of suspects is the person who made the obscene call; (4) if the individual who made the bomb threat over the telephone actually is the one who detonated it. Even these few examples should demonstrate the need for an effective SPID system. What we must deal with is the complexity of each event and the challenges of the identification task itself. Yet, as we will see, SPID can be successfully carried out under certain (even many) conditions, especially if a rigorous structuring of the approach and robust techniques are employed – but first, a brief overview of some of the problems to be faced.

PROBLEMS

UNIQUENESS

The basic problem with SPID is a horrendous one. It simply is *not* known whether or not every one of the 5–6 billion people in the world produces utterances which are unique to them and different from those of all the others. That is to say (technically), we really do not know if intraspeaker variability is always less (or smaller) than interspeaker variability and if this relationship is true for all situations and under all conditions. In other words, once the patterns are established for a given speaker, are they actually unique to them or will they vary around the resulting configuration in a manner that causes them to substantially overlap those of other speakers? The point being made here is simply that no one is sure that no matter what is done or felt, no matter how a person talks or under what conditions, they will *always* produce speech that is more like their own than anyone else's. While this aspect of the process constitutes a functional nightmare for anyone attempting to carry out any form of speaker recognition, there are ways by which you can cope with these and other problems. For one thing, you do not have to compare your target speaker (i.e., the unknown) with everyone else in the world. If it is a man, you immediately eliminate women and children. If he speaks in a particular dialect and/or language, you eliminate speakers of other languages and dialects, and so on. Further, suspects are very often located and made available for evaluation. Thus, you frequently end up with a reasonably small number of 'potentials'; a group in which the unknown probably resides. Now, what are some of the other problems?

DISTORTION

As you are aware, I already have suggested the existence of several types of SPID-related problems. The two of primary importance are system distortion and speaker distortion. A more complete description of their characteristics should be useful (even at the risk of being a little redundant).

System distortion

This category includes several kinds of signal degradation. One is reduced frequency response. That is, the signal passband can be limited when: (1) someone talks over a telephone line, (2) poor quality tape recorders are used to 'store' the utterances and/or (3) microphones of limited capability are employed. In these cases, important information about the talker is lost and these elements are not usually retrievable. In any event, limited signal passband can reduce the number of helpful speaker-specific acoustic factors. Second, noise can create a particularly debilitating type of system distortion as it tends to mask the talker's speech and, therefore, can obscure elements needed for identification. Examples of noise include those created by wind, motors, fans, automobile movement and clothing friction (especially if a body bug is used). The noise itself may be intermittent or steady state, sawtooth or thermal, and so on. It also must be remembered that *forensic* noise can exist in virtually any environment. This type of interference includes any sound at all (music or other speakers, for example) which will, in some way, 'mask' the signal of interest. Third, any kind of frequency or harmonic distortion also can make the task of identification more difficult (examples include intermittent short circuits, variable frequency response, harmonic distortion and so on). Both speech and speaker identity can be enhanced by application of a number of procedures; filtering and related techniques are particularly helpful here (an extensive review of these procedures can be found in Hollien (3)). However, you should be cautioned not to apply operations which will eliminate any of the speaker's idiosyncratic speech features.

Speaker distortion

The speakers themselves can be the source of many types of distortions. For example, fear, anxiety or stress-like emotions can occur when the perpetrator is speaking during the commission of a crime. They often will degrade identification as the speech shifts triggered by these emotions can markedly change one or more of the parameters within the speech signal (3, 4). So too can the effects of ingested drugs or alcohol; even a temporary health state, such as a cold, can mess up the speech you are attempting to process. Worse of all, the suspect may attempt to disguise their voice. If they are even modestly successful, the effect on identification can be serious. In any case, there are a number of speaker 'distortions' that can occur. If one or more actually do, the speech which is being analyzed can be degraded for identification purposes. Thus, these occurrences must be identified and then countered if at all possible. Finally, the 'open set' aspect of the identification task (see above) tends to confound the problem. That the known talker may or may not be the unknown talker, or that he may not be represented in the suspect/subject pool, creates problems on several levels. One of the more serious is that one member of any group will sound more like the unknown talker than will any of the others whether or not he actually is the same person. Imagine how this complicates the SPID process. To summarize, obtaining useful information about all of the cited factors and then knowing what to do about them, is of critical importance to SPID. These issues are what this book is all about.

A PERSPECTIVE

Given all the basic, theoretical and practical problems that will be encountered, what are the human, technical and environmental relationships which will permit the serious scientist or practitioner to attempt speaker identification in the first place? Indeed, what factors suggest that we can actually be successful in differentiating among voices? For one thing (3), certain theoretical constructs suggest we can do it. Data and logic also permit the assumption that certain elements within a talker's speech are idiosyncratic enough for our purposes. These several relationships appear to result from an integration of a person's natural anatomical/physiological features with his or her habitual speaking patterns. Indeed, a number of research projects have been carried out in order to study these very relationships. For example, attempts have been made (5–8) to compare the relevant importance of the 'source' (i.e. the voice or larynx) with the 'vocal tract' (the transfer system or the mouth/nose/throat) for speaker identification purposes. It was found that both these systems contribute and do so additively. Second, phonemic effects on the identification task also have been studied. It has been reported that the level of correct perceptual identification varies as a function of (1) the vowel produced, (2) the consonant–vowel transitions, (3) vocal tract turbulence and (4) inflections. Finally, research on voice quality, speech prosody/timing and many other speaking characteristics has permitted us to construct at least tentative working definitions of the identification process.

A large number of external events/elements can effect SPID accuracy: some will enhance efficiency, others can be detractors. These include social, economic, geographic and educational factors as well as level of maturity, psychological/physical states, sex and intelligence. Obviously, all of these elements can affect speech patterns and can do so in ways that make an individual's speech somewhat unique. Better yet, they can combine with the characteristics discussed previously to create recognizable sets of features. Indeed, there are so many elements and characteristics related to a person's speech production that it can be argued that the very complexity of the process will result in a relatively exclusive set of speaker attributes.

A further point can be made. If you measured and combined several of the many dimensions discussed, it just might be possible to discriminate effectively among talkers on the basis of profiles or sets of factors. Indeed, that is my position. I would argue that, while there may be no *single* characteristic within a person's speech which is of sufficient strength to permit that individual to be differentiated from all other talkers, the use of a group of features (or a profile) should provide the potential for relatively successful recognition. What is done is that you start identifying useful parameters and test them by themselves and in various combinations (see Figure 8.1 for a typical flow chart); you keep adding and testing them until you succeed in developing a procedure that is both robust and reliable. Of course, you cannot just go on adding parameters. If you do, you will run into the diminishing returns rule; it states that if you keep adding elements to a process such as this one, you eventually will saturate it. First, you will reach the asymptote (peak) of sensitivity, then the power of your procedure will start to decay. It could do so until the curve of your 'success' ends up in the negative. Hence, your first goal is to identify the best parameters that exist for SPID purposes and then combine the most powerful of them (and *only* the most powerful) into a single procedure. This postulation is a key one; indeed, it constitutes one of my major approaches and . . . it will serve as one of the bases for this book.

Of course, the trick is to find those parameters that make powerful SPID indicators. I believe that a good approach is to base them (and then the vectors) on those *natural* speech features employed by humans to carry out the ordinary, everyday processes of identifying people from their voices. It is my position that they attend to easily identified attributes of voice. Some of them are: (1) the pitch level of voice, pitch patterns and variability, (2) vocal intensity patterns, (3) dialect, (4) voice and speech quality, (5) prosody (the timing and/or melody of speech), (6) articulation, and so on. All we will need to do is organize them and train people and/or machines to apply them. Where did these cited elements or parameters come from? They result from both research and observation. That is, we have observed people over the years, plus what they did (and/or said they did) when they made identifications. We also developed and experimentally tested these parameter groupings or sequences. These efforts paralleled assessment of the early writings and research of other scientists (8–12) and we discussed relevant problems and issues with a number of practitioners (well, at least those in whom we had confidence). We continue to follow this plan. In any event, an effective approach quickly became obvious. As brilliant and genuinely helpful as the engineers were who analyzed the acoustic speech signal itself (usually for purposes of verification), it was the 'natural' speech features that we found both sensitive to speaker-specific patterns and resistant to many of the factors which degrade the process. Indeed, ordinary people 'did it' and they did it under conditions that sometimes seemed quite difficult. Thus, we reasoned that we should be able to control and refine the 'natural' speaking parameters for our purposes. If we could, we could then attempt to teach both phoneticians and computers to apply them successfully. If you read all of this book, you will learn about our triumphs and defeats and about how successful we have been.

TYPES OF SPEAKER IDENTIFICATION

As you know, this book is about various approaches to speaker identification. Since there are several, it would appear useful to list them before attempting to describe them in any detail. In doing so, please let me split the discussion into two parts: specifically, SPID by people and SPID by machines.

SPID BY PEOPLE

As you will see when you read the next chapter, all of the SPID accomplished down through the ages was carried out by human beings (until very recently, that is). A person heard a voice and then attempted to link it to a particular individual, i.e., the one whose speech they had heard. The process was as follows: first, they listened to the voice, then they carried out some sort of auditory-perceptual analysis of what they heard and, subsequently, they stored the relevant features in their memory. They may not have realized they were carrying out this process but they had to have done if they (later) recognized the speaker from his voice. In any event, we call this process aural-perceptual (AP)-SPID. As I indicated, until the twentieth century arrived, virtually all AP-SPID was carried out by people who had no formal training in this area. Thus, since there were no 'professionals', it was usually based either on a layman's familiarity with a particular voice or on his/her ability to remember a particular speaker. This general form of SPID existed until the present; it is only recently that we have been able to formalize the elements within the process and add two organized approaches to the general, unstructured process from the past. The first of these is earwitness identification and the other involves analyses by professionals who are specifically trained for that purpose.

Earwitness Identification

Earwitness line-ups or voice parades are not as common as eyewitness lineups or the use of 'mug books.' Nevertheless, they are a reality. This approach is applied when some person, a victim or an observer, hears the voice of another individual (usually a criminal) that they have not seen. Later, a 'suspect' is (somehow) located and law enforcement personnel ask the witness to attempt an auditory identification by listening to samples of that person's voice; i.e., is the suspect the same person that they originally heard. In almost all cases, the suspect's voice is recorded and embedded within a group of voices produced by other people. Occasionally, the procedure is conducted 'live' but it usually involves listening to the samples recorded on tapes or discs. While selection of the suspect does not 'prove' that he or she is the criminal (or voice originally heard), such an occurrence constitutes powerful evidence for investigational or trial purposes. An example, consider the case of the 'Small-town Librarian.' One night she received a telephone call just before she closed the library. The speaker on the other end of the line said: 'You bitch, I'm gonna fix your damn library tomorrow. You'll be out of a job and good riddance.' She called the police; they checked the library for a bomb. Nothing! Nor does anything happen the next day, or for weeks afterward. Just the call. Nevertheless, a crime has been committed and so the police check out a number of possible suspects. Two of them emerge as potential callers. Of course, forensic phoneticians are not called in to make the identification as there is no tape recording of the original telephone call. What the police simply did was establish an earwitness lineup. They recorded the voices of both the suspects and, then, mixed one of them with a set of five foil talkers and the other with a different set. The librarian heard both tapes and ultimately indicated that the caller was one of the talkers on the first tape. As it turned out, she was correct and the case was resolved by these two 'voice parades.' What would have happened if the librarian was not able to make the identification? Well, the investigation would have gone on and on (even though her lack of identification did not completely exonerate either of the two suspects). It would have continued until she either identified someone or the police ran out of leads. Earwitness identification will be reviewed in detail in Chapter 5.

Professionals

Most of the people in this category start out as phoneticians. A few have backgrounds in linguistics; fewer still in computer or audio-engineering. These individuals can be considered legitimate practitioners. Unfortunately, however, a number of charlatans have attempted to invade this field. Most of them are involved (even now) with 'voiceprints' (see Chapter 6) and, hence, are not very successful, but they are here, nonetheless. The group includes private detectives, a few law enforcement agents, technicians who work in music studios or have some type of 'audio' experience, plus others. As with most fields, impostors muck things up and, since they make few if any positive contributions, they will not be considered in any detail (see also Chapter 4, however).

As you might expect, the focus of this book will be heavily on forensic phoneticians and what they do. Chapter 4 provides some insight as to how they structure and employ aural-perceptual techniques when they use this approach. Later chapters contain reviews of some of their machine processing procedures. Of course, the tasks they must perform are governed by the situations they face. In a majority of the cases, they first receive an 'evidence' tape recording. It could be a bomb threat or an obscene call; an undercover agent might have recorded the conversation using a body bug (they are 'wired'). In any case, they have been given a tape recording of an unknown speaker. The task is to carry some sort of SPID but, before they do, they must obtain recordings of a suspect or several suspects. Appropriate exemplars may already be available but, if they are not, one or more must be made. (Incidently, procedures exist which will permit good exemplars to be obtained and appropriate instructions will be found in Chapter 4.) It is at this point that the professional must apply a set (or sets) of procedures so as to establish the relationships (whatever they may be) between the unknown and known (voice) samples. The method used may be aural-perceptual, computer aided or some combination of the two; foil voices may or may not be included. In any event, the forensic phonetician is at liberty to apply any procedure (or set of procedures) that will assist him in making efficient and valid decisions about the identity of the two speakers. What most of us do is to start with some form of an AP-SPID assessment. It will be (usually) followed by some sort of combined (perceptual–machine) processing.

In turn, there appear to be two schools of thought as to the most effective way to approach aural-perceptual SPID. One group stresses the segmental approach with the suprasegmentals somewhat subordinate, a second group reverses this focus. Segmentals refer to the speech sounds themselves. Hence, if the focus is on them, the practitioner studies the way the speaker produces the phonemes in his speech (see Figure 4.1 for a listing of speech symbols). For example, do they trill their /r/, substitute /d/ for /t/ or whistle their /s/? And just how are consonant clusters produced? Do they unnaturally prolong any of their vowels; do they use the /ɔ/ vowel? Questions such as these are the stock and trade of the 'segmentalists.' Both groups include analysis of the suprasegmentals among their procedures, but it is the second cohort that concentrate their efforts on these features. The suprasegmentals are those functions which underlie speaking. They include such characteristics as vocal fundamental frequency (F0) or pitch (is it the same for both the known and unknown speakers?), vocal intensity, prosody and speech timing, voice quality or spectra, etc. This type of specialist will consider the segmentals as they too are interested in the sounds of speech as well as dialect, idiolect and accent; however, they consider the paralinguistic elements to be more stable and speaker specific than the phonemes themselves. These approaches are reviewed at length in Chapter 4.

SPID BY MACHINE

The differences between speaker verification (SV) and SPID have been discussed briefly. All of the approaches to SV involve application of machine and/or computer procedures; so do a number of approaches to SPID. A review of several of the more relevant will be found in Chapters 7 and 8. The first of these two chapters focuses on certain of the earlier attempts (those initiated immediately after World War II). This discussion will be followed by descriptions of programs of more recent origin. The work at several laboratories will be reviewed and a few others featured. How one should go about meeting the SPID challenge by means of computer processing will be the theme of the final chapter. Specifically, details will be provided about an approach which my colleagues and I originated and developed over the past 35 years. We have named this approach SAUSI (Semi-automatic Speaker Identification system). Many people from many professions have worked on SAUSI; the more important of them were mentioned in the Preface. Over the years, the group has included phoneticians, forensic phoneticians, audio-engineers, computer scientists, linguists and psychologists; they have *all* contributed to SAUSI's development. Our approach is presented for two reasons. First, the system is now pretty well developed. Indeed, its users have enjoyed success with it. The second objective is just about as important as the first. How we formulated our objectives, how we selected our procedures, how we structured the experiments and how we carried them out is of relevance to this book and for a number of reasons. Thus, I will provide detail about the developmental process we established as well as the experiments we carried out in order to assess our constructs and ideas. You may also be interested in some of the surprises we experienced, our frustrations and how the dynamic process of research ultimately led to a technique which now enjoys a modicum of success. The word 'dynamic' is probably controlling here since it was the dynamics, plus exhilaration, associated with this research program that was particularly meaningful to us.

A FINAL NOTE

The admissibility of 'expert' testimony tends to follow certain rules. In the USA, for example, it is based on one or another of two tests. The older of the two is referred to as the Fry (13) test. Basically, it states that if a scientific method is to be considered valid (the courts usually refer to 'validity' by the misnomer 'reliability'), it must be generally accepted by members of the relevant scientific community. The second test is referred to as 'Daubert' (14, 15). It is somewhat more liberal than Fry as it gives the judge a greater latitude in deciding the testimony he or she can accept.

My reaction to these issues is twofold. First I am not a lawyer and, hence, am reluctant to advise anyone as to just how the courts will respond to any of the various SPID approaches. Second, I am an American and what little I know about legal systems or judicial structures is mostly confined to the courts in my native land. Accordingly, I will defer any discussion here to the relevant specialists and make only passing reference to these 'tests' throughout the book.

A FINAL, FINAL NOTE

It was difficult to find a place for this last item. (Can I put it here?) Anyway, it is about the references. You will see they are numbered and scattered (appropriately I hope) throughout the text. They are numbered so they will not intrude upon the flow of your thought. Second, the listings, are *all* placed (by chapter) at the end of the book, and for just this same reason. One other item. Virtually all of the items found in these reference sections will be cited in the text. There are just a few I did not cite but, since I found them useful and/or interesting, I included them as 'Further Reading.'

CHAPTER 2

HISTORY

INTRODUCTION

So, when and where did it all begin? It had to be a long, long time ago didn't it? As a start, lets consider the following yarn.

> It was really dark in the cave as wood was scarce and the coals from the fire were not even glowing any more. Gnarly was dog tired, he had been gone for 2 days and had come back empty handed. One-Eye had better tend the fire soon or he would have to try and borrow some embers from that ugly bunch down on the lower ridge. He was just wondering if One-Eye was going to give him something to eat when he felt the hairs on his back and his neck stiffen. Something or someone was inside the cave. Gnarly skittled toward the ledge; where *was* his axe? Just then he heard: 'Gawall, gawall, ugger' and nearly collapsed with relief. It was Twistjaw. 'Grunee' he replied so as not to get brained himself. Let's hope the old guy is bringing us a fat rabbit – or maybe a nice snake.

It is probably safe to say that Gnarly had to have carried out some sort of 'speaker identification' way, way back then. As a matter of fact, various types of SPID certainly have been going on for many thousands of years. Perhaps the process developed even before spoken language was very well organized. After all, a simple form of signal processing must have existed in even the earliest days of our history. For example, did the growl heard by Gnarly emanate from his mate, from his wolf-dog or from a great big cat looking to have him for supper? An accurate judgment in such a case would be pretty important to him, that is, if he wanted to survive. Of course, it is signal recognition of a simpler form than what we now call 'speaker' identification. Yet would not the development of such auditory processing procedures be useful in even a general sense? If I were Gnarly, I surely would want to be able to differentiate between a crow's mating calls and its warning cries. Logically, development of these skills should lead to even more complex types of auditory processing. To be able to discriminate between the mating grunts of One-Eye and those of old Thunderthighs might not just involve personal preference, it might also be helpful in the survival of the species. In any case, there is no question that speaker identification has been going on for a very long time.

EARLY HISTORY

Logically, you would expect that activity in the speaker identification area would intensify once language and speech became routine. If you do, you probably would be correct. You also would expect that appropriate references would be made once a basic system of writing had been developed. Of course, ancient references such as these might be a little difficult to locate. First, you would have to be literate in a number of these very old, and often extinct, languages. You then would have to find many, many appropriate specimens of the one you were studying (just how often do you think speaker recognition would be referenced?). Very few examples of these ancient languages survive, of course, even when you consider well-known systems such as hieroglyphics. On the other hand, the records left by Greek and Roman scholars are both marginally plentiful and readable (that is, if you are conversant with classical Greek and Latin). Better yet, useful translations exist in some cases. For example, Saslove and Yarmey (1) quote a translation of some writings by the pre-socratic philosopher Heraclitus wherein he warns us about earwitness identification. He writes 'Eyes and ears are bad witnesses for men since their souls lack understanding.' Sagacious is he not? The Roman philosopher Quintillian also proves 'helpful.' Of course, like Heraclitus with his eyes and ears having no souls, some of Quintillian's opinions are a little off the mark. For example, Hoffman (2) quotes him as saying '. . . a good speaker must be a good man.' Wow! That statement certainly could lead to an interesting debate. But, when he (Quintillian) gets around to speaker identification, he does a little better (3). He writes: 'The voice of the speaker is as easily distinguished by the ear as the face is by the eye.' His opinions here were certainly more positive than were those of old Heraclitus. Anyway, it appears that speaker identification existed as a recognized entity and did so from the time people began writing down their opinions about human behaviors and capabilities. As a matter of fact, if you are driven to do so, you probably could find lots of references of the type cited. But to what avail? Speaker identification happened and is still happening. It only takes these few references (plus a little logic) to establish the fact that it all started 'way back when.'

'SEMI'-MODERN TIMES

Things get livelier once we trundle our way up to the nineteenth century; well, either they do or the situation simply is one where more relevant documents survive. For example, there are a number of references to speaker identification among the legal records in Great Britain. And well there might be, for the admissibility of aural-perceptual SPID-based testimony can be traced back even earlier: at least to the year 1660, when voice identification was offered in the case of one William Hulet (4). Further, things in that country had developed to a point where Yarmey (5) has been able to identify and comment on a quotation by Jeremy Bentham who said 'witnesses are the eyes and ears of justice.' Of course, Yarmey correctly points out that sometimes these witnesses are 'accurate, complete and trustworthy; sometimes they are not.' Also, please do not forget a famous 1861 case in New York where the presiding judge permitted a witness to testify that he could recognize a particular dog by hearing its bark (6). In this case, a witnesses identified the defendant's dog as one of two that had killed his sheep. He said that the dog had an unusual bark ('coarse, harsh') and both the judge – and the jury – agreed on the basis that 'some people have such peculiar voices that they can be identified by acquaintances who hear them talk without seeing them.' It seemed reasonable to them that the same could be true of a dog's bark. As a matter of fact, before the nineteenth century ended, there was even talk about whether or not voices could be recognized over the telephone. However, in a relevant trial (7), the judge did not permit such testimony. He excluded it even though the witness in question demonstrated that he was familiar with the speaker's voice.

Things began to improve even further after the turn of the century. One of the most famous SPID cases of all time occurred in 1907 in Florida (8). It involved a rape – one where the defendant was previously unknown to the victim and could not be seen during the period during which the crime took place. He was black, she was white. She identified him on the basis of him having spoken two sentences to her: 'I have got you now,' and 'I don't want your money.' The judge agreed with the victim's testimony, explaining his decision by the following logic:

> 'The manner, time and place of his assault upon her threw her instantly into the highest state of terror and alarm, when all of her senses and faculties were at the extreme of alert receptiveness, when there was nothing within her reach by which to identify her assailant but his voice. Who can deny that under these circumstances that voice so indelibly and vividly photographed itself upon the sensitive plate of her memory as that she could forever afterwards promptly and unerringly recognize it on hearing its tones again.'

As bizarre as it may seem, this early decision is accepted by many courts, both within Florida and throughout the USA, as an appropriate legal precedent for the admissibility of earwitness identification. It is not as good a precedent for other types of SPID but it sometimes also prevails under those circumstances.

Then came the rest of the twentieth century. The next really big excitement occurred when, in 1933, Charles Lindberg's baby was kidnapped. As you probably know, Lindberg had been elevated to international hero status after he became the first man to fly solo across the Atlantic ocean. Hence, when his son was kidnapped, and later found murdered, many people in the USA joined with him and his wife in their rage and mourning. Indeed, the emotional level ran so high that later, when Bruno Hauptmann was arrested and indicted for this crime (9), there was great concern that the authorities would not be able to protect him. I can still remember one of my great-uncles telling me about the stress he experienced when he served as one of Hauptmann's prison guards (they were particularly worried about lynch mobs). Anyway, soon after the kidnapping, a man called and identified himself as the kidnapper. Intense negotiations were initiated at that juncture and they continued until the child's body was found. During that period, Lindberg apparently heard the kidnapper's voice twice: once over a telephone (an early model, one of pretty limited fidelity) and again in person but briefly and at night. Over 2 years later (during the trial), Lindberg testified that he recognized the voice of Bruno Hauptmann as that of the kidnapper. What a sensation his testimony created! No one doubted for a moment that he could and did make a valid identification – that is, except for the defense lawyers and a psychologist by the name of Frances McGehee.

Whether Hauptmann was guilty or innocent apparently was not at issue with McGehee (substantial physical evidence supported the notion that he was guilty, however). What interested her was the aural-perceptual identification Lindberg made over 2 years after having heard the voice of the kidnapper. In response, she conducted two studies (10, 11). They proved to be the first 'modern' experiments carried out on aural-perceptual SPID (they are reviewed in Chapter 3). She was able to provide insight about what might be expected of a lay witness and what can happen to their identification rates over time. Better yet, she reported experiments that were well designed and conducted. Indeed, and as you will see, contemporary research tends to substantiate many of her conclusions.

WORLD WAR II AND IMMEDIATELY AFTER

As you might expect, a number of important speaker identification-related events occurred during World War II. A few of those which occurred in the United States may be of interest to you. The first of these resulted from an assassination attempt made on Adolph Hitler; it occurred on July 21, 1944 at Wolf's Lair, his field headquarters in East Prussia. People became excited when word of this bombing crackled around the world – but . . . had Hitler been killed, with a double taking his place, or was he essentially unharmed as Joseph Goebbel's Ministry of Propaganda insisted. Obviously, British and/or US agents within Germany could have been asked to find out what had happened but this might take a rather long time. Moreover, an effort of this type might not have been successful at all. So, what could be done? For one thing, Hitler had given many speeches over the years and a substantial number of them had been recorded and stored – and *somebody* was still making speeches. Perhaps SPID (or non-identification) would work. Best yet, several groups of relevant scientists were available, ones that might be able make comparisons of the type necessary, i.e., between the old recordings and the new ones. One of these groups consisted of several phoneticians and engineers located at Purdue University, Indiana, USA; the team here was headed by Dr Mack Steer. For its time, his laboratory could be considered pretty much as state-of-the-art. Better yet, Steer and his compatriots already were at work analyzing the voices of a number of prominent speakers. Included among them were Theodore and Franklin Roosevelt, Neville Chamberlin, Beninto Mussolini and, of course, Adolph Hitler (12, 13). Steer had been conducting a SPID project on Hitler's voice relative to a speech he (Hitler) had denied making. Since this group already was up and running, they were given a contract requesting that they determine if the man who was now making the speeches was one-in-the-same as the Hitler who had made all of those other ones back in the 1930s and early 1940s. There was a problem in that they had to deal with a speaker that had been under psychiatric therapy for many years (14–16) and there is evidence that a voice probably will change as a function of certain psychotic conditions (4, 17–22). Another problem was the fidelity of their recorded samples was not all that great. Worst of all, they had to complete the project in a hurry.

Steer and his associates pulled out all the stops (M. Steer, personal communication). They used aural-perceptual procedures with both phoneticians and panels of auditors. They also used each and every processing system and device they had (or could lay their hands on) in order to assess any of the elements they thought might provide information. After combining and analyzing all their results, they came to the conclusion that Adolf Hitler was alive and functioning. Later intelligence proved them correct. You also should note that their efforts constituted one of the first cohesive, multivector, efforts in the SPID area.

Apparently, attempts at speaker identification also were going on at the Bell Telephone Laboratories in New Jersey, USA. The scientists there had already succeeded in developing one of the earliest sound spectrographs (the Sonagraph) as well as other relevant apparatus. Perhaps just as important, they had been able to recruit a number of top-flight scientists in speech communication and audio-engineering. What they actually did or did not do in our area of interest still is not clear (apparently much of it was classified) but some of the things they published and/or described certainly have bearing on speaker identification. One of their early breakthroughs was the development of a 'visible speech' machine or Sonagraph (23, 24). This apparatus was quite advanced for its time and, indeed, can be useful even today. It is of import also because it is the very device the 'voiceprinters' used to develop and apply their 'method.' Indeed, they probably did not even coin the name 'voiceprint' as this was done for them by the people at Bell Laboratories. That is, it was there that, in 1944, Gray and Kopp (25) wrote an in-house report entitled (you guessed it) 'Voiceprint Identification.' Relevant descriptions, plus an assessment, of the resulting voiceprint procedure can be found in Chapter 6; hence, they will not be further reviewed here. However, you should be aware that, at that time anyway, some pretty good people thought that they might have hit on a useful tool for SPID. Anyway, the people at Bell Laboratories have been working on speaker identification and verification for nearly 70 years now. As you will see, they have made some remarkable contributions.

STALIN AND HIS PRISONER SCIENTISTS

The next excitement actually occurred immediately after World War II, and not in the USA or Great Britain either. It came about because another twentieth century psychotic – Joseph Stalin – had achieved dictatorial control over Russia and adjacent countries. But to tell this story properly, it is necessary to start 5–6 years prior to the end of World War II. What had happened was that literally millions of people living under Soviet domination defected to the Germans when they invaded Russia in June, 1941; indeed, in one case, an entire army from the Ukraine did so. Later, the Germans captured huge numbers of loyal Soviet soldiers and civilians in their drive toward the cities of Moscow, Leningrad and Stalingrad. After the war was over, many of these prisoners – both the deserters and captives – returned, or were returned, to the USSR. At this juncture, Stalin was faced with a dilemma (at least from his point of view). Who among this mass of people had been loyal and who had not and how could he tell which was which? His solution was a simple one. Treat them all as deserters (whether they were or not) and imprison them – his military police could sort it all out later. However, not all of them were sent to suffer, and die, as slaves in the Gulags. Those individuals who were highly trained and/or educated in 'useful' professions were identified and sent to jails where they could be put to work at practical tasks. Included among these many groups were one or two that were forced to attempt development of systems for identifying speakers by voice. How well they functioned is not really known. However, in

1968, the famous author Solzhenitsyn (26) wrote about one such team of 'scientist' (phoneticians, linguists and engineers) prisoners in his novel *The First Circle*. The individuals he writes about were incarcerated in a jail near Moscow. There they were split up and assigned to a number of projects. In turn, one of the groups was tasked to create a workable speaker identification procedure. You can understand how important it would be for the masters of a police state such as the USSR to be able to identify their 'enemies' simply by voice analysis. In any case, Solzhenitsyn is quite amusing when he describes the imaginative strategies used by these scientists and engineers as they attempted to delude their supervisors into thinking they were making better progress than they were.

As you might expect, Solzhenitsyn takes the story yet a step further. Several of the group, (Rubin, Roitman and Smovlosidov) become enamored with what they were doing. When they were assigned to determine which of five suspects was the person who had committed a 'crime against the state,' they took on the project with verve. They joyfully analyzed the recordings made of the 'criminal' when he committed the 'crime' as well as the exemplars of the five suspects. After much analysis, they were able to eliminate two of these men plus (possibly) a third. They thought that one of the two remaining suspects probably was the culprit. However, they could not completely eliminate the other one because some of his speech characteristics were also like those of the perpetrator. Thus, when Major General Oskolupov showed up, they told him about both. 'That's fine,' said the General, 'I will have them both arrested!' 'But one of them is innocent!' cried Rubin. 'Innocent? . . . not guilty of anything at all!' replied the incredulous Oskolupov. 'The security service will sort this one out.' And, of course, they did, destroying both men in the process. Incidently, the term 'voice-prints' was used by Solzhenitsyn. Did he independently 'coin' this term?

As you might expect, substantive efforts in the SPID area continued in the USSR and now in present-day Russia. One of the current leaders here is Ramishvilli (actually a Georgian); he is still active (27–30). Even today, however, the problem of accurate speaker identification eludes solution in that country.

WHAT HAPPENED NEXT?

Things were pretty quiet during the 1950s, but a little research was carried out, much of it in the USA. This was probably because most countries in Europe and the Orient were attempting to recover from a devastating war, one that was so destructive that its scale is difficult to imagine here in the twenty-first century (difficult even for those of us who served in that war). Anyway, the energies and priorities of the inhabitants of those countries were directed toward sustaining life and rebuilding their respective economies. Then too, it was only later that changes in our social structure led to a greater need for SPID.

Most of the relevant research that was carried out during the 1950s and early 1960s will be reviewed in the chapters to follow. However, certain events of historical interest also occurred, some for the better and some for the worse. Moreover, a trend developed when the police started applying any SPID procedure they could get their hands on.

The thrust here took a number of forms. One involved an increased use of earwitness line-ups; these were patterned after eyewitness line-ups. This was because eyewitness identification had been in use for some time and 'mug books' had also become popular. Indeed, law enforcement personnel had become quite comfortable with these types of investigational techniques. It was during this period that personnel employed by many of these agencies began to assume that earwitness line-ups (or voice parades) would be just as effective as was visual identification. Unfortunately, they did not realize that there were substantial differences between the two approaches. For example, they were not aware that memory for heard acoustic signals could be quite variable: it was not the same as visual memory. Nevertheless, voice parades were organized and used but, when they were, problems arose. For one thing, no reasonable guidelines were available as to how to structure them or how to adapt what was known about eyewitness identification. Worse yet, very little appropriate research had been carried out. Thus, police departments were quite variable in how they developed earwitness identification and, hence, their use tended not be particularly rewarding. So many problems were created, a substantial number of professionals became chary about their use (4, 31, 32); these concerns exist even to the present day. The pros and cons of earwitness identification, the relevant procedures plus suggestions for their application, are considered in Chapter 5.

'VOICEPRINTS'

One of the major happenings in SPID also occurred in the late 1950s and early 1960s. That event was the assault on our field by the 'voiceprinters.' How did all this nonsense get started? Well, an engineer at the Bell Telephone Laboratories developed an interest in speaker identification in the 1950s. His name was Lawrence Kersta, an engineer who had spent most of his career assisting scientists with their projects. His interest appears to have stemmed in part from their work and in part from what he perceived to be a need for a useful (accurate, efficient) SPID system. It is without question that Kersta knew of the work reported by Potter and his co-workers (23–25); he might even have assisted them with their research. He also knew about the report on 'voiceprint' identification prepared by Gray and Kopp (5). In any case, he attempted to adapt their model for use by testing it. What he actually did, however, is a bit of a mystery. It probably would be fair to say that he initially attempted to see if the patterns on Sonagrams exhibited features (that is, ones beyond the phoneme patterns being uttered by the speaker) which could be used to identify individual talkers. He hoped, I am sure, that some of these characteristics were idiosyncratic enough for SPID purposes. How much work he did here is not known but apparently his observations were such that he felt justified in proceeding. Subsequently, he carried out some sort of a study. Just what he did here is not clear either – even after one reads his publication (33). What he may have done was to record the voices of some of the staff at Bell Laboratories and make Sonograms of certain of them. Then he probably asked these or other staff members to attempt to match the patterns found on these displays with those for yet other utterances made by these same people. In any case, Kersta claims that his subjects achieved 99% accuracy in correctly matching the known Sonagrams with the unknown.

Ordinarily, an article such as the Kersta's would have become but a footnote in SPID history or, at best, other investigators would have independently tested the approach and negated its use by having uncovered its flaws and inadequacies (unfortunately, these assessments did not come until later). Moreover, the 1960s intruded upon the early life of 'voiceprints' and things in the USA heated up quickly. It was only later that this problem spread to other parts of the world. In any event, it can be said that the US criminal justice system was nearly overwhelmed by the social unrest of the 1960s and the resulting increases in crime. One of the most challenging problems came from the use of telephones in criminal activity. Related chaos resulted from similar misuse of radio and especially television. The police were left desperately trying to find out who telephoned in the murder threat, who called 911 to take credit for the bombing, who (while visually disguised) admitted on television to having set the fires during the Watts riots. At first, there appeared to be no relief at all for law enforcement, at least, in the SPID domain. However, it was not long before they noticed the Kersta paper in *Nature* (10) and asked him for his help. He was, of course, only too happy to provide it. That he genuinely felt that he was making an important societal contribution seems true; however, there is some evidence that he later realized that what he was doing was flawed and could, ultimately, damage society. He continued anyway.

So, the use of 'voiceprints' exploded upon the American scene in the 1960s. It took years before the weight of the relevant research (plus court testimony by scientists) demonstrated the harm 'voiceprints' were bringing to law enforcement and the courts. The misuses of the procedure now are obvious, as is the damage that has been done by their use. Chapter 6 is devoted to this issue even though 'voiceprints' actually have become but a 'footprint' in history.

Finally, it must be said that a kind of heyday for speaker identification occurred during the 20 years between 1965 and 1985. Research still goes on but the emphasis here has shifted more and more toward speaker verification. Of course, the 'big money' resides with SV as even a passing familiarity with the Internet will demonstrate. However, while rather ironic, the SPID problem is still of the greater importance to society. The *verification* problem would quickly disappear if an accurate and reliable speaker identification method became available. Unfortunately, few in the SV area appear to understand this relationship. Then too, the challenge of SPID may be one that is simply too daunting for most relevant scientists.

Now, we should get on with the rest of the book. My goal is to tell (at least from my point of view) what has happened, what is happening and what may happen in the future. Discussion of these issues will be presented on a chapter-by-chapter basis.

CHAPTER 3

AURAL-PERCEPTUAL APPROACHES

INTRODUCTION

When one talks or writes about aural-perceptual speaker identification (AP-SPID), the focus is – and has to be – on the *listener.* The type of listener involved is of but modest importance, as are the characteristics exhibited by the speaker and the nature of the environment in which the utterances were produced. Accordingly, the focus of this chapter is on the listener and only the listener. In other words, the speaker is of consequence only when his or her behavior affects that of the listener. These same relationships hold as to when the utterance was produced (years ago or yesterday) or how it was produced (e.g. normally, disguised or stressed). All these relationships and occurrences are simply hurdles the listener must surmount in order to make an identification. So, please be advised that everything in this chapter revolves around the listener. As you might expect, things that will make it easier for them to make judgments will be included; so will those that make it more difficult. Of course, the behaviors which can be expected of the listener under a whole variety of conditions (memory for voices over long periods of time, arousal, hearing deficits, etc.) are also reviewed, but please permit me to be redundant: the controlling phrase here is 'the listener.'

The chapter is organized in sections that are hopefully both logical and readable. The first of these will be on what we know about a listener's ability to accurately remember a voice over varying periods of time; this discourse is followed by several about other basic issues. The strengths and weaknesses (for this task) exhibited by the human auditory system are then discussed, as are elements (acoustic and otherwise) related to the environment and the nature of the speaker. All this would be relatively simple except that we also have to consider the different classes of listeners, the different reasons for attempting AP-SPID and the different ways of doing it. For example, the listeners may be (1) members of the public, (2) people interested in the process (for some reason) but who are relatively uninitiated or (3) trained professionals (usually forensic phoneticians). While many of the elements present will affect them equally (or, at least, in a similar fashion), others will not. Then too, the listener may be responding to the speech samples as a witness in a voice parade or as a subject in a study. The task may call for a simple 'yes–no' decision about a side-by-side comparison of two voice samples or the selection of one voice out of many. You can see, I am sure, how even these few situations can complicate all those other relationships. Thus, while the overall focus of this chapter is on the basics of aural-perceptual speaker identification, certain of the discussions (in some cases entire sections) include perspectives on how one or more of these external elements/events can modify the relationship being presented. Finally, do not be concerned when you discover that this chapter is *only* about AP-SPID. Discussions about the use of computer-based procedures and/or 'mixed' approaches appear later.

REMEMBERING VOICES

First, please reconsider the discussion about the kidnaping of Charles Lindberg's child (see Chapter 2) and how Frances McGehee carried out research (1, 2) in which she attempted to assess his ability to identify the kidnapper (made 2 years after hearing the voice in question). You also should remember my contention that McGehee's efforts initiated *modern* research on AP-SPID: but what did she do, how did she do it and what did she find out?

In her first study, McGehee selected sets of speakers drawn from a subject pool of 49 individuals (31 males, 18 females). In her primary procedure, she had one of the speakers orally read a 56-word passage to the listeners, and do so while standing behind an opaque screen. These listeners were clustered into 15 different groups (for the different experiments) whose members were drawn from a total population of 740 students (554 males, 186 females). The identification task was simple; she had the members of each group first listen to the voice of the speaker. They heard his voice again (later) but, this time, he was randomly assigned to a kind of 'voice line-up' which also included five foil talkers (everyone spoke behind the screen, of course) who also uttered the same phrase. The listeners simply wrote down the number of the speaker they thought they had heard originally. Obviously, the foils were people the listener-subjects had not heard before. In any event, McGehee repeated this procedure after 1, 2, and 3 days, 1, 2, and 3 weeks and/or 1, 3, and 5 months (that is why she needed so many subjects).

McGehee reported data from both this main study and from a number of sub-experiments. That is, in addition to memory decay for voices (the primary study and the one of greatest interest to us), she also attempted to determine such things as whether men or women were best at recognizing voices, how various other parameters (speakers with foreign dialects, voice disguise, etc.) affected the recognition process, and so on. However, and as indicated, her key set of data came from investigations of the decay in the correct identifications which occurred over time. She was able to report scores of about 83% (correct) after a lapse of 1 day and, also, that this level was pretty much sustained for about a week. The first real drop in the correct identification scores came after 2 weeks (down to 68%), another occurred after 3 months (down to 35%). Finally, after 5 months, her subjects were only able to correctly identify the talker they had heard originally about 13% of the time (less than chance).

In her second investigation, McGehee (2) replicated much of her research on memory decay (i.e. for unfamiliar voices over time). However, in this instance she changed the procedure from one involving live speakers to that where recorded voice samples were used as stimuli. After all, working with live subjects hidden behind a screen is a little cumbersome. Nevertheless, her results were quite similar to those from the first set of experiments. That is, she found correct recognition for the recorded voices to be at the 85% level, whereas the mean for the live samples was 83%. These levels continued to roughly parallel each other; for example, mean accuracy for the recorded voices after 2 months was 45%, whereas it was 46% for the live ones. Again, she studied a whole series of other issues; however, they are of minimal import to us at this juncture.

You must agree that McGehee's research was pretty methodical. Indeed, it provided the first set of defensible data as to how the recognition process works. It also provided some basic concepts fundamental to the understanding of AP-SPID and specific information about what can be expected of an individual who is faced with an earwitness line-up.

A review of the relevant research that followed McGehee's will reveal that the findings reported by other authors tend to substantiate hers, at least in the main. Her research, as well as newer data, tend to support the idea that reliance on aural-perceptual identifications, particularly those of a previously unknown talker, may not be as robust as we would wish. However, few experiments in this area have directly replicated McGehee's and, therefore, our knowledge about this issue still is just a little sketchy.

What other data are available? In an early study, Bricker and Pruzansky (3) reported that, on day 1, they obtained 98% correct identification of speakers known to the listener when sentences were employed as stimuli. However, identification accuracy fell to 56% only a day later. This second-day effect would be striking except that it was confounded by the use of restricted speech samples (i.e. syllables) and unfamiliar voices. Nevertheless, their data, while somewhat tangential, were reasonably consistent with McGehee's. On the other hand, Yarmey and Matthys (4) reported somewhat different results. When they carried out a slightly different project on short-term memory for voices (tests of up to 1 week from the initial exposure), they found no significant reduction in correct identification. However, they did find an increase in the false positive rate and thus concluded that their subjects' ability to recognize speakers actually did deteriorate somewhat (because of this increase in 'false alarms').

Research of an even more appropriate nature also has been reported. For example, Clifford and his associates (5, 6) studied the 'decay' relationship by means of a procedure that paralleled McGehee's; they also found that identification accuracy was systematically reduced as a function of time. On the other hand, while Papcun *et al.* (7) and Saslove and Yarmey (8) also reported overall trends that generally agreed with those of both McGehee and Clifford, their decay slopes often were quite different. Moreover, they observed a few reversals among their data. Thus, while these authors generally substantiated the position that a listener's identification of a voice decays over time, they also established that it is not always possible to predict the exact pattern of these trends.

A couple of our own studies (9 and unpublished data) can be used to clarify several of these issues. The purpose of these studies was to test some of the basic patterns associated with identification accuracy plus generate insights about certain of the strengths and weaknesses of the earwitness procedure. We also tried to conduct the research under 'real-life'conditions. The listener-subjects were law school students who saw and heard the onslaught of an 'assailant' who burst into their classroom and for a couple of minutes abused a 'victim' (who had been 'planted' in the first row of the small amphitheater). The students then were assigned to groups (counterbalanced by where they sat) and, among other things, were asked to participate in both earwitness (recorded) and eyewitness (photographic) lineups at specific times of up to three weeks after the event. The decay in correct identification generally was what we expected, yet we found a quirk in some of our data. Basically, it was found that two of the four groups exhibited more correct identifications after a 2-wk delay than did the others for the earlier trials. Why did this happen? Was it coincidence? One might be tempted to say that the phenomenon was real and attempt to explain it on the basis of Brown's (10) argument that identifications associated with longer latencies might be easier to organize than those for shorter ones. Perhaps so but, if true, why did this pattern not occur with all groups in all studies? Nor were the trends consistent with the classic 'forgetting curves' suggested by Ebbinghaus in the nineteenth century (see ref. 11); he argued that much 'forgetting' happens quickly and that a decay curve, while somewhat muted, will be orderly as time lengthens. The second study in the series provided a somewhat different pattern. The curves here followed a more traditional form and, thus, were somewhat different from those found in the first. Accordingly, the data obtained from this (second) experiment were more consistent with McGehee's than are those from, at least, some of the other investigations.

So, what can safely be said about temporal decay of memory for voices? Well, there is no question but that the latency between hearing a voice and having to identify it can be critical as reduction in accuracy can be expected to operate as a function of time. However, it is not yet possible to specify exactly what this curve will look like in all instances or what can be expected of any particular individual. There are just too many variables which can affect the process.

NONCONTEMPORARY SPEECH

While it might appear more natural to continue the discussion of basic listener characteristics, there is a related (but somewhat different) issue that begs recognition at this point. It concerns the use of noncontemporary speech *samples* in speaker identification. That is, the term 'noncontemporary' SPID refers to where samples of a speaker's utterances are obtained at different points in time and then later subjected to some sort of an identification process. Thus, it is the talkers' speech (or potential changes in it) that creates the challenge. However, please do not be misled, the focus here has not shifted to the speaker. Rather, it still is on what the listener can do – in this case with comparisons of speakers wherein their samples are separated by periods of time.

It has been suggested that noncontemporary speech poses just as difficult a challenge to the speaker identification process as does the decay resulting from a listener's limitations in memory (12). Yet, the two issues actually are quite different and these differences can be appreciated by consideration of Figure 3.1. Here, the tasks involving judgments of noncontemporary speech samples are portrayed in the top panel; a typical earwitness line-up procedure (lower panel) defines the memory decay problem discussed in the last section.

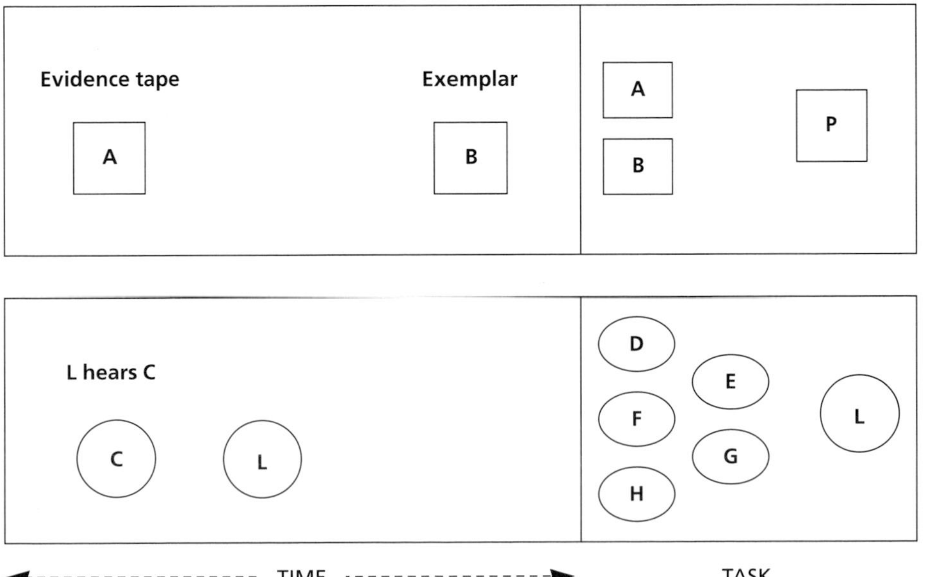

Figure 3.1

A portrayal of the differences between noncontemporary SPID (top box) and earwitness identification (bottom box). In the first of the two, a processor (P is an auditor or computer operator) attempts to determine whether or not the speakers heard in samples (A) and (B) are the same person. Note that it is the recordings which were made at different times. In earwitness identification, there are no recordings of the perpetrator's voice (C). Rather, the listener (L) attempts to remember his voice and pick it out of a line-up (D–H).

It is surprising but very little research has been carried out in which these 'noncontemporary' relationships have been studied. Of course, Endress *et al.* (13) did address it, at least tangentially, when they investigated the effects of aging on speaker identification. As with Suzuki *et al.* (14), they studied changes in certain speech characteristics but found no 'universals' even over long periods of time. Thus, it may be possible that there is but a single investigation in which the author formally addresses the effects of noncontemporary speech on the identification process. The report in question is one by Rothman (12) who studied this issue as part of a larger project. Basically, he recorded two dozen talkers and, then, had them re-record the same passage one week later. His experimental tape consisted of matched samples with one of the pair drawn from the earlier session and the other from the later one. Sometimes both were produced by a single talker, other times each was produced by a different person. He then had a group of listeners attempt to determine if the voices in a pair were the 'same or different' (an ABX design). His results were somewhat unexpected, as he reported that his mean correct identification scores dropped to 42% when the noncontemporary samples were presented. If accurate, these results are of substantial importance, since they indicate that use of nontemporary speech samples would be detrimental to the speaker identification process – especially if aural-perceptual procedures are used.

Then, in 1995, Schwartz (15) began to wonder if peoples' voices actually could change dramatically over relatively short periods of time. In order to assess this question, she carried out a pilot study that roughly paralleled Rothman's. Her results were not consistent with his even when she took the slight differences between their tasks into account. That is, he had placed some 'sound-alikes' among his pairs and she had not. In any case, her work led to a larger series of investigations which were carried out in an attempt to resolve the controversy (16, 17).

The procedures used in the first of these two projects were structured as four parallel experiments. Two of them involved relatively short speaking latencies; that is, speech samples were obtained, and then, obtained again, 4 and 8 weeks after the contemporary recordings had been made. A second group of talkers produced sets of samples 4 and then 32 weeks apart. The third and fourth studies involved comparisons for rather long delays, i.e., those of six and 20 years. The speakers for the first two of the experiments (i.e., those involving the 0–4, 0–8, 0–32 week differences) were normal, healthy males drawn from the faculty, staff and students at the Institute for Advanced Study of the Communication Processes, (IASCP), University of Florida. Those for the longer latencies (i.e. 6 and 20 years) were individuals who currently were available but who also had been talkers in earlier (related) experiments and, hence, had high-quality samples of their speech stored in the IASCP database. Since at least 10 talkers were required for each procedure, sufficiently large groups (where subjects met all past and present selection criteria) were found only in the 1989 database (6 years prior to 1995) and in that obtained in 1975 (a 20-year separation). The samples (consisting of 6–9 sec. sentences) were pulled and checked; the subjects were then rerecorded using the same speech material. A total of 149 auditors were used; they were distributed among (the listener) groups in sets varying from 30 to 41 members. The experimental task was structured as a randomized/counterbalanced paired comparison technique (ABX) with the listener indicating if the pair they heard was produced by one or two speakers. Between 68–74 token pairs were presented in four identical experiments; variation in design resulted only if a single time-pairing (for example 0–6 years) or two (for example 0–4 and 0–8 weeks) was administered. Listeners also were required to meet a number of selection criteria; including both a speech reception hearing test (SRT) (>92% correct) and a competency test. That is, they had to demonstrate that they could recognize which of a series of test pairs were produced by a single person and which by two different people at a level of 85% correct or better. These criteria were checked first and, if a subject did not reach the 85% level, their experimental responses were immediately discarded. (Actually, none of the auditors had to be eliminated for this reason as their correct scores were in the ranges of 90–100% and 87–100% respectively.)

The results of this research can be best understood by consideration of Figure 3.2. As can be seen, the subjects exhibited the expected 95% correct identification level for the contemporary speech; subsequently, their scores dropped (4-week condition) to an accuracy band roughly between 70% and

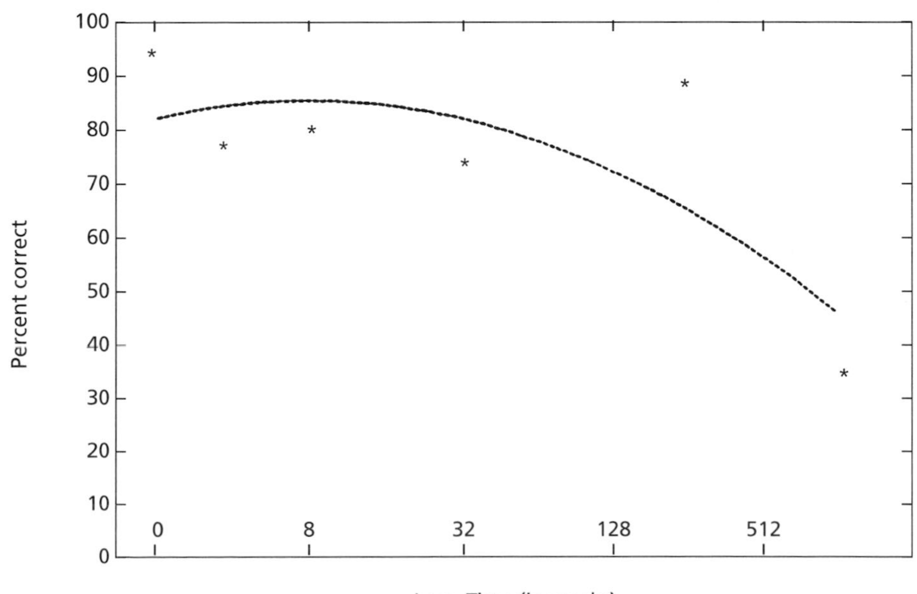

Figure 3.2
Graphic dispay of the mean scores from Hollien and Schwartz (16). The subjects responded to non-contemporary samples as a function of delays of from 4 weeks to 20 years. The contemporary baseline is the mean (95.1%) for all listeners. The fitted curve is a second-order polynomial.

85% and stayed there for up to 6 years. It was only after a 20-year separation that the judgments became unstable. This research demonstrates that using noncontemporary speech samples will have little effect on AP-SPID. At least they will not until very long periods of time have elapsed.

Once the primary relationship had been established, a number of additional questions began to surface. For example, why did a drop of about 20% in the identification scores occur between the contemporary utterances and those after a break of only 4 weeks? Why did a very sharp drop occur between the 6- and 20-year separations? Accordingly, we structured six experiments designed to address these questions. We have completed three (17). The aim here was to test for the potentially confounding effects of gender, of training and for (one set of) external variables. That is, the issue of gender involved the possibility that one or the other of the sexes might have performed differently than the other. This possibility is important since the female to male ratio ordinarily is at least 2:1 in university-based experiments of this type. The basis for the second question can be traced back to McGehee (1) who reported that the performance of her male listeners was markedly superior to that for her females. Down through the years, anecdotal, and tangential evidence (while mixed overall) occasionally supported her position. Of course, most of the more recent studies have not shown differences of this type (4, 5, 19), even though a mild trend can sometimes be seen. In any event, this study was patterned almost identically with the primary experiment, except that we compared the performance of 44 males with 44 females. When we contrasted their mean response, we found them to be almost identical. Hence, our results are in agreement with those from similar projects reported during the past 20–25 years: they certainly do not support McGehee's position. Since both sexes did equally well on the task, it is predicted that listener gender will have little to no effect on AP-SPID.

The second experiment in the series focused on training; it was based on the possibility that professionals would perform differently than student listeners (18, 20, 21). The question asked was: 'Might the drop-off between the judgments of contemporary and noncontemporary speech be due, in part anyway, to the *relative* inexperience of the student auditors?' Accordingly, we compared their responses to those obtained from a group of 'professionals' consisting of eight phoneticians with both advanced degrees and experience with speaker identification tasks. Replications were carried out for the 0–4 week and 0–20 year contrasts. The phoneticians did strikingly better at both tasks (see Table 3.1); this difference was, of course, expected (18, 20). In any event, the data underscored the fact that trained, experienced phoneticians can be expected to carry out speaker identification tasks in a manner substantially superior to individuals who do not enjoy similar backgrounds and experience.

Listeners	*N*	Contemporary (%)	Noncontemporary (%)
A. Latency: 4 weeks			
Phoneticians	5	100	89
Students	67	93	76
B. Latency: 20 years			
Phoneticians	8	100	74
Students	41	98	33

Table 3.1
Comparison of the responses of the experienced phoneticians with those of student listeners. From Hollien and Schwartz (17).

The third investigation in the series was designed to determine if (at least) one type of a 'distractor' could interfere with listeners ability to carry out accurate speaker identification tasks. There is some evidence that such might be the case (22–26). Except for the experimental factor, the procedures employed were virtually identical to those used in all projects cited here. That is, the experimental tape recording used in this case consisted only of pairs of speakers who were 'sound-alikes' (brothers, fathers and sons, and so on). We postulated that these built-in talker similarities would degrade the discrimination task, but if they did not, correct identification scores in the neighborhood of 75–80% would occur. However, a more serious reduction than expected occurred (note Figure 3.3). As can be seen, the listener groups performed appropriately when

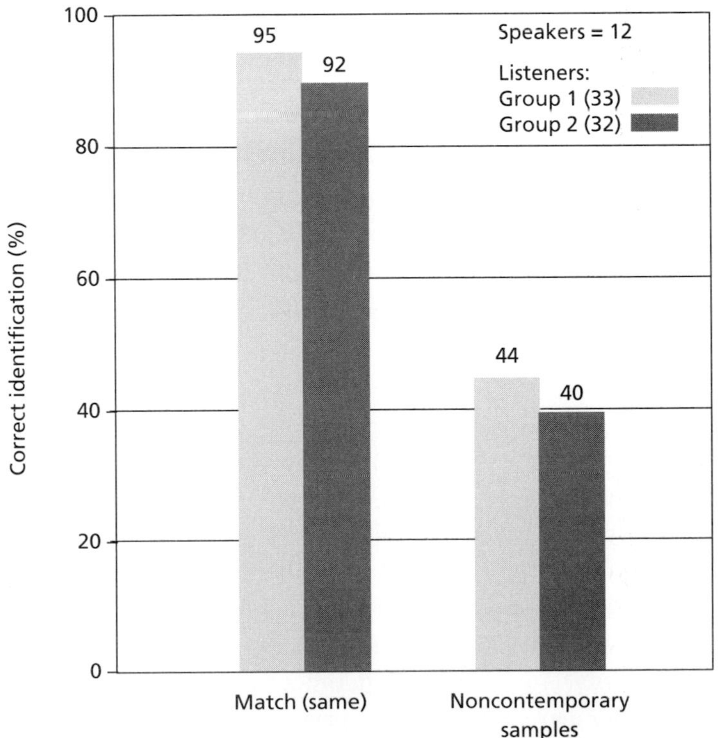

Figure 3.3
Correct identification levels for two groups of listeners who responded to both contemporary and noncontemporary speech samples with a 4-week time separation. The speakers were pairs of individuals who sounded like each other. From Hollien and Schwartz (17).

the contemporary utterances were presented (i.e., at the 94% level). However, their scores dropped sharply when the 'distraction' of sound-alike speakers was confounded with the fairly short time separation of 4 weeks. Note the marked reduction (to 42%); it is well beyond that which would be expected for the latency alone. Moreover, this level was close to Rothman's even though his delay was but a week and only about half of his speakers were sound-alikes. As stated, the research literature abounds with lists of possible sources of degradation (27–30): hence, at least some reduction in accuracy was predicted. What was not expected was the extent of the drop. Quite obviously, a number of factors here must be researched if human performance in this area is to be better understood.

In summary, the SPID experiments using noncontemporary speech have pretty much ruled out the (previously) predicted reduction in a listeners capability to identify individuals from samples made at different points in time. Rather, it appears that this factor can be expected to create only minor problems in the SPID process. Experienced professionals (at least) should be able to perform well even when the separations are in the order of decades. Of course, a particular individual might show behaviors sufficiently different from the group to be counted as an exception (or an outlier), but it would be expected that most people would exhibit the patterns reported above. Finally, it does not appear that machine processing will be greatly affected by the use of noncontemporary speech.

BACK TO GENDER AND TRAINING

Now that two of the major issues have been resolved – or, at least, reviewed – it should be possible to return to a more traditional form of discussion. But first, you undoubtedly will have noticed that two listener characteristics already have been introduced. They are listener gender and the effects of training. It should be useful to revisit them, at least briefly, even though they already have been partly covered.

GENDER ISSUES

As will be remembered from the earlier discussions, the relationships between gender and identification accuracy, while a little variable, did not lead to male–female differences. That is, while McGehee (1) suggested that male auditors can be expected to perform at levels better than those for women, a later study (23) tended to portray females as somewhat superior. On the other hand, most investigators have reported that, other things being equal, the sexes do not appear to differ a great deal with respect to SPID accuracy (4, 5, 17, 19,

30). But what does this tell us? It probably means that, when all the data are considered, men and women will perform equally well on perceptual tasks of this type. It is conceded, of course, that you might draw a person of one sex, or even a group, that is better (or worse) than the other but such would be the exception, not the rule.

At this juncture, it seems convenient to consider a reverse, but somewhat related, issue. The question here is: can listeners accurately identify the sex of the speaker? At first glance, the answer would appear obvious as, in most cases, this task should be an easy one. You simply listen to the speaker's fundamental frequency (F0) plus, perhaps, to the more subtle aspects of his or her vowel production. If you are careful, you should be able to identify the speaker's gender accurately and do so with but minimal effort. That is, you should be successful (31, 32), unless they are among that small population who have F0s and vowel formants that lie between those for men and women, or if they are transsexuals attempting to speak in a manner consistent with their new gender (33–35). Indeed, there is some evidence (37–39) that you can make reasonably accurate judgments of gender simply by listening to a speaker's consonants (or even, just their fricatives). However, please remember that identification of a speaker's sex is but a byproduct of the task at hand. The main job, of course, is to identify the individual. Nonetheless, the AP-SPID, as related to a person's gender, is a facet of the entire process; we must be aware of it if we are to develop a reasonably good understanding of this sector in the SPID domain.

TRAINING

The relationship between identification accuracy and training also was considered earlier; it will be reviewed again in Chapter 4. About now, you certainly must be thinking: 'Why is this author being so redundant?' Well, a discussion of training is germane to all three of these sections. Hence, where should I put it? Why, in all three places, of course.

First, you undoubtedly are aware by now that phoneticians ordinarily will do better (to much better) at perceptual identification tasks. They will do so especially if their training includes experience with forensics and if they intelligently structure the assessment procedures they use. In the section that follows, however, we are interested more in describing professionals simply as listeners rather than how they would go about doing their job. DeJong (27), among others, has addressed this issue. She suggests that 'while general training in Phonetics [will] increase identification accuracy only slightly, specific training in forensic phonetics [will] improve it considerably.' In support of this postulation, she refers to Hirson and Duckworth (40), Hollien and Thompson (41), Huntley (42); Köster (18); Nerbonne (43) and Shirt (21). Although DeJong's position is essentially correct, several of her references actually describe tasks that are only tangential to SPID. However, a number of core studies do exist and these are fundamentally relevant to the issue. If you will permit me to review three (two of which are also listed by DeJong), you should be able make up your own mind about the controversy (albeit a minor one) which exists in this area.

First, DeJong's argument that general training will only slightly favor the phoneticians in SPID tasks is pretty much based on Shirt's 1984 report (21). That investigator developed a procedure based on 74 recorded voices provided by the British Home Office. She then had 20 phoneticians and an equal number of untrained 'controls' carry out three fairly difficult listening tasks. A total of 40 phoneticians (not forensic phoneticians, however) were contacted; of the 26 who responded, 20 were used in the experiment. The speaker 'group' was large and the sample short but the auditors were permitted to use all the time they wished (1–14 h) in completing the task. Essentially, she found that, while the top 'naive' subject did about as well as the best of the phoneticians, the professionals, overall, did rather better than the untrained subjects. Thus, the contention here can be argued either way; i.e., that (1) phoneticians can be expected to do somewhat better at SPID than the lay public or (2) that training in phonetics results in only a minor advantage. However, it also should be noted that neither of the groups in the Shirt research apparently used the structured systems of the type ordinarily employed by modern forensic phoneticians. This limitation is a rather important one as it may be expected that judgments based on well-organized procedures will be superior to those which are restricted and/or general. This 'leveling' process may mute the differences between the two classes of listeners.

The second study finds Köster (18) reporting that his phoneticians did very much better at a SPID task than did his controls (students). These groups were contrasted in several experiments where all were asked to identify people that they knew. Again, unstructured procedures were used, as were rather short speech samples. However, in this case, not one of the phoneticians made even a single error. The third study (20) was carried out with native speakers of German. Talkers were six individuals who read a rather long passage (in German); the two listener cohorts consisted of 10 forensically experienced phoneticians and 17 untrained individuals. Eighteen samples (half over the telephone) were obtained for each of the six speakers; they then were randomized ($N = 108$) onto an experimental tape. The 27 listeners (both groups) were first provided training so as to familiarize them with the voices and then they were played the experimental tape. Their task was to identify each of the six speakers whenever their voices occurred. Schiller and Köster report that the phoneticians correctly identified the target voices (they called them 'hits') 98% of the time whereas the controls only achieved a level of 92% correct; the difference between these means was statistically significant. Listener selection of a foil as the target (an error) also was assessed. This 'false alarm' rate also was found to be different, i.e., 1% vs. 2%, respectively. Of course, this study relates more to earwitness line-ups than it does to basic research on AP-SPID. Nevertheless, it provides additional support for the position that formal training in the phonetic sciences is advantageous when one works in the area. Indeed, I have observed the dynamics of that relationship down through the years and have records of the performances of: (1) trained phoneticians, (2) phoneticians in training and (3) untrained controls when they attempted aural-perceptual tasks. The subjects with relevant training consistently scored higher than did the others.

In summary, it appears clear that trained professionals can carry out speaker identification procedures in a manner superior to that exhibited by untrained individuals. Phoneticians ordinarily can do so even under conditions where they (1) have but minimal training in *forensics,* (2) are unfamiliar with the talkers, (3) face an unstructured evaluation process and/or (4) are provided with only limited samples. It now appears clear that specialized training in forensics, plus the use of systematic and structured aural-perceptual procedures, will permit this class of professionals to perform reasonably well in forensic-based identification.

Yet another aspect of this situation can be assessed when the students who are used as listeners are considered. Subjects of that type simply are not typical 'lay' listeners, primarily because they are educated and often have backgrounds in phonetics, linguistics and/or speech. Moreover, before they are used, they usually have to demonstrate that they (1) have normal hearing, (2) are able to carry out the SPID tasks at reasonable levels of competency and (3) will perform well, at least when the task is optimal (contemporary samples, high-fidelity recording conditions, etc.). Thus, it can be expected that students ordinarily will perform better than will the lay public. These advantages undoubtedly serve to mute the separation between the student-subjects and the professionals. However, they still cannot be expected to match the performance of the latter group. Further, the differences between these two classes of listeners will be even greater when conditions are degraded in some manner.

Let us now proceed to new issues. For your convenience, I have attempted to group them into related clusters.

ISSUES INVOLVING THE SPEECH SAMPLE

At least two aspects of speech sample presentation appear to affect listeners when they attempt SPID: one is the size or duration of the sample and the other is its acoustic quality. Sample duration will be considered first.

When the nineteenth century US President, Abraham Lincoln was asked how long his legs were, he replied, 'Long enough to reach the ground.' The same is true in relation to the length of speech samples when they are used in forensic speaker identification. If you are attempting an analysis, you naturally will want them to be long enough to permit you to be successful. Künzel (44) for example, indicates that, as a rule, the German BKA (Bundeskriminalamt) requires that at least 30 sec. of speech be available if they are to attempt any type of speaker identification. There is no question that a sample of this magnitude is most desirable but can SPID be successfully carried out even if duration is compromised? Perhaps we can better understand the potential limitations here if we consider the available research. Most of it is at once off the mark and yet basic to it. Consider the following example; in 1954, Pollack *et al.* (45) published a study in which they report that identification accuracy can be improved by increasing speech sample duration but that these increases will only occur for periods of up to about 1200 ms (1200 ms equals 1.2 sec.). For longer periods, they say, accuracy does not seem to be related to duration but rather to the speaker's phonemic repertoire. These statements have bothered me for some time as I find it difficult to 'enhance repertoire' without also increasing the duration of the speech sample. Perhaps the discussion to follow will help in clarifying this relationship.

Consider what other researchers have reported (46–48). Several of them also have studied the effects of utterance duration on the identification task. They appear to agree with Pollack's group in that their data suggest that levels of correct speaker identification correlate with utterance duration only for brief periods of time and that longer productions are important because they permit listeners to sample a greater corpus of the speaker's phonemes, phrases, speech patterns, and so on (3, 30, 49). In fact, one of these authors (30) insists that the greater the opportunity one has to listen to a particular speaker the 'greater the accuracy of identification.' He supports his position here by indicating that he has found accuracy to improve when samples were increased from 3 min to 8 min (4, 50). However, he warns that the false positives often will increase in parallel with this rise in correct identification. He notes also that, even though rather long samples were used right from the start, the increases in accuracy were sustained as he continued adding to sample size. These data suggest that people unconsciously process and store what they hear in real time but keep adding to the sets as new stimuli are encountered. However, it also should be stressed that, even though listeners may quickly organize and store these memories, stable and efficient recall may take a while. As an example most of you have heard your Mom speak literally thousands of times. Thus, her voice should be easy to recognize. On the other hand, precise recognition of your new friend (from just his voice) may not occur for several weeks. Why? Primarily because it will take that long for you to process a large enough amount of his speech into a reliable system of memory patterns. So, how do these studies relate to sample duration? They suggest that, even though Künzel makes a strong point about sample size, the half-minute cutoff he specifies should not be considered absolute. Of course, the 10-sec. (or 10-word) minimum suggested by certain other forensic specialists may be less than marginal. Yet, it occasionally may be possible to evaluate samples falling (timewise) between these two boundaries, at least where the conditions are favorable.

The second issue in this section relates to sample quality or fidelity. First, it is a given fact that, if you cannot hear the person who is speaking (because of a signal which is too faint, noise which is too loud, or similar), you cannot make any identification at all. Moreover, listener performance will be limited if the speech signal can be heard but is seriously degraded by the presence of (1) multiple speakers, (2) whispered speech, (3) utterances in unusual voice registers (vocal fry or falsetto, for example), (4) speech materials of an obscure nature, (5) speakers whose utterances overlap, and so on. The identification accuracy even of known speakers can deteriorate under these conditions (46, 48, 51–53). These factors are presented first because they relate to the *quality* of the sample not its acoustic fidelity. Hence, they often are, but should not be, overlooked.

As would be expected, acoustic conditions can seriously damage sample quality. The two most harmful are noise and limited bandwidth. As we have discussed, noise can take many forms: it can be broad band or narrow band, steady state or intermittent. It can be 'noise' even though the signal is not aperiodic in nature. That is, competing signals such as speech by others, music, etc., can interfere with the AP-SPID process (or any form of SPID for that matter). Signals of this type are cleverly referred to as 'forensic noise.' In any case, noise in any form can mask or distort the speech signal produced by the talker you are trying to identify. The louder the noise, the greater the problem; the larger the number of its frequencies which reside within the speech band (defined as, roughly, 350–3500 Hz or 250–4000 Hz), the more serious the problem. As you can see, when the frequency band of the noise is combined with its strength and internal frequency patterns, the problem can become a complex one. For example, a loud, broad band, steady-state noise constitutes a greater threat to successful SPID than would a narrow band of low-energy, intermittent noise. However, while there is little question that the presence of noise can degrade the SPID process, a judicial use of filters (both digital and analog), plus other apparatus, can mitigate its effects. For a more complete discussion of this problem and its remedies, see the sections on channel distortions and speech enhancement in Hollien (28).

Another factor which can reduce speaker identification accuracy is that of

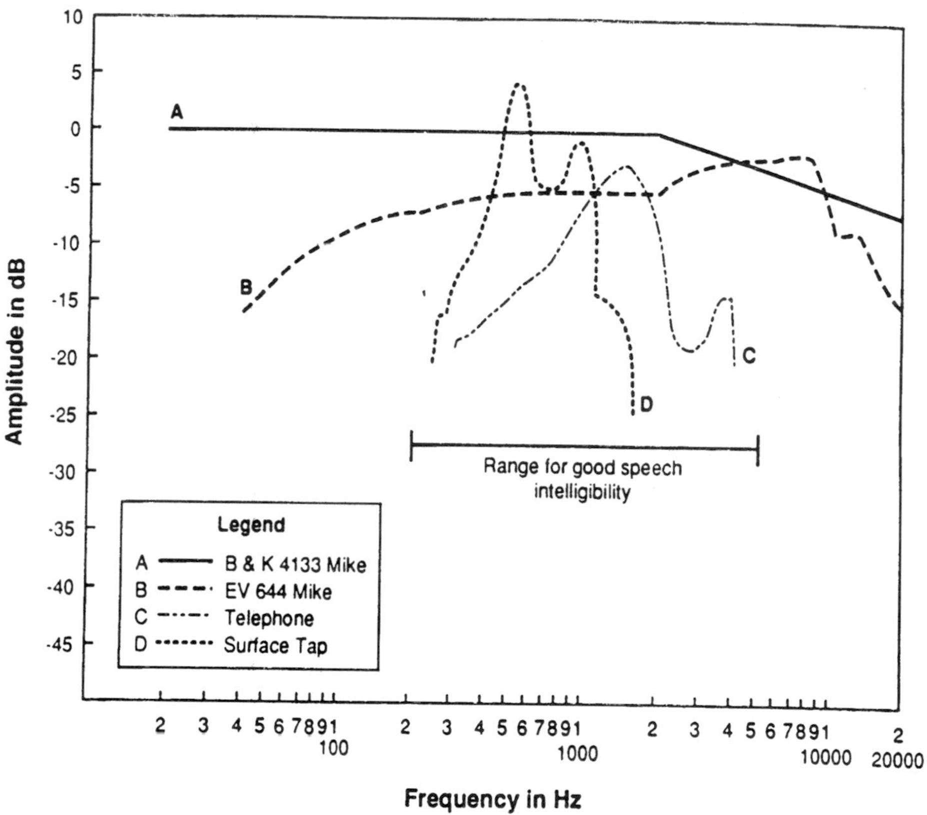

Figure 3.4

The frequency response of commonly used microphones. Note the variation in frequency bandwidth and frequency response within each band; both are important to speech transmission. These curves are based upon the means of the actual measurements of 2–4 copies of each microphone type.

limited signal (frequency) bandwidth. While this problem can result from operation of a number of electronic devices, its most common source is the telephone. Indeed, some telephone or microphone characteristics are so sharply limited (see Figure 3.4) that any signal passing through them will be degraded (28, 44) and speaker recognition rates can suffer. Techniques exist which can aid in mitigating the effects of limited frequency passband, but they are not as easy to use as those which can be applied to counteract levels of low energy (in that case, you turn up the gain and filter out the noise) or even most types of noise. On the other hand, the degrading effects of reduced frequency response are not usually as debilitating as are the others. Reasonably effective SPID can be carried out on speech obtained over a telephone link (28, 54–57) hence, this factor, by itself, will rarely preclude acceptable speaker identification.

FAMILIARITY WITH THE SPEAKER

We now come to the nasty issue of 'familiarity.' What happens to AP-SPID if the listener (always the listener, dear reader, always the listener) is 'familiar' with the speaker's voice? And, how does 'familiar' differ from 'very familiar' or, conversely, from 'kind of familiar' or 'just barely familiar'? Information provided by relevant investigators should permit us to make reasonable decisions here. First, however, it would be useful to consider how forensic phoneticians judge the layman who is about to become a SPID witness; that is, how we judge those individuals who say they are 'familiar' with a particular speaker's voice. You probably would opine that if the witness in question intimately knows the talker and their speaking characteristics, they should be able to identify that person and do so easily. True, but practitioners sometimes face the challenge of intelligently determining if that individual *actually* does know the talker and does so well enough to make the identification. It is not just that we must be accurate for the sake of both the witness and the suspect, we also must provide detectives, prosecutors, defense attorneys and/or trial judges with the information they need if, in turn, they are to be effective and responsible. In any event, it sometimes is necessary to assess the witnesses' (i.e., the listeners') strengths, skills, reliability, weaknesses and so on. If we find that they are competent to carry out the task, we can recommend that they simply do it. In these cases, there is no need to create an earwitness line-up or for the forensic phonetician to ply his trade either perceptually or by firing up their computers. If the witness in question is marginally competent, we then have to make an assessment as to whether they should be allowed to participate at all and, if permitted to do so, under what limitations. If we are to make responsible judgments, we must dip into the available research and our own experience. But, first, the research.

The question: what do we know about *levels* of familiarity and how do they affect the ability of a witness to make accurate judgments about speakers? Fortunately, a rather large body of research exists, one that addresses these assumptions either directly or, at least, tangentially. In turn, the results and findings here can be used to make the cited decisions. As a start, permit me to review a study we carried out some years ago (24). The objectives of this research were several: we sought to (1) assess the importance of auditors being acquainted with the talker's speech,(2) estimate their ability to resist the effects of disguise and stress and (3) determine if a foreign language can affect the recognition process. For the present discussion we will discuss only the first of these issues. The speakers for these experiments were 10 adult males that we recorded uttering 'standard' speech samples when speaking (1) normally, (2) under stress (electric shock) and (3) when attempting disguise. Three classes of listeners heard the sample under highly controlled conditions; they included

(1) a group of individuals who were very familiar with all 10 talkers, (2) a group of listeners who did not know the talkers but who were trained to identify them and (3) auditors who neither knew the talkers (they were 'trained' also) nor understood the language being spoken. As may be seen from Figure 3.5, significantly different performances were observed among and between the three cohorts. Note that the listeners who knew the talkers performed very well indeed (even in their response to disguise) and that none of the other groups approached their levels. These data certainly demonstrate that listeners who

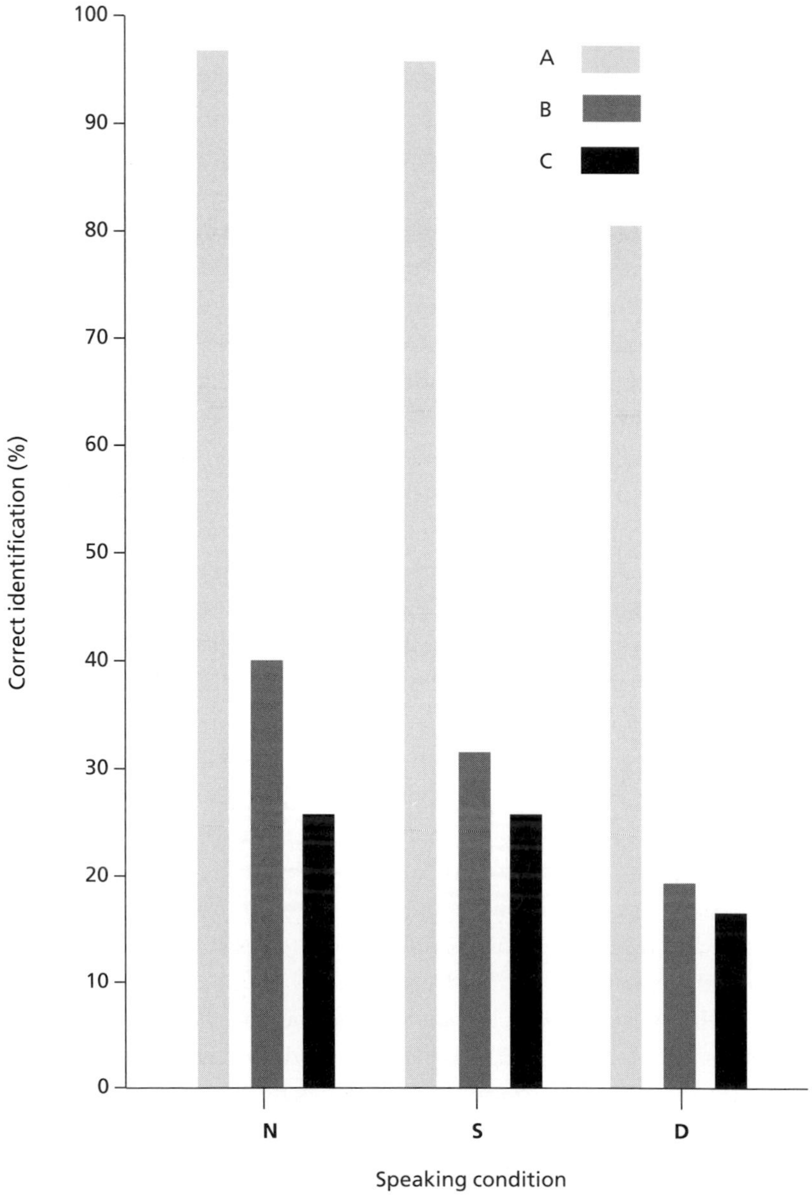

Figure 3.5
The mean (correct) AP-SPID of 10 talkers speaking under the conditions of N = normal, S = stress and D = disguise. Three listener groups consisted of: (A) individuals that knew the talkers very well, (B) listeners that did not know the talkers but who were trained to recognize them and (C) those that were trained similarly but did not know English nor the talkers. The task was to name each speaker for all six of his presentations out of a total of 60. From Hollien et al. *(24).*

know the speaker can be expected to identify them almost all of the time and do so even under difficult to very difficult conditions. Such was the case here; i.e., each 'experimental' talker had produced two samples each of the three types of speech (i.e. normal, stressed and disguised) for an overall total of 60 samples. All 60 were randomized and played serially to the listeners who had to identify the speakers *by name* each and every time they heard their voice. It was concluded that, if auditors could do well under these very tough conditions, it is reasonable that they should be able to achieve very high accuracy levels when conditions were optimum or near optimum. Thus, we feel that we have answered the first question in the affirmative. That is, people who are *very* familiar with speakers can accurately identify them.

While not all researchers report data as compelling as ours, many come close, at least, when conditions were favorable (58–63). Moreover, performances that are as good or better than these can be expected if the auditors are reasonably well trained (18, 20). However, the relationships cited are not as robust or clear-cut when other factors intervene. Hence, it still may not be wise to take the witnesses' claims at face value as these problems can lead to uneven performances. But, what are the boundaries here?

A fairly good 'rule of thumb' for establishing the familiarity of a listener with a talker, is that they should have good hearing and have heard the target speaker's voice fairly regularly over a period of around 2 years. This loose set of criteria is often employed in the courtroom (perhaps the judges involved are correct in their thinking but perhaps they are not). A second approach is one which may provide yet better guidelines. In this case, the ability of the listener/witnesses is tested directly. This procedure involves adopting the ear-witness line-up approach except that it is administered before the witness testifies. If they are correct in their judgments, the court can properly accept their testimony. Please consult Chapter 5 for information as to how to organize and carry out such a test.

The second group of listeners are those who are only 'somewhat familiar' with a person's speech or who have been 'trained' to recognize it. Unfortunately, they probably will not make reliable witnesses. Do you disagree? If so, please note Figure 3.5 again. As you will see, only those listeners who were intimately acquainted with the speakers provided high identification scores. The other groups did not do so even though they were 'trained' to recognize the speakers. Other research supports this relationship (64, 65). So we can test these people if we wish but both the lawyers and the courts will usually be disappointed with their performance. Occasionally, a listener of this type will be able to recognize a speaker even though they have not heard his voice very often at all. The problem is that you will not know just who these better listeners are and, hence, you (and the courts) can be misled.

Other events and factors can serve to reduce a person's competency to recognize familiar voices. Such degradation can occur if the utterances in question are distorted in some manner, are very short (65) or involve 'sound-alikes' (12, 16, 66). Yet, you certainly must agree that the research cited demonstrates that witnesses can be expected to accurately identify talkers if they know them very well. Moreover, if they do, they also should be able to make the identifications under somewhat difficult circumstances. Decreases in identification accuracy will correlate with reductions in familiarity. Please remember also that accuracy will vary somewhat depending upon conditions both internal and external to the witness. Finally, while these relationships have but minimal relevance to earwitness line-ups (Chapter 5) or where the professional is conducting a structured examination (Chapter 4), they are important when it is necessary to judge if an individual (in court or participating in an investigation) is familiar enough with the talker's speech to be able to identify them accurately.

PROBLEMS ORIGINATING WITH THE SPEAKER

To reiterate, AP-SPID is about what the listener does and how they do it. Nonetheless, some of the speaker's behaviors can affect (or disrupt) how well the listener performs when attempting a SPID task. Among the more important variables here are attempts at disguise (the speaker), the presence of psychological stress or emotion (either for the speaker or the listener) and the language being spoken (the speaker). But, before discussing them, it might be useful to consider a few speaker-related factors that sometimes are important but about which little can be done (usually anyway). The first concerns the size of the speaker population. Not very much specific research has been carried on this issue for, after all, it is logical to assume that the more speakers there are in a group, the greater will be the difficulty in identifying one of them. Some data which support this postulate are available but they were obtained when investigators varied population size for other purposes. Conversely, the smaller the population from which the target speaker must be selected, the 'easier' will be the task. Trying to select a single talker from a pool of 50–60 suspects will not just take a lot longer, it will also be much more difficult to do correctly. Conversely, if the suspect pool consists of only two or three suspects, the task will not be as formidable. The problem here is that you do not have functional control over the size of speaker population.

Another area that is difficult, if not impossible, to control, but which can have a material effect on identification accuracy, is the uniqueness of the speaker's voice. A voice that has few (if any) distinctive features will be less recognizable (and harder to separate from the crowd) than will one that exhibits one or more idiosyncracies (7, 49, 50, 67–69). For example, a lisp is difficult to disguise;

if you have one it will mark you. Kay Francis (a prominent US motion picture actress in the 1930s) was sometimes referred to as 'Kay Fwancis'. People did so because she exhibited a /w/ for /r/ substitution. Her voice was fairly recognizable anyway but it did not matter because she usually could be identified from just that single element. Both DeJong (27) and Köster (18) recognize the fact that distinctive voices are easy to identify; so do Papcun *et al.* (7) who studied the issue when they investigated recognition decay for unfamiliar voices. They report that the speakers who were classed as 'hard-to-remember' were more often confused with others than were those who were classed as 'easier-to-remember'. These authors use the term 'prototype' in order to classify those voices that exhibited idiosyncratic (or 'extra') features. While such individuals may not be unique in all respects, the idiosyncratic characteristics that they do possess can make them most identifiable. In any event, if a speaker's patterns in some way differ from the norm, identification robustness can be materially increased. Forensic phoneticians may not be able to control this factor but it can work for them.

This statement (i.e., the one immediately above) can be illustrated by a case I refer to as 'Brother-My-Brother.' It took place some years ago and proved to be one of those odd events that can happen to anyone as they trundle their way through a career. It serves to illustrate the effect unique voices can have on the speaker identification process.

It all started when a couple of families – *entire* families – began warring with each other. Both seemed to have a pretty good case for their side but, since they appeared to really hate each other, they attacked in ways that were both honorable and a little bit shady. Kind of like the Hatfields and the McCoys, I guess. Worse yet, one of the families was Jewish and the other was not. Thus, when members of the Jewish family began to receive really fearsome threats over the telephone – threats that were couched in the kind of anti-semitic rhetoric that undoubtedly was directed at Jewish families by the Nazis – the police were called in. Their investigation was 'aided' by the fact that several of the family members thought they recognized the caller as the head of the other clan. The accusation appeared to be supported by the fact that he exhibited a couple of rather unique speaking characteristics, and similar ones could be heard in the speech of the caller. Accordingly, he was arrested, indicted and tried for what would now be called a 'hate' crime.

Through all of this, the man was adamant about his innocence. He conceded that his voice sounded like the one on the telephone, but he *insisted* that he had not made any of the calls. It simply was *not* his voice. His position here appeared pretty much irrelevant as most individuals accused of a crime claim not to have committed it. That he was a leader in his community also was irrelevant; leading citizens sometimes commit crimes. Nevertheless, his attorney acceded to his wishes that an 'expert' be retained to compare his voice (from an exemplar) to that of the person who had made those truly dreadful telephone calls.

When I first listened to the tapes, I was struck by certain distinctive speech features – two in particular – that could be heard on all of the samples. One was an odd distortion within a common consonant cluster and the other was a rather unique prosodic (or timing) characteristic. These two idiosyncracies resulted in 'voices' seemingly so distinctive – and so alike – that, at first, I thought the defendant was pretty stupid for wasting his money. Nonetheless, I went to work on the samples and, to my surprise, began to discover differences between the voices heard on the exemplar and evidence tapes. When I listened to them casually, they seemed to have been produced by a single person. When I carefully analyzed them, different patterns in the relationships began to emerge. In short, it ultimately became clear that the speech actually had been produced by two different individuals. I then was asked to testify about my findings. Needless to say, I was a little uncomfortable in explaining just how the distinctive characteristics common to both speakers (and easily heard) created the *illusion* that one person had produced all the tapes. It was easier, however, to demonstrate the between-speaker differences. Hence, before long the jury appeared to be learning how to look at the (often subtle) features that were different and, thereby, determine that the two samples undoubtedly were produced by two people. It was hard work and by the time the lunch period arrived, I was ready for a break. As I left the witness stand and approached the defense lawyer, I noticed the defendant's family crowding around him. Then, suddenly, I heard that voice from the evidence tapes. I looked over and saw a man talking to the defendant. Without thinking I said (apparently in a very loud voice), 'that's the man who made the telephone calls!' You can just imagine the uproar that followed. To make a long story short, the man I heard was the defendant' s brother. His speech contained not only the incriminating speech characteristics noted, it also proved to match the other aspects of the caller's speech production. Needless to say, the relevant principals and attorneys spent the lunch period in the judge's chambers.

So, what had happened? The brother was a recently released mental patient (yes, this is a *true* story) who had been 'trying to help out' his relatives in their conflict with the other family. He cheerfully admitted that he had made the calls and his description of what he had said made it clear that he was, indeed, the culprit. The moral of this little tale? Distinctive speech characteristics can be of great help to the SPID process, but do not let them seduce you into an 'analysis' that is anything but rigorously thorough. If I had been sloppy in this instance, the businessman in question might have been convicted for something his brother did. The brother? I am not sure but I think I heard that he had been re-institutionalized.

DISGUISE

The first, and more important of the speaker-based problems, is that of voice disguise. The phrase 'more important' may be too mild in this case since, if the speaker is good at it, the effort can be markedly detrimental to effective SPID of any type. Accordingly, this issue has been the focus of a number of research projects. Sometimes the experimental questions asked are about its effect on voice line-ups, other times the focus is on basic AP-SPID or on which of several forms of disguise are the more effective. What rarely is considered, however, is how one goes about detecting and counteracting such tactics. Neither has very much been written about the strength or severity of the disguise. Accordingly, this discussion will not be just a review of disguise behaviors, I also consider how effective they can be and provide a few of the countermeasures that can be applied to reduce their impact.

Perhaps the most devastating form of disguise is an external alteration of the motor speech act by application of an electronic device. These systems can alter speech so dramatically that it will appear to have been created by a machine or, perhaps, by a 'monster' of the type often found in the movies. Gone is information about fundamental frequency and gone are the usual cues about vowel formants and articulation; even timing can be blurred. Very little research on these systems has been reported (70), but the little data available have pretty much demonstrated that SPID attempts on machine-distorted speech are futile. About the only good news is that, when used, they are easy to recognize.

Another type of disguise which can sharply degrade the SPID process is one where the talker speaks in a whisper (26, 30, 49). What happens in this case is that whispering tends to eliminate (or at least reduce) information about fundamental frequency (F0) or heard pitch (level, inflections, etc.). It also reduces the available information about vocal intensity, voice quality and, to a lesser degree, prosody or speech timing (primarily because of compensatory over-articulation). Comparing whispered speech to whispered speech is not all that easy and whisper-modal voice comparisons are even more challenging. Whispering can certainly stress almost any form of speaker identification.

A number of types of speaker disguise have been studied (8, 13, 24, 40, 65, 71). They range from the use of bite blocks or pencils (72, 73) to shifts in phonatory level (26, 68, 72) and to free disguise (24, 26, 74). All these investigators have found that any attempt at disguise interferes with the identification process, at least, to some extent. To illustrate, Reich and Duke (26) studied the perceptual effects of a number of different types of disguises; they report that strong nasal speech and free disguise were most damaging. Hollien *et al.* (39) tend to agree with them at least with respect to free disguise but point out that listeners who know the talkers are still able to correctly identify them about 80%

of the time and that they can do so even under fairly difficult conditions. However, Masthoff (72) casts gloom on this picture as he reports that listeners experience increased difficulty with the identification task when more than one speech characteristic is varied simultaneously. Of course, multiple speech shifts usually are what happens when a speaker employs free disguise. If successful (and many will be), their efforts can degrade the identification process whether it is aural-perceptual, machine based or both.

So, are there any remedies? There are a few, but first it is important to determine if the talker is attempting to alter, or not alter, his or her speaking mode. The good news is that Reich (74) has discovered that people can usually tell when the speaker is attempting voice disguise. Even better, attempts at disguise do not appear to be all that common. Yet, if criminals think that their 'speaking identity' is important, you may be sure that they will consider attempts at disguise. If their decision is in the affirmative, they will endeavor to thwart the examiner's efforts by obscuring or changing their speaker-dependent features. The criminal often will be more successful during the period when they are committing the crime than later, when their (speech) exemplar is being made as, in the latter instance, you will have some control over what they do. Nevertheless, you should attempt to discover if they are trying (or have tried) to modify their speech. It is important to be aware of this problem at all levels – when evaluating the evidence tape, when talking to them (if you do) and/or when making or assessing the exemplar. A search for speaking inconsistences sometimes can be helpful, especially if they aid in determining when 'breaks' in the attempted voice disguise occur. For example, if the suspect's speaking patterns change markedly at some point, the added set of characteristics might provide information about his normal or ordinary mode of speaking. Indeed, it is very difficult to consistently disguise ones voice over long periods of time. If the sample is short, the problem can be severe. If the sample is reasonably long, there may be ways to identify which parts are 'normal' and which parts are not. This determination alone can reduce the effectiveness of the attempted voice disguise.

Other people can sometimes aid with the SPID process, especially if they are willing to do so. In the case of the 'Killer Liked Red', the murderer's violence was triggered by the color of his victim's dress. He would rape them and then stab them to death with a hand tool. After a while he either began to repent or at least grow weary of his perversions. At this point he started calling the police and asking them to stop him. He attempted voice disguise in his early calls but later reduced this effort. Thus, when he ultimately was arrested; a voice match with the telephone confessions was possible. Unfortunately, when faced with life in prison, the defendant recanted and claimed to be innocent. He had his lawyers challenge the entire SPID process as well as the specific procedures employed. The issue became moot, however, because his wife apparently realized that the voice heard on the later tape recordings was his and said so. At this point he pleaded guilty. It is always nice to have your judgments verified even if the process is not a scientific one. The point here, however, is that someone who knew the target voice aided the SPID process.

Somewhat better control over the situation is possible if the disguise attempt comes after the suspect has been identified and arrested but subsequently endeavors to thwart the speaker identification process. In this case, procedures for getting the best exemplar recording possible should be followed and protocols for doing so have been developed by a number of practitioners. For example, the criteria established by P. A. Hollien (75) have been found to be quite effective; a copy of these instructions is included in the next chapter. Note especially, that this author recommends a rather long verbal interchange. That is, if disguise attempts seem possible, the suspect should be required to produce a lot of speech and different types of it (reading, conversation, etc.). If necessary, attempts even should even be made to 'stress' them a little. In any event, just as a good polygraph examiner can sometimes coax a confession out of a suspect, a good forensic phonetician often can inveigle the speaker-suspect to produce utterances in their normal speaking mode. Here also, individuals who have heard the suspect speak under ordinary conditions can be asked if the voice on the tape recordings is typical of his or her everyday discourse.

Over time, the forensic phonetician learns skills that can assist in developing good investigational materials for SPID. Such endeavors are not, as yet, an exact science. However, as long as he is aware of his limitations, and the hazards inherent in the process, reasonably effective SPID *may* be carried out even in the face of attempts at voice disguise.

STRESS AND EMOTIONS

This issue is a rather nasty one. Not because it creates particularly difficult problems for the listener but because so little is known about how these conditions actually affect the SPID process. Of course, some general principles have been established as to how stress and emotions will change the characteristics of speech and voice. However, just what they do to speaker identification itself has not yet been studied in any great detail. Let us start with psychological stress. The primary thrust of my discussion here will be about: (1) how stress, plus arousal, affect voice and (2) what these relationships *might* do to the SPID process. Before proceeding, however, please let me point out that, while our discussions about psychological stress will focus on what this behavior does to a speaker's performance, the condition of arousal can affect either the listener or the speaker.

Psychological stress involves anxiety, fear and perhaps anger and fatigue (76,

77). A reasonable definition of this condition (78) is that it is a 'psychological state which results in response to a perceived threat and is accompanied by the specific emotions of fear, anxiety and/or anger.' Scherer's definitions (79–81) are similar, except that he adds that the sources of these effects may be either internal or external and that adaptive or coping behavior usually can be expected. An additional question must be asked at this point. What is arousal and are stress and arousal interrelated? Arousal often is defined as an excitation to action from the state of rest or that it will cause the individual to rapidly become more alert in their response to a stimulus. Thus, as far as we can tell, they are related; that is, while stress may or may not be a component of arousal, the reverse nearly always is true.

What are some of the speech/voice characteristics associated with psychological stress? Well, if you were to compile and summarize what is known, you probably would end up with the composite found in Figure 3.6 (28). Portrayed in the figure are the shifts which usually take place in an individual's speech

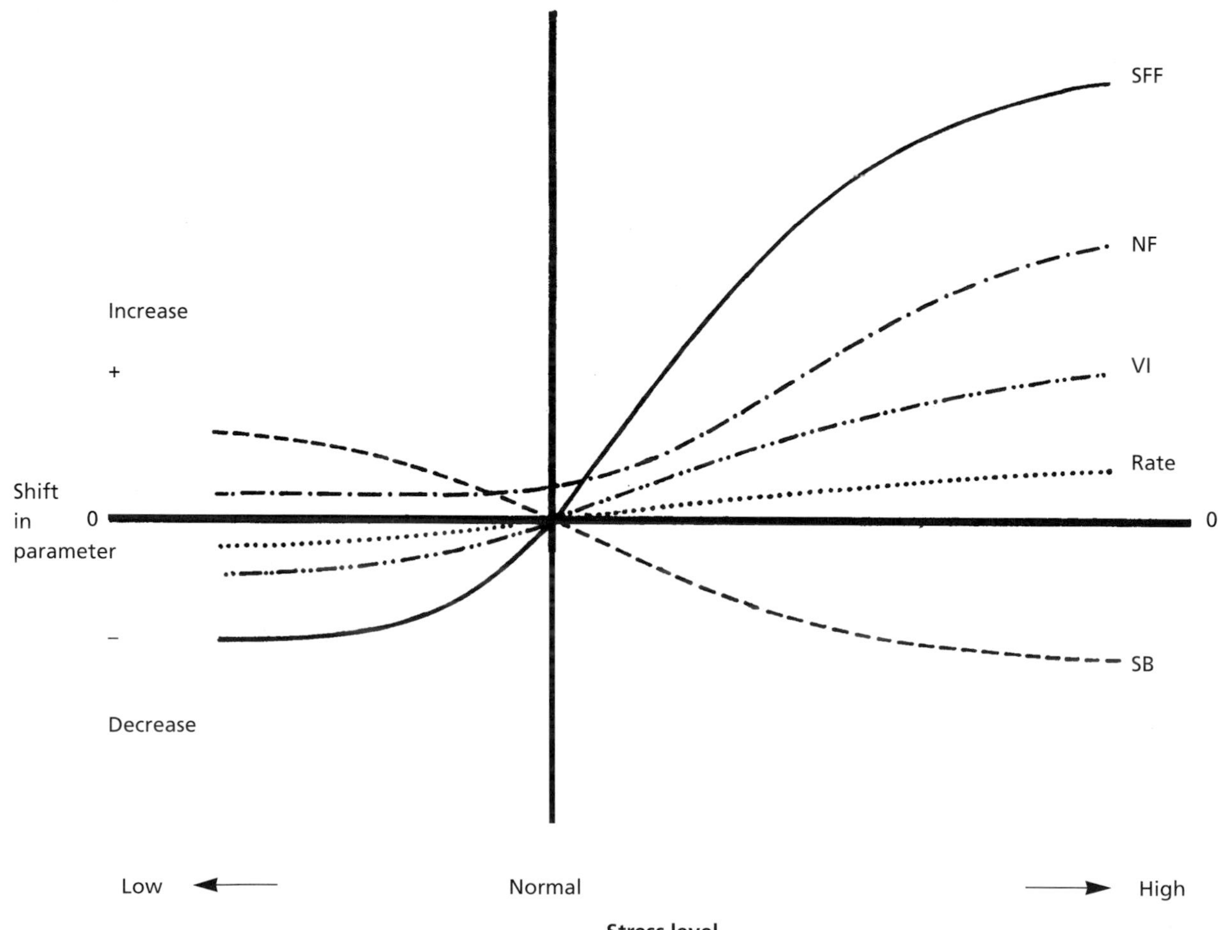

Figure 3.6

Model of the most common shifts in the voice as a function of increasing psychological stress. SFF is speaking fundamental frequency, NF are nonfluencies, VI is vocal intensity, and SB is the number of speech bursts per unit of time. Adapted from Hollien (28).

when that person is stressed. As you can see, voice fundamental frequency (F0 or SFF) will rise, as do the number of nonfluencies. Vocal intensity and speaking rate increase a little and a stressed person tends to talk in longer but fewer speech bursts. As you can see, if a criminal was recorded during a crime, their speech would probably shift in direction from its norm (or neutral state) toward the predicted patterns. Then, later on, if you made a recording of the criminal when he was not particularly stressed, these factors would have shifted back toward their norm and, hence, the SPID process could be somewhat compromised.

Compensatory steps can be taken if the problem is identified and if analysis of those speech parameters or vectors which are less likely to be affected is upgraded. However, a complicating factor is that a small number of people who experience stress will not show these characteristics at all; they even might shift them in other directions. A good example is what happened at the US Navy's Sealab-3 operations in 1969. In retrospect, the project appeared doomed from the start. It was underfunded and hurried, it was in competition with NASA, and there had been a serious shift in command from diving specialists to fleet officers. Most notably, Captain George (Pappy) Bond had been transferred from his prior position to project medical officer. By the time the habitat – under 600 feet of very cold seawater – was to be opened and put into operation, the helium gas used as part of its internal atmosphere had caused leaks. In turn (and because of them), the chamber had to be overpressurized. When the initial team descended, they found that this internal overpressure prevented them from opening the hatches and, hence, they could not enter the habitat. When they tried a second time, they were facing a combination of numbing cold, extreme fatigue and great ambient pressures. It was during this second attempt, that the project's diver-engineer convulsed and died. Worse yet, the remaining three divers quickly reached a point where they were in physical danger and, owing to the severe distortion to their speech caused by the helium and pressure (HeO_2/P), it was almost impossible to understand their calls for help. Pandemonium broke loose topside on the mother ship, Elk River. The various personnel whose voices were recorded all exhibited characteristics of very high stress. That is, except for one person. Suddenly and dramatically, Pappy Bond's voice came over the communication net. He assumed command, organized/calmed the teams, and had the other three aquanauts safely aboard the mother ship's decompression chamber within an hour. The point? Every element within his voice and speech was shifted *away* from (not toward) those characteristics seen in Figure 3.6. Here was a person under unimaginable stress who, when he spoke, violated all of the strictures usually associated with psychological stress in voice. Incidently, he was immediately recognizable to those of us who knew him but then, his speaking characteristics had not materially shifted away from normal.

The related issue here is that of arousal, a condition that can affect either the speaker or the listener. When the speaker is aroused, the condition probably operates in a manner similar to stress. However, the confounding effects may be a little different when the listener is considered. In our research (22, 82), we found that aroused listeners tended to be somewhat better at SPID than people who were not aroused. The two groups we studied did not show statistically significant differences between their performances, but the trend was unmistakable. The tendency was probably muted because the level of arousal was somewhat confounded by the psychological stress experienced by some of the subjects (the procedures administered upset part of one group). Although less clear cut, Yarmey (30) also reported findings that were somewhat similar to those cited. However, his study employed earwitness lineup protocols rather than those consistent with basic research in AP-SPID. Finally, Mayor and Komulainen (83), argue that, as practitioners, they have observed that the victims of extreme violence exhibit high arousal states; they also indicate that they are very accurate at identifying speakers. However, the observations are based on only a small number of witnesses – those who made identifications – rather than on all the victims interviewed.

To summarize. The forensic phonetician should be able to identify – *must* be able to identify, is more accurate – the psychological relationships discussed above; they also should be able to counteract them, at least to some extent. We now know that arousal will tend to enhance a listener's ability to identify speakers and that most individuals will exhibit certain shifts in their speaking characteristics when stressed. When these relationships are detected, compensatory procedures should be applied.

ACCENTS, DIALECTS AND FOREIGN LANGUAGES

The following relationships may or may not enhance identification of the target speaker. What happens depends greatly on the reason the investigation is being conducted, the nature of the procedures employed and the person or persons responsible for the probe. Consider dialect: practitioners very often seize upon the dialect or dialects heard in forensic speech samples and use them as part of their assessment of the speaker's identity. It is appropriate for them to do so. Subsequently, they analyze the dialect suprasegmentally (84, 85), segmentally (sometimes phoneme by phoneme) and in terms of its strength (25, 29, 44). Determination is then made as to whether the dialect is regionally based (within a language, of course) or results from the effects of a foreign language (i.e. the speaker's native language). At this point, the professional compares the dialect found on the evidence tape (the unknown speaker) with that on the exemplar (the known). A finding that both are 'natural' and alike is usually of modest significance. After all, the samples in question could have been produced either by a single speaker or by two different individuals speaking the same dialect. Since many thousands of people could exhibit that particular system, a match simply could not be made on this type of evidence alone. Such comparisons are only really helpful if the dialect is so narrow and so unique that it would be found in but a tiny population of speakers. Conversely, if a different dialect is found in each of the two samples, the analysis becomes quite significant. The presence of two different dialects strongly suggests that the speakers themselves are two different people.

While there is little question that dialect alone can be used as a SPID aid (even by lay listeners), the illustration to follow should provide some insight as to just how this type of assessment can be misleading. Indeed, reliance on dialect alone is especially hazardous when the analysis is a quick and/or casual one (i.e. when neither the time nor appropriate support are available to permit a thorough comparison). In any event, let me be specific. Some time ago we carried out a series of experiments on dialects; the results of a couple of them can be found in Tate (86, 87). Basically, what we did was to study perceptually both speakers and mimics of a Southern American dialect. We did so in order to determine whether this attribute would either enhance or degrade efforts at speaker identification. An attempt to discover if speakers' could use dialect as a voice disguise were also among the project's goals; hence, both trained (actors) and untrained imposters were studied. Speakers who normally spoke with Southern American dialect were recorded, as were the two types of imposters (they uttered the speech materials in both their ordinary dialect and in Southern American). The tapes were then presented to three listener groups, the first cohort spoke in the target dialect (Southern American), the second did not and the third consisted of professional phoneticians and phonologists. All were asked to identify the speaker. As expected, the phoneticians did better at all the different identification tasks, especially at identifying the imitated dialect as deceptive; further, the actors were best at imitating it. However, none of the imposters were able to convince a majority of the listeners that they actually were Southerners. On the other hand, faking a dialect did not appear to interfere very much with the speaker identification process. That is, the scores for the imposters were a little poorer, but not significantly so, when they faked the Southern dialect. Moreover, the listeners said that they were aided somewhat when the dialects were strong.

The effects of foreign dialects on SPID also has been studied (88, 89). Indeed, McGehee (1) included a substudy of this type in the research she carried out in the 1930s. Her results tended to suggest that foreign accent had little effect on the AP-SPID process. Moreover, Goldstein *et al.* (90) agree with her, at least to some extent. That is, the Goldstein group found no differences when their listeners attempted to identify white American, black American and

Chinese speakers (the sample was a long sentence). The recognition of the Chinese was poorest but not significantly so. However, these patterns were exacerbated when the investigators replicated the research with the stimuli reduced to a single word. In addition, their results appear to show relationships that are a little different from those reported by Tate; that is, in their case, the presence of foreign accents had a detrimental effect on the SPID process. It should be noted that the Southern dialect was regional not foreign in the Tate research and the listeners were generally familiar with it. Hence, the two studies may not be directly comparable.

The Schiller and Köster (91) research tends to be more consistent with that reported by the Goldstein group, as does that reported by Thompson (92). These investigators studied English and Spanish, reporting that they always found that listeners did better when they attempted SPID with speakers producing their own language. Again, it is possible that the listeners in our research responded differently because they were presented a regional dialect in their own language. In any case, the presence of foreign dialect does not preclude success in SPID.

Language is a little different as most investigators have come to the conclusion that listeners find it difficult to identify talkers when they are speaking a language other than their own. Köster *et al.* (93) and Köster and Schiller (94) have demonstrated these relationships with the English, German, Spanish and Chinese languages. Köster and Schiller (94) indicate that, while they have found that their 'experts . . . perform much better' than do lay subjects, they still are apprehensive when confronting the problem. Perhaps they have a point but, as I have argued many times previously, the professional does not attempt to make a swift judgment after having heard only a few phrases uttered by the target speakers. The systematic evaluation carried out by the forensic phonetician is much more thorough: it can be exhaustive. The phonetician enjoys extensive training and experience in the area, the availability of many types of tests and equipment, as much time as necessary to conduct the evaluation, and so on. Moreover, the phonetician will be cautious, unbiased and professional when conducting evaluations in this domain.

Finally, what can be said about the *basic* effects of accent, dialect and language. Well, under certain conditions they (especially dialect and accent) can actually aid in the process. In most instances, however, these (especially language) will operate to reduce accuracy. Why do they do so? First, they undoubtedly operate to distract the listener; second, they tend to mute speaker-specific idiosyncracies; third, subtle but useful nuances in the language itself can be masked or lost; and, fourth, they tend to reduce the number of available segmental contrasts. In contrast, no-one has shown experimentally that foreign languages and/or dialects/accents will have a negative effect on SPID when it is carried out by means of appropriate semi-automatic (computer) procedures. We have had experiences of this type with a semi-automatic speaker identification system (SAUSI) and the paralanguage vectors on which it is based (see Chapter 8); in no instance did we experience added difficulty when processing Polish, Spanish, German or Japanese speakers. Thus, it appears that the more serious effects of foreign language and dialect are pretty much confined to AP-SPID by nonprofessionals. The professional may wish to consult with native speakers of the target language but they need to be no more wary of these challenges than with those in other areas.

MORE ABOUT THE LISTENER

It would seem a little strange to include a section on 'the listener' when the chapter is almost entirely about them. However, a few relationships exist which simply cannot be tucked away under any of the other subheadings. They include listener hearing, listener ability and listener age. The first of these, listener hearing, is almost self evident. If the person in question cannot hear acoustic signals, they simply cannot carry out any form of AP-SPID. While DeJong has found that high levels of auditory capability do not correlate particularly well with prowess in speaker identification, there is no question but that this process will be impaired if the listener or witness is experiencing any but the mildest of hearing problems. A minor conductive hearing loss, with no neural component, will probably not interfere to any great extent with the AP-SPID process, especially if high-quality amplification is available; neither will mild neural losses (especially those involving frequencies above 4000 Hz). However, appropriate safeguards can be met here simply by administering a speech reception hearing test (SRT) to the listener. One procedure is to present him with a standardized SRT test at a 'normal' sensation level (about 60 dB). If the subject scores in the 90–100% range, he or she probably can understand speech well enough to make adequate judgments. If the tapes to be heard by the person with a loss are of poor quality or if they score well below 90% on the SRT, a more complete audiological assessment may be justified. This probably would be necessary before a decision could be made as to whether or not the auditor in question is competent to make decisions about utterances heard.

The second issue to be addressed concerns a listener's natural ability to carry out AP-SPID tasks. This relationship involves more than just listener validity and reliability which, in themselves, can be difficult to assess (42, 95, 96). What is of primary importance here is the listener's basic ability to successfully carry out these tasks. For one thing, investigators have observed that, while most auditors exhibit the capabilities necessary for successful AP-SPID, they also display a great range of related skills (25, 27, 28, 97–101). But why this variability? Again, very few researchers have addressed this particular problem. One of the few who did so is DeJong (27). While her research is more completely reviewed in Chapter 5 (where it is most relevant), two of her findings are of consequence here. Basically, she found only two relationships that were robust enough to be called predictors of good SPID ability. They were (1) 'factors that require high level cognitive processing' and (2) 'a high degree of musical ability.' Could it be that the top people in this area are bright musicians? My quip here is much too simplistic, of course; nonetheless, DeJong has opened (and contributed to) a new and important area.

Finally, what about the age of the listener? Is age a factor in predicting (generally anyway) just how good a person will be when they attempt speaker identification? Well, first off it appears that adults (of both sexes) can be expected to perform better than children or elderly adults (5, 23, 97, 100, 102). Infants do not respond with any real accuracy, yet, both Friedlander (103) and Mehler and associates (104) report that some SPID occurs in infants even within the first few months of life. Later, Saito *et al.* (105) studied the ability of children to identify (by voice) their preschool classmates plus some previously unknown children. They report that the average level of correct identification grew from about '20% for 3-year-olds, to 29% for 4-year-olds and 49% for 5-year-olds.' This trend is a rather strong one, is it not? It would appear that, while children are not as good as adults in identifying even known speakers, they should be as successful as they grow older. That is just about what happens (106, 107): by about the age of 10 years, children may reach nearly the same level of competency as adults. However, anyone (including law enforcement personnel and the judiciary) who deals with SPID should be especially cautious when the earwitness is a child or an older adult.

SUMMARY

Before ending this chapter, let me list some of the factors which suggest that useful speaker identification is a possibility. These are the pros which operate in support of the process and can be used as its basis. Following the pros is a list of the cons. They are the parameters or hazards which tend to reduce success in the area. Finally, a series of multiparameter vectors (i.e. complex systems) is provided. They are ones which I believe should be incorporated into the organizational structure of any AP-SPID procedure.

SOME PROS

The parameters or relationships to follow are those which will enhance the perceptual identification task.

1. Speakers who are known to the listener are the easier to identify than those who are not.
2. Unique voices, or those with strong idiosyncratic features, can be identified at very high levels of accuracy.
3. Correct identification level is (better) maintained if the listeners' perception of a talkers' speech is reinforced from time to time. This relationship holds both for listeners who know the speaker and those who do not.
4. Larger speech samples – and those of better quality – permit more accurate aural-perceptual identifications.
5. Listeners can be quite variable in their ability to make speaker recognition judgments. However, some are naturally quite good at this task; they often can be identified by pretesting.
6. Listeners enjoy better success at SPID when they employ the 'natural' speaking characteristics exhibited by humans.
7. Phonetic training enhances success in identifying speakers by voice. Training in forensic phonetics upgrades it further.
8. Accents and dialects can be used to advantage in the process; the presence of foreign languages usually cannot.
9. A structured approach to speaker identification will operate to raise accuracy.

THE CONS

Certain relationships operate to reduce precision in aural-perceptual speaker identification; several of the more important ones follow.

1. Identification will be more difficult if the speaker is not well known to the listener.
2. The greater the number of talkers in a group, the more difficult will be the SPID task.
3. Both system and channel distortions can degrade SPID accuracy.
4. Degradation of talker utterances (especially by disguise) will tend to impair the identification process.
5. Talkers who sound alike can be confused with each other, even by listeners who know them.
6. The greater the time delay after hearing a talker, the more difficult will be speaker identification.

FEATURES USEFUL IN IDENTIFICATION

Evaluation of appropriate relationships inevitably will lead to the postulate that humans attend to certain features within the speech signal and use them in the recognition process. A number of these features have been identified (28, 108) they include the following (by category).

Heard pitch

These parameters include pitch level (high, medium, low), pitch variability and the patterning of pitch usage. Many individuals exhibit habituated structures and patterns, ones that can aid the listener with identification. The acoustic parallels to pitch are, fundamental frequency of voice (SFF, F0) and the shifts/variations within its distribution. Many types of measurements (i.e. of level, variability, phonation-time ratio, etc.) are available for the physical assessment of these parameters.

Articulation

The basic focus in this area is on perceived consonant production (both individually and in clusters) plus the observed vowel formant levels and relationships. A critical aspect of this assessment involves the idiosyncratic production of these speech sounds. That is, to be useful in the identification process, an individual's phoneme production should be, at least, somewhat unique or a little different from that of others. These assessments functionally interface with a number of related speech components. For example, relationships exist between this vector and dialect and between it and measures of coarticulation. Hence, there is little question but that it is profitable to evaluate articulatory characteristics for AP-SPID purposes.

General voice quality

It is well known that the overall quality of a sound-producing mechanism materially aids in the identification of the instrument which is providing the auditory percept. For example, if the same person played the same note (at the same intensity) first on a clarinet and then on a violin, you would be able to either identify each of them (from these signals alone) or, at least, determine that they were two different instruments. The same strategy can be utilized in voice recognition. Again, it is the perception of those acoustic events making up the signal which provide the appropriate information. In humans, it is the signal produced by the source (i.e. the voice emanating from the larynx) combined with the modifying effects of the vocal tract (the oral/pharyngeal/nasal cavities and articulators) which provides 'voice' quality. Thus, the configuration of the entire vocal tract creates the patterns in wave composition (or spectrum) which ordinarily will make you sound more like yourself than other people.

Prosody

The timing of a person's utterances (sometimes referred to as the temporal patterning of speech) can affect the ability to make identifications. Sometimes it seems almost easier to assess these parameters perceptually than it is to carry out quantitative analyses. What we do is listen to how slow or fast a person talks and how smooth or choppy is his word train. In short, the timing and melody of a person's speech can be used to provide cues which establish identity.

Vocal intensity

So far, vocal intensity, while identified as a recognition feature, has not been investigated extensively enough to permit a good understanding of either its general nature or its sensitivity as a speaker-specific parameter. As a matter of fact, what we do know about vocal intensity and its constituent parts suggests it is not a very robust identifier of speakers. Moreover, it is very difficult to determine *absolute* intensity level. The reason for this is that even small variations in the distance or angle between the talker's head and the pickup microphone can result in rather substantial (but erroneous) variations in energy level. Nevertheless, it is obvious that we listen to how loud a person speaks and how they vary vocal intensity when they talk. Accordingly, it is theorized that, if processing can be controlled, perceptual evaluation of this parameter can be useful for speaker identification purposes.

Speech characteristics (segmentals)

This category extends beyond 'assessment of segmentals' and articulation (see above). That is, it starts at analysis of phonemes and continues to the study of: (1) dialect, (2) unusual use of linguistic stress or affect, (3) idiosyncratic pronunciations, (4) coarticulation and (5) speech disorders and similar problems. Incorporating segmentals into an AP-SPID procedure or system is not difficult; they are simply listed along with their means and ranges. Indeed, some forensic phoneticians feature approaches based on their use; all of us include them among our procedures.

. . . AND, FINALLY

By now it should be clear that people who identify each other by voice do so only after carrying out a substantial amount of auditory processing of the voice signal heard. This processing may be completed quickly or over long periods of time. It is accomplished nonetheless and the results of all that processing are stored effectively, or not so effectively, in the person's memory. Thus, a listener may employ all, or only some, of the many (speaker) attributes and relationships listed above when making an identification. However, these perceptions are all most people have to work with; hence, the processing may be quite limited if they are forced to base their decisions on only one or two of the available relationships, or when some of the critical ones are degraded or distorted. Nevertheless, if a sufficient number are available, they can provide a reasonably robust basis for AP-SPID (109) and do so for either the average person or the professional. They certainly will provide a basis for the forensic phonetician in his or her endeavors to carry out 'top-flight' SPID. That is, they will if these individuals combine these elements and organize them into an appropriate system – and then further combine them with procedures where properties of the acoustic signal are extracted and used in a composite SPID. Please note also that these features/elements can be used as the conceptual structure for machine approaches (see Chapter 8). Perhaps the most remarkable thing of all is that many people use them to make identifications under circumstances which are arduous.

How does all of the above relate to law enforcement? Well, as has been pointed out, the information provided by this review can (1) assist in the development of earwitness line-ups, (2) permit the courts to establish boundaries as to what is, and is not, acceptable and (3) provide a structured basis for conducting all types of forensic-related SPID. Indeed, a good understanding of the nature of AP-SPID will materially aid in the development of machine-based SPID systems.

CHAPTER 4

THE PROFESSIONALS

INTRODUCTION

So far we have defined speaker identification, discussed its history and reviewed some of the relevant research about how people make identifications of the auditory type. This chapter is about the professionals who work in the area and how, at least some of them, approach SPID tasks. You will also be introduced to a few of the disagreements and controversies that currently exist. However, please note that certain of the areas and/or issues are so important and well defined that they will be accorded chapters of their own. The next chapter is about the nature, practices and controversies associated with earwitness identification. That following focuses on 'voiceprints' (pretty much *all* controversy there) and the thrust of the final two chapters will be on machine/computer approaches. Nearly everyone cited in those last two chapters is a professional of some sort or another. The same is not true for many of the individuals found in Chapters 4–6.

What, then, is this chapter all about? Basically, it will include descriptions of the professionals who conduct speaker identification evaluations. As you will see, some of them limit their activities to aural-perceptual procedures (AP-SPID); most of us combine AP-SPID with some sort of machine processing and a smaller number concentrate on computer-based algorithms alone. All three approaches have their merits but, in this chapter, I will still cling (primarily anyway) to descriptions involving an aural-perceptual slant. After all, the thrust of the final two chapters is on machine processing and those of us who want to conduct a combination of perceptual and machine procedures simply select those elements that we consider most useful.

This chapter will also introduce you to some of the major procedures and techniques developed by a variety of professionals; a discussion about how well they work will usually be included. I will start with descriptions of forensic phoneticians (and their backgrounds) as well as their strengths and weaknesses, plus some of the disagreements (or at least cautions) that currently exist. However, before doing so, let me describe the various types of people who *attempt* forensic speaker identification. Indeed, if you were to examine all the different classes and types who do so, you would find that they fall into a number of categories and, collectively, exhibit great disparities in talent and training. You also would discover that, individually, they reflect a very broad range of opinions about SPID. Indeed, their assertions range from 'Hey, its easy; anyone can do it' to somewhat negative statements about who should or should not be permitted to practice in the first place (especially in real-life situations) and/or, if any of the research reported can be considered forensically acceptable.

THE PRACTITIONERS

The first of the several groups of 'practitioners' consists of a class of people I consider to be at the very bottom of the competency scale. They include all of the essentially untrained types mentioned previously. Unfortunately, this group is a fairly large one. There might even be as many of these as all of the others put together. Included among this 'low end' bunch are private detectives, some law enforcement agents (who are trained in forensics but not in SPID), recording studio technicians, some musicians, audio technicians, fingerprint specialists, etc. However, they all appear to have one thing in common: they seem to think that speaker identification is something which is fairly easy to master. They argue that you often recognize family members, entertainers and other speakers with whom you are familiar and you usually do so with little effort. They then insist that they can do it too and, further, that they can operate above your level because they add their 'special' methods to the process. There is even an organization that encourages people of this type to work in the area, it is called the International Association of Identification. If you listen to speeches by their members or read their reports (1), you would soon be convinced that about all you have to do to be a successful SPID practitioner is to: (1) have a high school diploma, (2) join their organization, (3) take one of their 'special' 2-week courses and (4) be supervised for a period by one of their 'accredited' members. If only it were that easy. Worse yet (as far as I can tell, anyway) most, if not all, of these people subscribe to some form of the 'voiceprint method.' As you probably have guessed by now, the great bulk of them are charlatans and, even though some of them are convinced they can do it, their ministrations can be most hazardous. It is a little difficult to ignore them (they just keep popping up) but, except for the chapter on 'voiceprints', I intend to do just that.

It is a little difficult to deal with the second group of 'practitioners.' They are mostly professionals from areas that are related to, or associated with, speech communication. These people are usually well trained in their own speciality but, at some point, they are seduced into attempting SPID. Linguists, speech pathologists, physicians, audioengineers, some musicians and even some 'voice scientists' can be found in this general group. A few are intuitively pretty good at SPID; however, most lack enough of the necessary background in acoustic and physiological phonetics, audition, engineering and/or the forensic sciences to operate effectively. I tend to treat these people gently, primarily because they are professionals in their own areas and usually are quite ethical. It is appropriate, however, to keep their attempts in perspective.

Next, it appears necessary to recognize the work and opinions of that fairly small cadre of electrical, audio and/or computer engineers who are interested in our particular type of 'identification.' Please be advised, however, that another (and much larger) cohort of engineers exists in speaker *verification* (SV). This larger group operates extensively with techniques which permit direct analysis and/or processing of the acoustic signals which are created by human speakers. They tend not to be trained, or interested, in human behavior and, of course, they work in rigorously sterile environments. These (SV) professionals are individuals of great talent and training; indeed, it would be wonderful if some of them could be persuaded to join one or another of the SPID teams which currently exist. If they did, progress in both SPID and SV undoubtedly would be upgraded and rapidly so.

Now back to that much smaller group whose members focus on SPID. It consists of individuals who operate in a number of different ways. The activities of some of them simply parallel those of the verification specialists, except that they attempt to take their signal processing techniques into real-life situations. Others cooperate (to some extent) with 'our' type of specialist (i.e. the forensic phoneticians) and, hence, add a little to information about the SPID process. There also is a subgroup here whose members seem to believe that only individuals with their particular skills should be permitted to carry out SPID tasks of any kind. Indeed, some of them (2–5) have suggested that phoneticians should not engage in any type of SPID analyses. It appears that they feel that identifying speakers from voice is their provence and, even though they seem to recognize that it is a challenge quite different from verification, they still tend to approach the problem as do many of the engineering specialists working in that area. Some phoneticians have answered this particular challenge by conceding that engineers are more skillful than they are when it comes to mathematics and electronic equipment. However, they also argue that they (the phoneticians) have the edge when it comes to human physiology and behavior as well as the rigor of experimentation. Accordingly, they opine that it is the engineers who should 'back off.'

Unfortunately, the criticisms leveled by each of these two groups (about the other) are fairly accurate (6, 7). Generally, engineers are pretty much system-linked, which is why so many of them gravitate into SV in the first place. It is within that domain that they can control the acoustics of the environment, specify the equipment to be used (usually of very high quality) and select the stimuli to which the speakers respond as well as the number, type and extent of the samples used. Moreover, SV procedures involve 'closed' sets, i.e., the speaker is a member of the relevant population and wants to be authenticated as being so. Thus, almost any engineer would be comfortable working with SV. That is, while the vagaries of human behavior tend to be of only minor consequence to them, they do have insight into appropriate engineering processes and can develop all types of potentially useful algorithms. These strengths are impressive but, since they are quite narrow, they operate to reduce effectiveness in the identification area. The problem becomes even more challenging when they have to shift from their typically descriptive research approach to one involving experimental procedures.

On the other hand, phoneticians are not so magnificently accomplished either. Since they often lack many of the skills and understandings outlined by the engineers, they tend to drift more into the area of identification. Here, an investigator's control over the acoustic and physical environment is usually minimal; human behavior can be both variable and unpredictable. Yet, most phoneticians are at home in an environment of this type. Many of the (human) behavioral elements are already known to them and can be factored into (or out of) their various approaches. Then too, the challenges and 'unknowns' associated with SPID tend to excite them.

AN ASIDE ABOUT FORENSICS

Permit me to interrupt the narrative here to address an issue that transcends all aspects of practitioner background. That is, several authors have pointed out that any individual who wants to work in the SPID area must become conversant with the forensic sciences in general and the nature of criminal cases/investigations in particular (8, 9–12). Indeed, Champod and Meuwly (9) stress that it is necessary for the practitioner or scientist to advance their understanding beyond a simple appreciation of forensic investigations. They urge us to learn all we can about the courts (the system, the judges and juries, the prosecutors and defense lawyers) and how to ethically and fairly present evidence in ways that will permit reasonable judgments and decisions to be made. They are correct, of course, as the way in which the relevant data are presented can be especially important. For example, let us pretend that you have contrasted the speech of an unknown talker with that of a known suspect and have done so on the basis of 10 speech characteristics. Let us pretend also that you have recorded your 10 judgments as percentages and, based on these determinations, have decided that the two samples were produced by the same person. You judge that the data you have generated permit you to be about 80%

confident that you are correct. Of course, the value you have calculated may not be a mathematical probability; rather, it might be simply an estimate of your confidence level (i.e. that you are correct in your assessment). But, does 'I am 80% sure' mean you can argue that your conclusion is beyond a reasonable scientific doubt? The lawyer (not *you*, however) who wants the two samples to be uttered by one person (often they are the prosecutor) will argue that it is. The lawyer on the other side will stress that, on the basis of your 80%, there will be about 20 people out of every 100 who could be the unknown talker. Indeed, under these conditions, Champod and Meuwly (9) argue that you would have to apply a Bayesian statistical framework to your data before you could present any conclusions or opinions at all. Their approach is a good one, of course; nevertheless, before I recommend that we fully adopt that particular procedure, I would like to see more research conducted on how well it works (for SPID) under both controlled experimental conditions and in real life.

I also agree that it is unwise to first state and then defend a set of conclusions. I recommend that the practitioner carefully present (1) how they conducted the examination, (2) the nature of each of the factors assessed, (3) how they were measured and (4) the specific results obtained. Of course, that is the easy part, explaining what the data mean often is not so easy. What the 'expert' has to do here (hopefully in an interesting manner) is to first indicate how each of these relationships fits into an overall pattern and, then, how they relate to research in the field plus real life situations. Incidentally, Champod and Evett (13) refer to this approach as 'verbal' rather than mathematical. It is also necessary to explain why some of the scores are weighted (if they are). It is only then that what has been done can be put together and the conclusions presented. If the 'expert' explains the process and his results properly, the jury can then use the materials intelligently; if not, they may be dazzled into errors. In any case, it is they, not the expert who are the decision-makers.

A final caution here. It concerns dangers that can arise as the practitioner becomes experienced and/or a particular case proves to be an 'easy' one. Let me illustrate this problem by reviewing 'The Case of the Not-So-Clever Cop.' It is about a detective in a nearby state who, in his middle years, was confronted by a personal financial crisis of substantial proportions. Of course, it is not unknown for disasters of this type to descend on people; some handle them well, others are crushed. Policemen have been known to sometimes resort to criminal activity when stressed by calamities of great magnitude, and the individual in question took this route. However, he employed a slightly different method than do most others. That is, instead of engaging in theft, drug trafficking or the like, he resorted to blackmail. He would first determine if an investigation was directed at a financially well-to-do individual. If it was, and if he obtained appropriate evidence, he would approach the suspect with promises to suppress the investigation, but only for hefty payments. Many of his 'victims' cooperated. However, some of them rebelled and, as a result, a series of tape-recorded telephone conversations were gathered. What was required of me was to match – or not match – the voice on his exemplar with those found on a number of the telephone conversations.

This case was sent me just about the time I had settled into a nicely structured approach to SPID, had successfully completed a substantial number of cases – plus several relevant experiments – and was pretty much 'feeling my oats.' Better yet, the suspect's voice was incredibly unique, so was the voice on the evidence tapes, i.e., both unique and very much like that on the exemplar. Indeed, all of the major speaking characteristics were quite similar; none were dissimilar. Moreover, both voices exhibited three idiosyncratic characteristics (one segmental and two suprasegmentals) and these three were the same for 'each' of the speakers. What an easy match – and such a strong one! Only a verbal report was required and I gave it. Subsequently, I was deposed. It was only then that I realized I had cut corners and, as a matter of fact, actually short-changed the prosecution, the defendant, the process and myself. Fortunately, I was able to organize what I had done (I already was using a structured approach) as I went along. Even more fortunately, other types of evidence became available. But having the defendant capitulate and 'plead' before the trial began was of little consolation. I had performed only minimally, had slighted my ethics to some extent and certainly had operated unprofessionally. It all had happened because I had become too cocky and had an easy, easy case. Of course, this case occurred a long time ago and, best yet, no harm was done. Still, I think of it every time I agree to take on a new investigation. Each of them, each client, deserves nothing less than a best effort. Of course, there is no panacea as to just how you can block yourself from slipping into a similar situation. Self-discipline and adherence to top-flight ethics are probably your best defense.

THE FORENSIC PHONETICIAN

We now come to the group to which I belong; they form the core group in the SPID field; hence, they are basic to many of the sections in this book. I will cheerfully concede that there are a few professionals who both work successfully in SPID and violate at least some of the strictures listed below. However, even these individuals will exhibit enough basic academic training and real-world experience to operate proficiently and ethically. In any event, the career track followed by most of us was to first become a modern (or 'experimental') phonetician; it was only then that we were able to branch out. While a large percentage of us hold the doctorate, all will have won advanced academic degrees in the phonetic sciences. As basic to our speciality, we have had to become fundamentally conversant not only with acoustic, physiological and perceptual phonetics but also with audition (especially psychoacoustics and auditory physiology), basic linguistics (especially phonology), experimental design and statistics. It also is important that members of our specialty have a good grounding in computers, the behavioral sciences and electrical engineering. Add to all this, a need to understand the forensic sciences and the legal system and you have a program which presents a pretty formidable challenge. Yet these areas are open to any individual who is interested in forensic phonetics in general and SPID in particular. Training opportunities in all the listed areas, except those related to the forensic sciences and the courts, are already part of various academic programs in the phonetic sciences. Thus, the transfer route to forensic phonetics involves only a specialized course or two in forensics plus practical training with attorneys and law-enforcement personnel. Of course, some hands-on experience with criminal investigations and trials is also helpful but that can come later.

It should be possible to evaluate forensic phoneticians once they have completed their primary training and logged some experience in forensics and with the courts. That is, it should be possible to do so once they are beyond the intern phase. Table 4.1 lists some of the characteristics and accomplishments that can be evaluated. Success with all are desirable; for items 1, 2, 5, and 9 it is mandatory. The problem, of course, is how these criteria and the practitioners ability to meet them are evaluated. At present, most of the assessments only can be subjective. The elements making up forensic phonetics have been outlined by Hollien (10, 14); SPID is one of the basic areas within this speciality.

Finally, are you aware that forensic phoneticians have their own society? It is called the International Association of Forensic Phonetics. We have a journal;

Table 4.1

A listing of the requirements which appear to permit assessment of a forensic phonetician's capabilities. They are structured to transcend any of the approaches employed. All specialists should be able to demonstrate the following.

1. Good hearing acuity; i.e. auditory sensitivity that is adequate for the task.
2. A reasonable level of correct identification. It should be available and acceptable. It also should have been assessed under a variety of experimental conditions.
3. Techniques which are appropriate for obtaining the recorded exemplar samples (for the comparisons).
4. That the criteria, established for task validity, are appropriate, and that they are especially so with respect to (a) the minimum acceptable length of both evidence and exemplar samples and (b) the minimally acceptable recording conditions.
5. Sampling and scaling techniques (developed for the evaluations) which are both objective and defensible.
6. Procedures which permit the use of 'control' talkers (i.e. foils).
7. Quantification of some, or most, of the procedures employed.
8. Application of confidence or probability levels; ones which can be quantitatively established.
9. Procedures which permit reliability measures to be applied.

currently it is called *Forensic Linguistics, The International Journal of Speech, Language and the Law* (I, for one, certainly hope that this title can be streamlined soon). It is published by the University of Birmingham Press, located at The University of Birmingham, Edgbaston, Birmingham, B15 2TT, UK. The current IAFP officers also can be contacted at that address.

APPROACHES TO THE SPID PROBLEM

Most forensic phoneticians approach SPID within the context of one or another of three philosophies. That is, they either stress the aural-perceptual procedure, the machine or computer techniques or, as most of us do, apply a mix of both. This chapter is devoted primarily to the first of these three procedures. Work in AP-SPID has now progressed to a level where, if it is properly structured, it can be applied pretty much as a stand-alone technique. However, it must be conceded that phoneticians will be even more effective if they supplement the perceptual approach with appropriate machine procedures.

DEVELOPMENT OF THE AURAL-PERCEPTUAL APPROACH

As it turns out, modern AP-SPID procedures were developed (primarily anyway) in three countries; i.e., in the USA, the UK and Germany. The thrust started right after World War II and development was roughly parallel in each of the three countries (at least after Germany recovered from the war) with only a few exceptions. The first of these was that, initially, the AP-SPID research and practice conducted in the USA was somewhat overshadowed by the furor surrounding 'voiceprints.' However, the 'voiceprint' controversy stimulated additional research. It is for this reason that most of the early SPID investigations were carried out in the USA (primarily, but not exclusively at the Bell Telephone Laboratories, MIT, the Haskins Laboratories, the University of Iowa, the University of Florida and UCLA). Thus, the early practitioners here based their procedures on what the American research programs had to offer and, hence, the SPID techniques developed were based more on research than on what could be learned from practical forensic experience or traditional phonetics. It should be noted that the US and UK phoneticians varied markedly in their philosophies toward SPID and did so because of their basic differences with respect to phonetics in general. As Pickett (15) succinctly points out, the 'Americans are more concerned about speech science. The British focus on the phonetic alphabet and how to use it.' Consistent with his remarks are the forensic phoneticians from the UK who lean toward 'segmental' SPID and the Americans who typically stress suprasegmental approaches.

Thus, the SPID thrust in the UK took a path somewhat different from that in the USA. Another reason it did so is that the UK is much smaller than the United States (it has a land mass roughly equivalent to the US state of Kansas) and has a far better system of communication among academics. The strong basis in what can be called traditional phonetics and phonology led naturally to a focus on the segmentals (especially those involving *narrow* phonetic transcriptions). In turn, the progress made here, coupled with the good internal communication, soon led to a positive response by British law-enforcement agencies. Moreover, since administrators in that sector seemed to be more enlightened about the possible development of forensic phonetics than were those in most other countries, the UK practitioners appear to have achieved earlier acceptance than did those elsewhere.

As you might expect, the German effort matured later than did the other two. After all, their first priority after World War II had to be the restructuring of their country and its economy. However, once active, the professionals there were able to move rapidly – especially by avoiding many of the early errors made in the United States. Germany also is much smaller than the USA and their Bundeskriminalamt (BKA) tends to interact with their scientific community in a far more enlightened way than the American FBI does with ours. Hence, the Germans were able to draw from the sometimes painful developments experienced by the Americans and British and were quickly able to embark on reasonable SPID programs. Researchers in other countries contributed of course; but their efforts tended not to be programmatic.

Approaches based on traditional phonetics

The AP-SPID approaches developed by the British have been well reviewed by both Nolan (16–18) and French (19, 20). Those by others (especially German phoneticians) have been discussed by Künzel (11, 12) and by Braun (21, 22).

The authors cited above go to great lengths to warn of the hazards in using segmental approaches in particular and aural-perceptual procedures in general. (Please remember that segmental analysis involves assessment of the individual sounds, phonemes and syllables that make up the words and phrases of a language.) When reading their warnings, however, I was struck by the fact that their negative feelings appear to be based on problems a little tangential to the primary thrust of the approach. That is, there have been a few instances where a feature was misinterpreted or some element within a dialect overlooked. While small errors such as these may be critical to a given investigation, they appear to be but a minor threat to the AP-SPID approach itself. Other problems with the segmental approach have been articulated by individuals both inside and outside of the phonetic sciences. They suggest that the relevant segmental elements (relevant to SPID, that is) simply have not been identified,

THE INTERNATIONAL PHONETIC ALPHABET (revised to 1993, corrected 1996)

CONSONANTS (PULMONIC)

	Bilabial	Labiodental	Dental	Alveolar	Postalveolar	Retroflex	Palatal	Velar	Uvular	Pharyngeal	Glottal
Plosive	p b			t d		ʈ ɖ	c ɟ	k ɡ	q ɢ		ʔ
Nasal	m	ɱ		n		ɳ	ɲ	ŋ	ɴ		
Trill	ʙ			r					ʀ		
Tap or Flap				ɾ		ɽ					
Fricative	ɸ β	f v	θ ð	s z	ʃ ʒ	ʂ ʐ	ç ʝ	x ɣ	χ ʁ	ħ ʕ	h ɦ
Lateral fricative				ɬ ɮ							
Approximant		ʋ		ɹ		ɻ	j	ɰ			
Lateral approximant				l		ɭ	ʎ	ʟ			

Where symbols appear in pairs, the one to the right represents a voiced consonant. Shaded areas denote articulations judged impossible.

CONSONANTS (NON-PULMONIC)

Clicks		Voiced implosives		Ejectives	
ʘ	Bilabial	ɓ	Bilabial	ʼ	Examples:
ǀ	Dental	ɗ	Dental/alveolar	pʼ	Bilabial
ǃ	(Post)alveolar	ʄ	Palatal	tʼ	Dental/alveolar
ǂ	Palatoalveolar	ɠ	Velar	kʼ	Velar
ǁ	Alveolar lateral	ʛ	Uvular	sʼ	Alveolar fricative

VOWELS

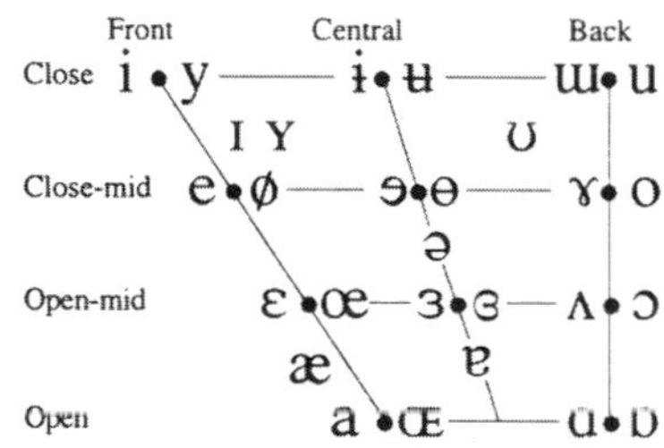

Where symbols appear in pairs, the one to the right represents a rounded vowel.

OTHER SYMBOLS

ʍ Voiceless labial-velar fricative

w Voiced labial-velar approximant

ɥ Voiced labial-palatal approximant

ʜ Voiceless epiglottal fricative

ʢ Voiced epiglottal fricative

ʡ Epiglottal plosive

ɕ ʑ Alveolo-palatal fricatives

ɺ Alveolar lateral flap

ɧ Simultaneous ʃ and x

Affricates and double articulations can be represented by two symbols joined by a tie bar if necessary.

k͡p t͜s

DIACRITICS Diacritics may be placed above a symbol with a descender, e.g. ŋ̊

̥	Voiceless	n̥ d̥	̤	Breathy voiced	b̤ a̤	̪	Dental	t̪ d̪
̬	Voiced	s̬ t̬	̰	Creaky voiced	b̰ a̰	̺	Apical	t̺ d̺
ʰ	Aspirated	tʰ dʰ	̼	Linguolabial	t̼ d̼	̻	Laminal	t̻ d̻
̹	More rounded	ɔ̹	ʷ	Labialized	tʷ dʷ	̃	Nasalized	ẽ
̜	Less rounded	ɔ̜	ʲ	Palatalized	tʲ dʲ	ⁿ	Nasal release	dⁿ
̟	Advanced	u̟	ˠ	Velarized	tˠ dˠ	ˡ	Lateral release	dˡ
̠	Retracted	e̠	ˤ	Pharyngealized	tˤ dˤ	̚	No audible release	d̚
̈	Centralized	ë	̴	Velarized or pharyngealized	ɫ			
̽	Mid-centralized	e̽	̝	Raised	e̝ (ɹ̝ = voiced alveolar fricative)			
̩	Syllabic	n̩	̞	Lowered	e̞ (β̞ = voiced bilabial approximant)			
̯	Non-syllabic	e̯	̘	Advanced Tongue Root	e̘			
˞	Rhoticity	ə˞ a˞	̙	Retracted Tongue Root	e̙			

SUPRASEGMENTALS

ˈ Primary stress

ˌ Secondary stress ˌfoʊnəˈtɪʃən

ː Long eː

ˑ Half-long eˑ

̆ Extra-short ĕ

| Minor (foot) group

‖ Major (intonation) group

. Syllable break ɹi.ækt

‿ Linking (absence of a break)

TONES AND WORD ACCENTS

LEVEL			CONTOUR		
e̋ or	˥	Extra high	ě or	˩˥	Rising
é	˦	High	ê	˥˩	Falling
ē	˧	Mid	e᷄	˦˥	High rising
è	˨	Low	e᷅	˩˨	Low rising
ȅ	˩	Extra low	e᷈	˧˦˧	Rising-falling
↓		Downstep	↗		Global rise
↑		Upstep	↘		Global fall

organized and tested for such purposes. They argue that no-one knows precisely how effective these techniques can be under any conditions at all, much less under the great variety of those found in the forensic milieu. It is also suggested that, even if they were structured, virtually no useful data are available about how well (or how poorly) they operate to provide valid SPID.

It also appears, to date anyway, that little structuring has been accomplished. Some phoneticians are still trudging along their own trails and use whatever contrasts they feel will be effective. Perhaps an even more serious problem is that only a few of them have made a formal attempt at organizing, defining and testing the approaches they have developed. An exception here is Nolan (16) who structured a model founded on traditional phonetics theory; i.e. he built his approach on the framework of British pronunciation. Accordingly, he refers to it as the Received Model. Nolan is a little disparaging about phoneticians who refuse to organize their procedures but concedes that it is difficult to do so as language, voice and speech are extremely complex. Anyway, he makes the attempt and his results are rather good (albeit, quite complex). But, before discussing the pros and cons he articulated (and those of the other individuals cited above), permit me to provide an overview of the segmental approach.

First, please remember that the description to follow includes only the segmental approach to AP-SPID. At this point, little-to-no consideration will be given to the suprasegmental or paralinguistic approaches or to any of these procedures when combined with machine processing. The method discussed here is one which involves narrow phonetic transcription of the speech found on any tape, be it evidence, exemplar or some other. What is meant by 'narrow' is that the fine detail of vowel and consonant pronunciation will be obtained and compared (20). The codes or alphabets used for this purpose are those established by the International Phonetic Association who published their most recent set in 1993 (see Figure 4.1 for a listing of the symbols). As you can see, this system is a rather complex one. It is designed to permit specification of any of the sounds, symbols, words and phrases associated with any of the thousands of languages that exist in the world today. The successful use of this system will depend on (1) your personal talent, (2) good hearing, (3) knowledge of the language and its dialects and (4) how effectively you can apply this system when profiling a person's speech.

Now, back to Nolan. If you are unconvinced that this approach involves some rather substantial challenges, consider some of his examples. He writes about the structure of a 'segmental strand' (or sequence) by outlining the 'phonetic properties the speaker has to achieve when producing the utterance.' As an illustration, he selected the word 'teal' and specifies it using narrow phonetic transcription. He then defined this word as 'an aspirated alveolar stop with slightly affricated release (followed by) a diphthong gliding from a half front,

Figure 4.1 (opposite) The international phonetic alphabet is the product of the International Phonetics Association. (Centerfold, J. Internat. Phonetics Assn, *F. Nolan, Ed., 1995, Vol. 25.)*

half close to just short of close front, and (completed by) a strongly pharyngalized lateral.' Note that Nolan's definition is for a single, short, three-phoneme word. Elegant but complex. One of his later examples involves how a CV utterance (i.e. a consonant followed by a vowel) can be used to differentiate between two speakers who otherwise 'have phonetic *systems* which are identical in every respect.' That is, he shows how his two speakers produced the CV combination in slightly different but discernable ways. These are the contrasts which can be used as building blocks to establish that two speakers are (or are not) a single person.

One of the most powerful aids employed by this particular group of forensic phoneticians involves regional dialects. The presence of any particular dialect can be segmentally established by the procedures they employ, and nicely so. However, if they find that both speakers have the same dialect, they then must apply other tests to determine if they (the talkers) are the same or different people. Conversely, if the dialects can be shown to be different for the two speakers, strong evidence exists that they actually are two different people. Unfortunately, regional dialects are not as distinct today as they have been in the past; hence, they are no longer the powerful indicators they once were. Dialects, however, are but one tool among many for segmentalists.

While this review could be extended, it appears sufficient to say that, even though the segmental approaches can be robust, they also have their weaknesses. Specifically, they are very complex, they require the availability of a relatively large corpus of speech material and they can suffer from subjective evaluations. However, their strength is much enhanced when they are coupled with suprasegmental and/or machine approaches.

Approaches stressing paralinguistics

As you will remember, an AP-SPID approach introduced earlier in this chapter was one where analysis was focused on the assessment of voice, speech timing and the like. The bases used in establishing these procedures have been drawn more from experimental phonetics than they have from the traditional field. The relevant parameters here are often referred to as suprasegmentals. And, while they are the basis of the procedures to follow, I should hasten to explain that the segmentals will not (and cannot) be ignored. It is just that the emphasis on narrow transcription is reduced and the segmental analyses are blended in with those focused on the suprasegmentals. It is, of course, a matter of choice, but the phoneticians here reverse the order used by the first group; i.e. those who are comfortable with traditional phonetics and dialectology, and those who stress the segmentals and employ the suprasegmentals in support roles. I would suggest, however, that the approach to be described in the following paragraphs better lends itself to a combination approach – i.e., one where they (the suprasegmentals) are assessed both auditorily and acoustically. For example, it is important to be able to determine that a pitch level, which appears to be very low for a male, is not an illusion but actually has a mean F0 of 94 Hz. It also is useful to confirm acoustically that the vowel you heard as /a/ is actually an /a/. In any event, the aural-perceptual approach to follow has been structured and, to some extent, tested. It has been employed successfully (sometimes on its own) over the last 10–12 years.

First, its characteristics. The procedure involves listening critically to the evidence and exemplar tapes; it then requires individual (and repeated) assessment of a number of the speech features found on them. Next, a series of responses are made; these are graded on a continuum (0–10) ranging from the point where the paired samples are very likely to have been produced by two different people (0–3) to where it is most probable that they were uttered by a single person (7–10). As you would expect, the speech samples to be compared consist of words and phrases drawn from the evidence and exemplar tapes; they are placed in pairs (both text dependent and independent) and transferred to a 'test' tape recording. At the risk of being redundant, may I indicate again that the listening procedure involves first attending to the evidence and exemplar tapes, then to the 'pairs tape' (usually 25–30 of them) as many times as necessary to permit a judgment to be made about a *single* relationship (i.e. about pitch variability or about the use of the vocal fry voice register, for example). As stated, the parameters are considered one at a time with the next one in the series not assessed until a decision has been made about the one being judged.

As you can see, the structuring of these comparison tapes can be quite challenging. Of course, since the speech on the evidence tape is not under your control, about all you can do is clean it up and use what it contains. On the other hand, you should be able to regulate the utterances on the exemplar tape in order to ensure a good repertoire. My wife and colleague, P. A. Hollien (23) has developed a set of guidelines for obtaining good exemplars. I have found them quite helpful and want to 'share' them with you. I had a little trouble working out just where to place them as this listing does not comfortably fit in anywhere. Yet exemplar recordings are of particular importance to the issues under discussion. Hence, they are placed here.

PREPARING AN EXEMPLAR TAPE RECORDING

The materials that follow were developed by Patti Hollien and her staff for use by personnel at her consulting firm, Forensic Communication Associates. They were structured, applied and critiqued over a period of 8–10 years prior to their finalization in 1992. Please note that they can be used to generate good exemplars either 'live' in a one-on-one interview or over the telephone. The criteria which were established for this purpose follow.

The recording environment

The room in which the recording is to be made should be quiet and non-reverberant (i.e. not a 'bright' sounding one). A room with plaster walls, little furniture, no carpeting, etc., will tend to produce reflections, reverberations, etc., and these conditions can distort the subject's voice. In addition, a noisy environment will both mask and otherwise degrade speech.

The recording equipment

Only high-quality tape recorders should be used as low fidelity systems often will distort a speaker's utterances. The use of a good quality microphone, one which is external to the recorder, is also desirable. The operation of all systems should be checked prior to the session to ensure that the equipment is functioning properly. Only new, high-quality tapes should be used.

Live recordings

A test recording should be made prior to initiation of the exemplar session. It is necessary to conduct one in order to ensure that the entire setup is appropriate. Either the microphone or the tape recorder should be placed on the table directly in front of the suspect (especially if it is voice activated). As with all interviews, it is important to record the date, the time, the place (the recording was made) and the participants present during the session. All information should be recorded before the exemplar is made and appear both on the tape itself and in a written log. Once the recording procedure has been completed, a section of the tape should be rewound and replayed. This procedure will permit verification that a proper recording was made. Incidently, if the recorder has both an input and tape monitor, the quality of the recording can be checked during the session by listening to the latter channel through a headset. Finally, after the session is over, the tape should be taken from the unit, labeled and, for tape cassettes, the tabs removed. Some important do's and don'ts include: (1) do not 'overdrive' input level; (2) do not allow the tape itself to come into contact with any other electronic device or machinery; (3) do make a high quality copy of the exemplar tape as soon as possible.

Telephone recordings

Except for tape recorder placement, the procedure for making an exemplar recording over a telephone is almost identical to that for live recordings. In this instance, the recorder is not placed in front of the subject but rather at the appropriate remote location (i.e., coupled to the receiving telephone). It is also necessary to obtain and use equipment which will permit simultaneous reception of the subject's speech by both the investigator (over her headset) and the taping system.

Speech material needed

It is most desirable to obtain three different types of voice samples, especially if the exemplar is to be useful in all possible comparisons. The sequence here is to first identify the tape recording and the participants. The exemplar session is then carried out. The subject should be first engaged in extemporaneous speech, then asked to read/repeat some of the material on the evidence tape and, finally, read sections from a newspaper or a magazine. It is advisable to repeat these tasks. The examiner should endeavor to discover if the speaker is attempting voice disguise and, if so, extend the session while trying to counter their efforts. The materials cited above include the following.

- **The extemporaneous speech.** Attempts should be made to reduce subject stress. To do so, the examiner should engage the subject in conversations on neutral topics. The goal of this procedure is to obtain as natural an exchange as possible between the examiner and the subject. Normal or ordinary speech is the goal. The subject should be kept talking for as long as possible and the examiner should resist speaking any more than is absolutely necessary.
- **The evidence text.** It often is desirable to have the subject read or utter sample words or phrases, especially those that have been either reported by the victim or found on evidence recordings. Moreover, it is important to prevent the subject from reading these samples in a monotone or while attempting voice disguise. Multiple recordings often are necessary here; sometimes it will be useful to excite or stress the subject (i.e. to break down attempted disguise or to parallel the environment in which the original recording was made).
- **The reading material.** Any easily read material will suffice. The purpose is to obtain as large and as complex a repertoire of the subject's speech as possible. Attempts at voice disguise can sometimes be foiled by this procedure.

A final caution

As indicated, subjects sometimes attempt to disguise their voices when making an exemplar tape recording. They often do so by speaking in a very soft voice, or in whispers, or in a monotone. Do not permit them to do this. Rather, attempt to motivate them to speak in a normal manner. These suggestions should aid you in developing a usable comparison tape. Unfortunately, you cannot control the material on the evidence tape and you will find that it (not the exemplar) will create the greatest difficulty. Additionally, it may exhibit channel distortions (noise, telephone frequency, etc.) or speaker problems (excitement, stress, several speakers, simultaneous speech, intoxicated speakers, whispering, etc); worst of all, it may be very short. It is important that you recognize and counter (as best you can) these problems. If you do and if you are able to extract a number of phrases and words from both tape recordings, you should be able to create a good pairs tape.

THE PAIRS TAPE

You may, of course have your own way of making an exemplar recording. Once it is finished, you can initiate construction of the pairs tape. The goal here is to create a string of utterances that will provide paired samples of the speech of both the unknown (U) and known (K) talkers. Ideally, this tape would consist of (1) eight to ten sentence-length text-independent phrases, (2) six to eight equally long sentences or phrases of the same (or nearly the same) words found on the evidence tape, (3) 10–12 short phrases taken from both tapes and (4) 10–12 samples of paired words (even though they may be drawn from different contexts). The roughly three dozen pairs of utterances can then be played over and over with the examiner first listening to a phrase/word uttered by U and then a second spoken by K with the two tokens in each pair separated only by about a second. Note also that construction of the tapes must permit flexibility. For example, it should be possible to add new pairs or subtract others plus reverse the pattern (especially if the evidence tape is short) so that K is compared with U. By this means also, a second unknown speaker (or a third, or a fourth) can be added to the tape, any of the samples can be switched out for comparison to other voices, and so on. However, the tape recording's construction *must* permit the examiner to conduct the evaluations in an orderly manner.

A STRUCTURED APPROACH

As has been stressed a number of times, the procedures developed must be based on the best available evidence and logic; moreover, all of the constituent operations must be repeatable. In short, the most sophisticated and complete test vehicle possible should be structured, applied and evaluated under controlled conditions. In addition, it is helpful to carry out experiments (or, at least, descriptive research) in order to determine its robustness, and to ensure that it is both valid and reliable. Since the AP-SPID procedures will often be carried out in concert with machine processing, it also is important to contrast the accuracy of each of these approaches against the other. Finally, the success rate (often referred to as the hit rate) should be established for anyone attempting to use it. It is best to do so by having each of these people participate in AP-SPID experiments. If this is possible, the scores obtained should be supplemented by those from real-life situations. If relevant experiments are not possible, the data from the field assessments (alone) must suffice. Of course, it is recognized that field data are not generally scientific and there always is the temptation to view these efforts in a more favorable light than they warrant. Nonetheless, the assessment and retention of those data is most desirable.

The AP-SPID approach to follow is highly structured (10, 24). In certain instances, it has been successfully employed as a stand-alone procedure. Moreover, some research (primarily descriptive) has been carried out both on it and on several of the workers who have applied it in real-life situations. Data from these activities will be provided after it has been described. Be advised that this procedure is not being touted as an end-all to the AP-SPID problem, neither is it being sold. Indeed, if you judge it useful, you can obtain it just by reading the next few pages (you have my permission to use all or any part of it).

The task now is to determine just how this suprasegmental dominant AP-SPID vehicle can be used in evaluating speaker identity. It should be remembered, of course, that segmental evaluations will be included or added, as may acoustic analyses. The process is best understood by consideration of Figure 4.2. You will note that it is based on the assessment of up to 20 scaled comparisons. In turn, these judgments lead to decisions about a match (or a non-match) and its associated confidence level. The estimates are made of a series of parameters clustered around the speaking characteristics of (1) pitch, (2) voice quality, (3) intensity variation, (4) dialect, (5) segmentals, (6) prosody and (7) possible disorders. Each of the individual parameters is assessed on a 10-point scale.

The procedure specifies that the examiner listen to a large number of sample pairs, in a paired comparison (ABX) mode (sometimes in the presence of control samples or foils; sometimes separately), contrasting the unknown talker (U) with the known (K). These comparisons are made *one* feature or parameter at a time. For example, the pitch *levels* heard in the U and K samples are compared over and over until a judgment can be made about their similarity. Once a score is assigned, the examiner can go on to assess pitch *variability* (separately of course); later, the pitch usage *patterns* are compared. To reiterate, the examiner does not proceed to a subsequent category or parameter until a final judgment is made about the particular feature under consideration. While it is not necessary to follow the specific order found in Figure 4.2, it is important to assess factors systematically.

Next, let us consider how these judgments are scored with respect to their observed similarities or dissimilarities. A 10-point scale is provided for this purpose. The scores on the low end are used to suggest substantial differences between these voices and those on the high end a close relationship. Thus, if a decision falls within the 0–3 range, it can be said that there is evidence that the utterances (being quite different) appear not to have been produced by a single person. The converse is true for those in the 7–10 judgmental range. Scores

Figure 4.2
The AP-SPID form developed for use with the suprasegmental SPID approach being described (10, 24).

FORENSIC COMMUNICATION ASSOCIATES

Case Name: FCA REF:

Aural-perceptual Approach to Speaker Identification

Score Sheet: 0 = U–K least like; 10 = U–K most alike

			SCORE	RANGE
1.	PITCH			
	a. Level	0 . . . . 5 10		
	b. Variability	0 . . . . 5 10		
	c. Patterns	0 . . . . 5 10		
2.	VOICE QUALITY			
	a. General	0 . . . . 5 10		
	b. Vocal Fry	0 . . . . 5 10		
	c. Other	0 . . . . 5 10		
3.	INTENSITY			
	a. Variability	0 . . . . 5 10		
4.	DIALECT			
	a. Regional	0 . . . . 5 10		
	b. Foreign	0 . . . . 5 10		
	c. Idiolect	0 . . . . 5 10		
5.	ARTICULATION			
	a. Vowels	0 . . . . 5 10		
	b. Consonants	0 . . . . 5 10		
	c. Misarticulations	0 . . . . 5 10		
	d. Nasality	0 . . . . 5 10		
	e. Other	0 . . . . 5 10		
6.	PROSODY			
	a. Rate	0 . . . . 5 10		
	b. Speech Bursts	0 . . . . 5 10		
	c. Other	0 . . . . 5 10		
7.	OTHER			
	a. Nonfluencies	0 . . . . 5 10		
	b. Speech disorders	0 . . . . 5 10		
	MEAN		______	______

here provide fairly robust evidence that a single individual produced both samples. Finally, and as would be expected, scores falling between 4 and 6, while not very compelling, tend to support the possibility of a match. That is, while these judgments are somewhat neutral, they serve to suggest that, since the voices are not strikingly different, they *may* have been produced by only one person. Please note, if foils are used, it is necessary to conduct a one-on-one evaluation for each foil with both U and K.

Of course, a *single* polarized score, (of say 2), does not mean that the paired utterances were actually produced by two people. Neither does a score of 9, taken alone, demonstrate that both samples were produced by a single speaker. To illustrate: a value of 8 for dialect might not be very compelling if it (i.e. the dialect) was quite common for the geographical area in which both U and K reside. On the other hand, a dialect score of 2 would be rather persuasive (but not controlling) by itself. It is difficult to imagine that a person would (or could) speak in a particular dialect under one set of circumstances but sustain a second in a different situation. In any event, the judgment procedure is continued until all the contrasts possible have been made; it is necessary to do so before any additional steps are taken. However, please note that it is not necessary to make judgments about relationships which do not exist. That is, if a speech disorder is not heard in either sample, this category is simply omitted. It is rare that the paired samples can be compared for all 20 parameters; rather 12–16 assessments ordinarily are possible.

The *entire* process must then be repeated a number of times (usually on different days) and individual means obtained from all trials. Of course, some variability can be expected from run-to-run. For example, the unknown speaker's voice may sound more like the known's (with respect to a given feature) for one set of pairs than it does for another and/or the examiner's internal focus may shift a little from sample to sample or from run to run. Hence, exactly the same score may not be repeated each time for a given speech feature (parameter). However, if variability is limited, the mean of several independent trials will provide judgments which are more persuasive than will that for a single decision.

Once all of the scores have been tabulated and the entire process replicated two or three times, the means for each parameter judged can be calculated. It is at this juncture (i.e., before the overall mean and range are calculated) that all values should be checked for possible weighting. In most instances it is not necessary to do so. However, please note the dialect example provided in one of the preceding paragraphs. In the first instance, U and K came from the same dialect region, and it showed. In that case, dialect weight might be reduced a little. In the second example, the speakers on the two samples exhibited strong differences in dialect; in that case, the parameter should be given greater weight. As another example, greater weight should be given if a speech disorder is present. That is, if it is observed in both samples, weighting should be added to that (already high) score. If, on the other hand, a speech disorder is found on only one of the recordings, that (low) score should be emphasized. Finally, it is sometimes necessary to reduce the importance of a polarized score if it is clearly caused by differences in the situation or the environment. For example, it is difficult to make accurate pitch level decisions when one of the samples was made during the high stress associated with the commission of a crime and the other after the perpetrator has been caught, is depressed and under interrogation.

TWO EXAMPLES

Figures 4.3 and 4.4 provide examples of real world cases (24). They were carried out at the behest of attorneys in two different criminal cases. I also made certain acoustic measurements in both instances and they provided confirmation of the aural-perceptual evaluations. First, please consider Figure 4.3. Generally negative scores, or essentially a non-match, can be found in that instance. A strong relationship (i.e. toward a match) can be seen in Figure 4.4. Please note that each example provides a summary of three complete runs carried out on different days.

Consideration of Figure 4.3 will reveal that a match could not be made and the confidence level (not a mathematical probability, however) associated with these negative conclusions exceeds 70% (i.e. the possibility that the two samples were produced by one speaker is only 29 in 100); indeed, if consistency is considered, this confidence level would be even higher. Note also the parameter values. It can be seen that, while there were some modest U–K similarities (especially with respect to nasality, general vowel usage and vocal fry), consideration of two fairly powerful (but negative) relationships would suggest that the samples were produced by two different individuals. The first is dialect. As has been discussed, it is a characteristic which tends not to be very important when they are similar but provides a robust (non-match) cue when (two) different dialects are present. Further, the strength of the non-match would be enhanced if it can be shown that K was not attempting voice disguise and such was the case for this example. Ordinarily, segmental analysis of phonemes heard in the two samples would have been carried out. However, in this instance the contrast was so great that further analysis was not considered necessary. The second strong indicator that U and K were different women was that U exhibited a mild but observable /d/ for /th/ substitution. While this problem did not reach the level of a speech disorder, it was discernible nonetheless. Note also that variability among the judgments tended to be quite low and only four of the features

FORENSIC COMMUNICATION ASSOCIATES

Case Name: **State vs. Jane Doe** FCA REF: **1491**

Aural-perceptual Approach to Speaker Identification

Score Sheet: 0 = U–K least like; 10 = U–K most alike

			SCORE	RANGE
1.	PITCH			
	a. Level	0 X===X . 5 10	2	1–3
	b. Variability	0 . . X . 5 10	3	3
	c. Patterns	0 . X=X . 5 10	2	2–3
2.	VOICE QUALITY			
	a. General	0 . . X===X 10	4	3–5
	b. Vocal Fry	0 . . . . 5 X . . . 10	6	6
	c. Other	0 . . . . 5 10	NA	NA
3.	INTENSITY			
	a. Variability	0 . X=X . 5 10	3	2–3
4.	DIALECT			
	a. Regional	0 X=X . . 5 10	1	1–2*
	b. Foreign	0 . . . . 5 10	NA	NA
	c. Idiolect	0 . . . . 5 10	NA	NA
5.	ARTICULATION			
	a. Vowels	0 . . . . X=X . . 10	5	5–6
	b. Consonants	0 . X===X 5 10	3	2–4
	c. Misarticulations	0 X . . . 5 10	1	1*
	d. Nasality	0 . . . . X=X . . . 10	6	5–6
	e. Other	0 . . . . 5 10	NA	NA
			U shows a /d/ for /th/ substitution	
6.	PROSODY			
	a. Rate	0 . . . . X5 10	4	4
	b. Speech Bursts	0 . . X=X 5 10	3	3–4
	c. Staccato (K only)	0 X===X . 5 10	2	1–3
7.	OTHER			
	a. Nonfluencies	0 . . . . 5 10	NA	NA
	b. Speech disorders	0 . . . . 5 10	NA	NA
	MEAN	Mean of three runs; no foils.	29%	25–35%

*Double weight

Figure 4.3

Evaluation of a woman who, as it turns out, was not the criminal (from ref. 24). However, please note that an error in that article has been corrected. The lateral /s/ was displayed by the woman's sister (who was not it either).

Figure 4.4

Assessment of a male suspect who, as it turns out, was the perpetrator.

FORENSIC COMMUNICATION ASSOCIATES

Case Name: **State vs. John Doe** FCA REF: **1475**

Aural-perceptual Approach to Speaker Identification

Score Sheet: 0 = U–K least like; 10 = U–K most alike

			SCORE	RANGE
1. PITCH				
	a. Level	0 . . . . 5 . **x===x** 10	**8**	**7–9**
	b. Variability	0 . . . . 5 **x=x** . . 10	**7**	**6–7**
	c. Patterns	0 . . . . 5 . **x=x** . 10	**7**	**7–8**
2. VOICE QUALITY				
	a. General	0 . . . . 5 . **x===x** 10	**8**	**7–9**
	b. Vocal Fry	0 . . **x===x** 10	**4**	**3–5**
	Slightly more fry by U c. Other	0 . . . . 5 10	**NA**	**NA**
3. INTENSITY				
	a. Variability	0 . . . . 5 **x=====x** 10	**7**	**6–9**
4. DIALECT				
	a. Regional	0 . . . . 5 . **x===x** 10	**8**	**7–9**
	b. Foreign	0 . . . . 5 10	**NA**	**NA**
	c. Idiolect Both 'Lilt'	0 . . . . 5 . . **x=x** 10	**9**	**8–9**
5. ARTICULATION				
	a. Vowels	0 . . . . 5 **x===x** . 10	**7**	**6–8**
	b. Consonants	0 . . . . 5 **x===x** . 10	**7**	**6–8**
	c. Misarticulations	0 . . . . 5 . . . **x** 10	**9**	**9**
	Both d. Nasality	0 . . . **x======x** . . 10	**6**	**4–7**
	e. Other	0 . . . . 5 10	**NA**	**NA**
6. PROSODY				
	a. Rate	0 . . . . 5 . **x===x** 10	**8**	**7–9**
	Relatively fast b. Speech Bursts	0 . . . . 5 **x=x** . . 10	**7**	**6–7**
	c. Choppy	0 . . . . 5 . . **x** . 10	**8**	**8**
7. OTHER				
	a. Nonfluencies	0 . . . . 5 . . . **x** 10	**9**	**9**
	Show similar articulation problems b. Speech disorders	0 . . . . 5 10	**NA**	**NA**
MEAN		Neither of two foils matched U or K.	**74%**	**66–81%**

(pitch level, general voice quality, consonant assessment and K's staccato rate) showed as much as a three-point variation. Moreover, a similar number of parameters (pitch variability, vocal fry usage, misarticulations and speech rate) exhibited no variability at all. In short, when the multiple evaluations of the 14 features were collapsed onto a single scale, the only conclusion that could have been drawn was that the samples were produced by two different women. Another woman was arrested about 6 months later and confessed to the crime by means of a plea bargain. Not scientific data, but confirmation to a degree.

Figure 4.4 also was drawn from a real-life case. In this instance, a match was possible with the decision being made at a reasonably high (but not *extremely* high) level of confidence. Note also that both U and K were compared to samples from two foil speakers (in those cases the scores were strongly toward a non-match). As can be seen from the figure, the U v. K judgments were quite positive with only vocal fry usage an exception. The lowest mean score for any of the other features was at least at the level of 6 (i.e. those for speech bursts and nasality); further, 16 of the possible features could be assessed (both the evidence and exemplar tapes were long and of reasonably good quality). On the other hand, greater than desirable evaluation-to-evaluation variability can be observed. Indeed, judgments for two of the features (nasality and intensity variability) were spread out over four categories (4–7 and 6–9 respectively) and seven others showed a three-point spread. This variability was found to be due (in part anyway) to: (1) the extensive amount of speech available, (2) disguise attempts by the suspect (especially early in the exemplar) and (3) differences in the speaking environments. Nevertheless, the two sets of utterances quite probably were produced by the same talker. Again, external evidence (including computer-based 'acoustic' measures) pretty much confirmed the relationship.

A NOTE ON ADMINISTRATION

This approach is one which, while subjective and flexible, requires some rigor in its administration. It is necessary to develop a reasonably large number of U–K sample pairs and, then, spend some period of time assessing them. It is important to complete the entire set of judgments in one sitting and score each of the similarities and dissimilarities on the 10-point continuum. It is also important that the entire process be independently repeated one to three more times, preferably on different days. If the impact of any of the factors is increased or decreased by weighting, it is necessary to record carefully the reasons for doing so. In any event, while this approach is not a trivial one (especially if it is supplemented by acoustic analysis), it will suffer if criteria for its administration are not rigorously observed.

TEST ASSESSMENT

In my estimation, it is not quite legitimate to develop an approach to something (to anything for that matter) and not test it. The problem, of course, is how you can conduct a fair and impartial evaluation of something you have developed yourself. Activities of this type simply are difficult to carry out. Yet, you must attempt validation of your work. If you do not, you are subject to Nolan's (17) justifiable comment that AP-SPID approaches lack standards. Moreover, if you turn to the basic research for guidance, you will be disappointed as test evaluation is only a very minor part of it. For one thing, most of the studies designed to test a person's ability to identify speakers by hearing their voices usually involve only a single exposure to very short samples (10, 14, 25–35). The task is sometimes even more complex than that (36–39) but short samples are the norm. In contrast, data from the studies reviewed in Chapter 3, can be used to argue that it is possible to structure an AP-SPID procedure in such a manner that it can be reasonably valid and efficient. They support the proposition that, even though you will not always be able to achieve satisfactory results, intelligent decisions can usually be made – that is, if careful processing is carried out.

Nonetheless, it is important to establish the validity and reliability of any test vehicle. We have done so here, at least to some extent. Please consider Table 4.2. The data seen in section A were drawn from laboratory experiments. None of these (laboratory) trials used machine-based supplements of any type. Note that an incorrect judgment was made in only one instance. In that case, the voices were difficult to assess and the examiner reported only a 57% confidence level. The data in section B were drawn from real-life criminal cases. As far as can be determined, no errors were made. However, the support for section B precision can hardly be called scientific, since the outcomes are based on confessions, plea bargains and convictions rather than on experimental data.

Table 4.2

A summary table of laboratory assessments and real-life criminal cases where the AP-SPID procedures described in this section were evaluated. These data were collected over the past 23 years; while they result from the efforts of four examiners, nearly two-thirds were completed by the author.

Type	*N*	Confirmed	Confidence level	
			Mean	Range
(A) Laboratory				
Match	10	9	81	57–88
Elimination	4	4	88	86–90
(B) Field[1]				
Match	8	8	77	65–84
Elimination	2	2	79	77–81

1. A further 12 cases were processed but no information about their outcome was available. Note also that over half of the field cases were supplemented by acoustical analysis.

A second set of comparisons also are available. They involve how well the calculated confidence level obtained from our AP-SPID agreed with those produced by panels of listeners and, especially, with those generated by our acoustic processing method (SAUSI; see Chapter 8). The data from this assessment may be found in Table 4.3. Admittedly, the sample is a small one. However, the AP-SPID and SAUSI scores are quite comparable and this finding suggests that the AP-SPID technique, if carried out with precision, may just be robust enough to use even if no other procedures are available to supplement it. Finally, note the scores from the panels; they proved to be a little better than expected. True, the powerful paired-comparisons technique was employed (i.e., ABX or A = hear a sample, B = hear a second sample, X = decide if they were spoken by one or two individuals). Nonetheless, the results are a little surprising as the samples used here were fairly short (7–12 s long) and the people on the panels had to make their decisions rather quickly.

Comparison	N	AP-SPID	Panel	SAUSI
U-1 vs. K	1	19.6	11.3	13.0
U-1 vs. U-2		80.1	71.2	73.4
U vs. K	2	78.3	74.2	81.5
U vs. K				
Match	4	76.8	–	83.0
No Match	2	14.4	–	11.7

Table 4.3

Summary table of comparisons among three different approaches to speaker identification. All values are in either per cent confidence level (AP) or probability level (SAUSI)

Finally, it is clear that anyone carrying out AP-SPIDs should be aware of just how well they can do it. Personally, I have been fortunate in this regard because, over the years, I have been included as a subject in literally hundreds of experiments. These investigations have included a number that addressed issues in SPID. The per cent correct (or hit rate) for those studies where I still have records may be found in Table 4.4. The performances here are not perfect to be sure. Additionally, I believe that there are other phoneticians who could do (or have done) just as well as I have; perhaps they have performed (snarl) even better. The point is that anyone doing this type of work *must* provide evidence of both their native hit rate and the success rate they have had with actual cases. If they do not have this information available, they should put themselves to the test, as research of this type is fairly easily accomplished. All they will need is a good tape recorder, earphones, access to a number of voice samples and a neutral referee.

Table 4.4

The author's correct identification (or nonidentification) scores from 34 different experiments over a 29-year period. The first category (i.e., identifying speakers from a pool of speakers) is a much more difficult procedure than is the second (ABX).

Type of experiment	*N*	Per cent correct	Range
Select Speaker			
Laboratory	6	90.6	87–95
Low Fidelity	9	83.1	73–90
Pairs (ABX)			
Laboratory	12	97.3	94–100
Low Fidelity	7	89.3	86–96

THE USE OF PANELS

As with the section on exemplar tape recordings, it was difficult to find a home for this topic; indeed, I was not comfortable with any of the other possible positionings. Yet, a number of forensic phoneticians actually use panels as a supplement to their primary procedures – at least they do from time-to-time. Thus, permit me to review these procedures before I close the chapter.

In practice, the forensic phoneticians who employ panels will use one or both of two classes of auditors: (1) highly trained professionals (i.e. phoneticians) and/or (2) semi-trained or untrained laymen. As would be expected, the data obtained from the professionals usually are quite robust and can provide a great deal of useful information about the speaker's identity. However, it also is important to include the second group – at least those who can demonstrate their ability to successfully carry out the task. That is, before this class of auditors is used, they should be required to show that their responses will be valid. They must demonstrate that they can: (1) follow instructions, (2) hear the samples presented them, (3) correctly identify pairs (of samples) produced by the same speaker and (4) determine when the samples in a pair were uttered by two different individuals. To meet these criteria, each volunteer should be given a hearing test and then (after hearing a few exemplars for purposes of familiarization only), be presented a number of sample pairs on a quasi-random basis. To qualify as subjects, all auditors should pass the hearing test (92% or better) and demonstrate that they can recognize when a pair of samples was produced by the same person, or by two different talkers – at a level of 85% or better. It is suggested that this approach is a reasonable one as either the subjects demonstrate that they can properly carry out the task or they are not included in the subject pool. A paired comparisons technique (ABX), the open selection procedure or what is referred to as a blind sort approach can be employed as the test vehicle. Any of them will provide a reasonably good basis for the decision-making process.

Sometimes the use of panels in a forensic context is challenged when their data are presented in court. Indeed, opposing counsel will argue that the use of such data constitutes 'hearsay.' However, that description is not a correct one as the scores do not constitute third party opinions at all. Rather, they result from subject responses to perceived stimuli by means of a time-honored approach to scientific investigations of human behavior. Indeed, the argument can be shown as functionally incorrect simply by a review of basic stimulus–response (S–R) procedures or by documentation drawn from thousands upon thousands of experiments wherein investigators have used this method in research. In reality, the subject is used as a meter, just as any electronic apparatus might be. Thus, the responses from the panel members are just like those from other 'meters.'

The use of panels does present some very real problems, however. These tend to stem from several inherent relationships. First, it is an expensive and cumbersome technique, second, a sufficient number of forensic phoneticians may not be available to populate the first group (or they may be so widely dispersed that appropriate experimental control is difficult) and, third, it is an awkward procedure to use in the field. Thus, for all its strengths, this technique does not enjoy widespread application.

EPILOGUE

So ends my discourse about the professionals – who they are and what they do. If you are interested in developing your own skills here, you should read some of the books and articles which have been cited. The road may be a long one if you are just starting out but not quite as long if you already have background in some of the relevant areas. Moreover, our area does not, as yet, exhibit a sophisticated structure and that is one of the reasons this particular chapter was written. It is my personal hope that the International Association of Forensic Phonetics will take on the job of establishing *specific* criteria relative to the background and proficiencies a person must have before being recognized as competent in the field. The IAFP committees are off to a good start but now it is time for them to lay down the hard rules necessary. Hopefully, they will do so in the near future. Until that time, I guess that I will just have to be one of those 'gadflys' who challenge those who would assume trappings they do not deserve.

Finally, you will remember that I left you in the lurch at the beginning of Chapter 1 (remember my story 'Women Can Be Stupid Too'?). What happened to that young woman who threatened the judge? Well, I pulled out all the stops in response to his request as I reasoned that it simply *had* to be someone else. However, after completing the AP-SPID procedures described above, plus several drawn from SAUSI, I could only conclude that she was indeed the culprit (AP-SPID = 88% confidence level; SAUSI = 91% probability). My efforts proved to be academic, however, as she admitted that she made the call. I eventually learned that she became the 'guest' of the State of Florida for a period of 18 months.

CHAPTER 5

EARWITNESS LINE-UPS

INTRODUCTION

Problems associated with earwitness line-ups, or voice parades, are of growing concern. First, this form of speaker identification is becoming somewhat more common than in the past; second, in some cases (perhaps many), the procedure is being conducted by individuals that are only marginally competent; and third, adequate criteria for their proper use have not as yet been fully established. However, earwitness line-ups do exist. Since they are a form of SPID, and a complex one at that, we should learn about them.

DEFINITION

Just what, exactly, is an earwitness line-up or a 'voice parade' (as they are sometimes called)? It is where a person who has heard, but not seen, some individual attempts to identify them by listening to their voice. However, these utterances (i.e. those made by the target speaker) are not simply directed to the witness for a judgment of 'It's him' or 'It's not him'. Rather, the voice is presented (or should be anyway) in a field of other voices – usually five to eight – and the witness is asked to identify which among the group belongs to the subject or suspect. An example would be where a woman was raped in a dark place by a man she could not see but heard when he talked to her. When, some time later, a suspect is identified (by some means), his 'voice' is brought before her for identification. All she has available in order to make this identification is her memory of the voice she heard. Naturally, it would not be one with which she is routinely familiar for, if that were the case, she would have long since told the police who he was. An earwitness line-up is therefore created for her by the following procedure. First, the suspect's voice is recorded (an exemplar), then recordings of several other speakers (foils or distractors) are added to the tape. Once complete, it is played for her. If the suspect is guilty *and* she can identify him from his voice, he can be brought to trial. Sounds like an eyewitness line-up doesn't it? It is to some extent, yet it is not exactly the same and herein lies the first of several problems with earwitness identification.

THE FIRST PROBLEM

The fact that voice parades resemble eyewitness line-ups creates almost as many problems as it solves. Accordingly, it would appear useful to consider both the similarities and the dissimilarities between the two procedures. However, it is first necessary to provide some perspectives about eyewitness identification. As you are undoubtedly aware, the process of *visually* identifying a criminal from a pool of individuals is a practice of long standing. It can occur 'live' – i.e. where the suspect is placed in a line-up with four to six other people and the witness attempts to pick him or her from the group – or it can be based on a 'mug-book line-up' (i.e. a set of photographs). In the second case, the witness looks at books crammed with photographs of possible perpetrators and tries to find the correct one (these mug-books remind me of Claude Rains when he said: 'Round up the usual suspects' in the motion picture Casablanca).

There is little question but that eyewitness identification can be quite important to the conduct of a criminal investigation or a trial. Indeed, Buckhout and Freire (16) pointed out that 'the crucial point in many criminal investigations occurs when a suspect is formally identified by a witness in the showup, lineup or photo array.' They are joined by Loftus (2) and van Wallendael *et al.* (3) who suggest that eyewitness testimony can be of considerable importance to a jury, regardless of the circumstances under which the crime was committed. In fact, Buckhout (1), argues that the ability of a witness to visually identify a criminal is one of the very foundations of the criminal justice system. Such testimony is not just important, some people believe it to be virtually infallible. Thus, it goes without saying that, since earwitness line-ups are patterned somewhat after visual identification procedures, they too can be considered both important and valid. I will concede that they often are important. Unfortunately, however, neither the eyewitness nor the earwitness procedures are as robust as you might think. There are problems with both and, worse yet, there are as many dissimilarities between them as there are similarities. You are not convinced that eyewitness identification is not as powerful as you might believe it is? Let us consider some of the positives and negatives inherent in the approach.

PERSPECTIVES ABOUT EYEWITNESS IDENTIFICATION

As you might expect, anything approaching a complete discussion of eyewitness identification would require a book of some magnitude. Indeed, the field is already replete with them. Accordingly, this review will be but a brief outline of some of the relevant pros and cons about the process.

First, you might be interested in an eyewitness research project reported by Loftus (2). She writes about an experiment where a simulated crime was committed and a suspect tried by a student jury. Surprisingly, 68% of the student jurors voted to convict the 'defendant,' even though the single eyewitness, who was shown to have only 20/400 vision, was not wearing glasses at the time of the 'observed' crime. Rattner (4), plus a number of other investigators, emphatically agree with her. To illustrate further, Buckhout (5) also simulated a crime before a class of student 'witnesses,' they later were shown two videotaped line-ups. He found that, in some cases, less than 15% of his subject-witnesses identified only the criminal, and did so without impeaching their choice by also choosing a second, but innocent, person. At their best, the witnesses were mistaken over 40% of the time. In another example, Buckhout and Figueroa (6) demonstrated that they could bias witnesses by misaligning certain photographs in a 'spread' or by the verbal instructions they provided. In all fairness, it must be said that the effects these investigators created were not particularly powerful and, hence, the witness probably would need substantial biasing before the process was significantly degraded. Nonetheless, the effect was there and it was operative.

Other projects support the idea that eyewitness line-ups can be less effective than you would wish. Some of these relationships can be summarized as follows:

1. Race: individuals generally are better at identifying members of their own race than other races (5, 7);
2. Sex: females tend to be better at identifying females whereas males do not show much of a gender bias (7);
3. Attractiveness and distinctive features: individuals who are substantially more or less attractive than the general population appear easier to identify (8); so are faces that can be considered distinctive (9, 10);
4. Age: older individuals tend to be somewhat more identifiable than younger people (7);
5. Clarity of observational field: poor lighting, poor eyesight and so on reduce accuracy (5).

While approval (i.e. a 'positive' environment) tends to enhance identification accuracy, factors such as high similarity among the foils or presentation unfairness (especially that of misinformation or 'suggestive' information) tend to reduce correct identification levels (11–15).

As can be seen even from this brief review, the strengths and weakness of eyewitness identification have been studied and many of the pitfalls related to their use are known. While it is, perhaps, not as powerful a tool as is often thought, it still can be useful if employed with rigorous and intelligent controls (16–20). Moreover, the procedure can be reasonably accurate if the various environmental and behavioral factors are favorable and the investigator understands which relationships and/or events can degrade or enhance the process.

EARWITNESS VERSUS EYEWITNESS

The second problem to be faced is that a number of professionals apparently favor the eyewitness process as a model for earwitness identification (21–30). Several argue that both involve the use of a sensory modality and that they are structured in a similar fashion. Others seem comfortable with the procedures because they (apparently) believe them to be both similar and equal. In some ways, but not all, these authors are correct in their thinking.

At the other extreme are those individuals who argue that voice parades are an inadequate or inappropriate approach to SPID (31, 32). Still others appear uneasy with their nature and application (33–38) or with the ways in which they often are carried out (39, 40). I ignored this area when writing my 1990 book (33) and (later) in a chapter on Forensic Phonetics (41). At that same time, however, a number of practitioners were attempting to codify and upgrade the approach (21, 29, 39, 42–51) and the police were also quite active in this area. In any case, a controversy exists.

Now back to the eye–ear contrast. As stated, many of the similarities between the two procedures are obvious; both involve the use of sensory modalities, the memory of human characteristics or behaviors, confrontational situations, the process of selecting (or identifying) a person from a group, and so on. In other instances, the two may or may not be parallel. Examples are where the witness saw the assailant, the witness heard the assailant (alike), the witness saw the mugger, the witness overhead a drug dealer making a sale (different) etc. Moreover, they are dissimilar in even more fundamental ways. That is, differences exist in: (1) how the (auditory/visual) memories are processed; (2) how a voice is structured (or categorized or analyzed) as opposed to how visual features are assessed and stored; (3) the ways in which fear, anger or arousal can affect the two identification processes; (4) the ways in which poor eyesight and hearing disabilities relate, and (5) the native abilities and attributes which support good visual analysis/memory in contrast to those which make some listeners better at identification than others. As you might expect, this list could be extended with neat parallels observable for some factors and very serious differences for others. In short, it is unreasonable to postulate that eyewitness and earwitness identification mirror each other. On the other hand, and because of the similarities noted, forensic phoneticians involved in voice parades certainly should be cognizant of the nature and structuring of eyewitness procedures. They also should have an appreciation of the successes, failures and controversies articulated by the forensic psychologists working in that area. It is particulary important to have reliable information about the practical problems encountered when eyewitness line-ups are attempted (1, 4, 5, 10–12, 15–17).

Finally, we should not take the position that somehow the workers in the older field are the masters and we are but the students. We certainly can learn from them but even more important to us are the scientists in our own area who have provided a great wealth of information about speaker recognition in general (its strengths and limitations) and the aural-perceptual process in particular. This information can often be directly applied to problems associated with earwitness identification. In short, we need to know what they are all about, how they work and, especially, about the research and practice upon which they are based.

AN ADDITIONAL ISSUE

One criticism leveled against earwitness lineups (and against eyewitness identification in general for that matter) is that they are unreliable – that people simply are poor witnesses. How often have you heard a detective on TV say something like 'Give me 10 witnesses to a crime and I'll give you 10 different descriptions of it!' As a matter of fact, some critics ask why anyone bothers to ask witnesses anything at all? But, is the situation really that bleak? Perhaps not. Interrogation (of all types) is conducted because investigators can often sift through the information they obtain and make sense out of it; other times it provides them with leads. Moreover, there have recently been a number of advances in relevant areas. Improved interrogation techniques now exist, more is known about memory and about how witnesses may react to a given situation. We are better informed about AP-SPID and information also is available about environmental situations and how they can upgrade or degrade perceptual judgments. Let me give you an example, I call it 'A Big Noise on Sunday.'

From time-to-time the Beech Aircraft company requests that my son Kevin and I evaluate certain events about which they think we can legitimately provide them with useful information (these requests usually are associated with an incident or crash). Ordinarily, we can either do so or, at least, make appropriate observations; often experiments are run to test their (or our) theories about what actually happened. One such incident occurred on a pleasant Fall Sunday morning not too long ago. A pair of military fliers on a 'cross country' took off from the commercial airport outside a middle-sized US city (where they had overnighted); they were flying a Beechcraft T-34 two-seat military turboprop trainer. They crashed immediately after takeoff and the disaster was heard by over 50 people (and seen by nearly half of them) who lived in an area either near the airport or at the end of the runway. Why did it happen? We were contacted only after the 'usual' causes had been shown not to be operative. Perhaps clues could be obtained from the sounds the plane made, or from the witnesses. Our team was provided technical details of T-34 operation, the NTSB (National Transportation Safety Board) findings, statements by the witnesses and, of course, a reconstructed scenario of the flight. As you might expect, a reading of the witnesses' statements revealed all kinds of descriptions and what appeared to be many contradictions. Indeed, taken as a whole, what they said they heard (and saw) was pretty confusing. We were asked to digest all available information and then go to the crash site in order to (1) re-interview the witnesses about both their auditory and visual impressions and (2) make sound level measurements, plus tape recordings, of a number of controlled fly-overs by a T-34. We were permitted to specify the number and characteristics of these flights (that is, we could do so within reason). We first reorganized the witnesses' reports into sets based on where the people were located at the time of the crash. We then set up the sound level meters and tape recorders at the centers of these several areas with another of my sons, Brian, handling the most sensitive of them. What became apparent almost immediately was that, when the witnesses were grouped by location, their observations showed reasonable agreement and, more importantly, began to make sense. That is, nearly all of them said that they heard either a very loud bang, an impact sound or a brief but very loud roar. Where they actually were located also seemed to control what they visually observed when they looked up to see what had created the disturbance and where it was coming from. The question then became 'What caused that big roar?' especially since the T-34 engine was found not to have malfunctioned. Moreover, turboprop engines are quieter than radials or jets; they do not 'roar' as loudly on takeoff. Finally, since all of the people interviewed lived near the airport and were used to noises associated with aircraft traffic, their attention would not have been attracted unless something rather unusual had happened. In addition, while turboprops make noise, loudness is usually reduced not increased when they malfunction. Yet, this particular plane made such a loud noise it induced dozens of people living in a trailer park close to the end of the runway to rush from their homes to see what had happened. Moreover, the pilots operating our test aircraft simply could not make the kind of noise the witnesses said they had heard. A dozen of them cooperated by listening to all the different sounds we were able to make. They said that none of them were like those they heard on that fateful Sunday. By the end of our evaluation, we were pretty sure that their opinions were accurate. As a matter of fact, they materially aided us with the solution (sorry, but the parties involved have asked that we keep it confidential). What is important here is that the (witness) reports were both stable and helpful. That is, they were once we had determined (1) where they were located at the time of the accident, (2) their field of view and (3) the time elapsed between when they were attracted to the event auditorily and then could locate the T-34 visually. My personal opinion (based on this example and other like experiences) is that witnesses often are given less credit than they deserve. Perhaps some of the problem here is due, in part anyway, to the people who interview them.

So much for the example. It now would appear useful to take the information found in Chapter 3, add what we know, specifically, about earwitness identification and structure some sort of criteria about how it should be done.

RESEARCH ON EARWITNESS LINE-UPS

It is almost impossible to disassociate the relationships we are discussing from those reviewed in the previous chapter. After all, the processes used here are both auditory and perceptual. However, earwitness line-ups are restricted in the sense that: (1) the target voice will not be known to the witness; (2) there always is a latency (sometimes one that is quite large) between the point in time where the listener first heard the perpetrator's voice and when the earwitness line-up is held; (3) the witness will rarely, if ever, have received training fundamental to SPID analyses; (4) the process is controlled, almost rigid, and (5) all kinds of emotional/personality variables can influence it. Moreover, you will recall that some people are simply better at remembering voices than are others and this is an important uncontrolled variable. Thus, the list goes on and on and, as you can see, it intrudes into many areas that are only quasi-related to SPID. So how can the relevant issues be organized so they will not result in just randomly presented statements, or a simple review of Chapter 3 (and a redundant one at that)? My approach will be to divide the material into several functional categories. They consist of the relationships which are: (1) controllable, (2) partly controllable and (3) uncontrollable. A subsequent section will focus on procedural controversies and, finally, you will be presented an outline focused on how the earwitness line-ups can be structured.

CONTROLLABLE RELATIONSHIPS

The following issues or events should be pretty much under the control of the people who establish, administer and interpret the voice parade.

Witness familiarity with the suspect

It is not enough just to say that, if the witness knew the speaker, the case would have been long since resolved. This is true, of course. However, there are other relationships which also are relevant; they are related to, but have a somewhat different slant from, those discussed in Chapter 3. For one thing, van Lancker and her colleagues (52–55) suggest that the cognitive processes which underlie the recognition of familiar voices differ from those used in identifying unfamiliar ones. Specifically, while familiar voices invoke a discrimination process which can be likened to a pattern recognition task, the perception of unfamiliar voices taps into one which involves feature analysis. This latter process is much more difficult to carry out than is the former and, as such, may result in greater error. In addition, since naive listeners are not trained to differentiate among voice parameters, they have to rely on a rather global set of criteria when they attempt voice judgments (56). This strategy poses an extra problem when the target voice differs from the other voices with respect to a parameter which is not in the listener's response set. An understanding of these features permits the investigator to appropriately structure the line-up as well as intelligently assess the judgments obtained.

Administration and control of line-ups

A controversy exists here. Künzel (47) insists that only qualified forensic phoneticians should be permitted to structure and conduct earwitness line-ups. He takes this position in reaction to a serious problem. Specifically, there is now ample evidence that the individuals who conduct these earwitness line-ups can vary widely with respect to their competencies. Indeed, they include such divergent individuals as police officers (some of whom are seriously unqualified), law enforcement personnel (only some of whom have studied the process), social workers, handwriting specialists, fingerprint examiners, private detectives, security personnel, eyewitness specialists, speech pathologists, linguists, psychologists and phoneticians of all types. Virtually no cohesive structure exists relative to how they should conduct/interpret these procedures, and there should be. That is, those who are not qualified should be excluded and those who are competent (basically, anyway) should be provided with appropriate operational criteria and guidelines. However, is Künzel correct in insisting that *only* forensic phoneticians control the process? He is in an ideal world, but it also is necessary to be practical. Indeed, there are some countries and/or regions in this world that cannot claim the services of even a minimally trained phonetician, much less a specialist in forensic phonetics. Morever, there are other types of forensic specialists who could handle this task; even some law enforcement personnel are competent. For example, a Canadian law enforcement officer (49) has reported a sequential (10) approach that appears superior to the traditional simultaneous line-up (see below). So, what would appear to be the best solution to this particular controversy? The key, of course, is education. Specifically, appropriate operational criteria and procedures should be developed and disseminated, and selected personnel trained in their proper administration and assessment.

Witness expectations

Problems have resulted from the witnesses' assumption that the criminal – or, more accurately the criminal's 'voice' – will be among the persons/voices in the line-up. This issue has been recognized for some time (57–60). For example, we

(58) found that 'innocent' talkers were sometimes selected as the criminal. Worse yet, very few listeners took the option of indicating that the target voice was not present in the line-up even when they realized that such was the case. This problem also is addressed by Milroy (61) who warns that listeners' expectations (as to the identity of the unknown voice) can sharply influence their performances. As stated, this factor is especially critical as earwitnesses can be persuaded that the criminal is among the suspects for no reason other than they believe the police officers would not ask them to come in and identify a voice if they did not have the perpetrator in custody (14, 57). This bias can be countered, however, if the examiner informs the witness that the voice line-up may *not* include the alleged criminal.

Test structure and administration

These elements are, of course, under the control of those individuals (and their staff) who carry out the voice parades. They are discussed in greater detail later. What is reviewed here are those relationships which provide the undergirding of the process plus others which interface with AP-SPID in general. Some of the more important of these are:

(a) **Sample size.** One factor that can be appropriately controlled is sample size. As you will remember from Chapter 3, a number of investigators have observed that sample length can be an important factor in SPID (33, 44, 62–65). Indeed, data had become available as early as 1954 (66) which indicated that identification accuracy improved with increasing sample duration (at least for a while) and greater sampling provided additional information about the speakers phonemic repertoire (63, 67–69). Another relationship. While increased sample length may improve listener scores for filtered speaking conditions, these relationships are quite complex and are especially so for speech over telephone links (39, 70–75). In short, however, the larger the speech sample, the better for the listener (it does not matter if they are professionals or lay witnesses). That is, the greater the repertoire of speaking events, the greater the fund of contrastive information. In any event, good control can be exercised over sample length or duration.

(b) **Sample quality.** Note from Chapter 3 that sample quality also is important. Again, reasonable control can be exercised at the identification end of the process even if it was impossible to do so during the confrontation (for example, severe noise may have been present even if the perpetrator was close to the witness or the telephone link may have been a poor one). Control of quality can be quite important especially across the line-up samples. A number of investigators have observed that listener's performance can be hampered, even for known speakers, when the signal is degraded by increasing the number of speakers, substituting whispered for normal speech, using different types of speakers, using different speech materials and so on (35, 45, 48, 58, 67–69, 72, 76–85). Suggestions as to how to control sample quality will be found in subsequent chapters.

(c) **Foils.** The number and nature of the foil or distractor voices used in the line-up is important too and many aspects of this element lend themselves to control. That is, since witnesses' ability to cope with the identification task correlates with the number of talkers in the group, the number of 'foil talkers' will affect their accuracy in making judgments. Hence, the number of foils or distractor voices used in a voice parade should be kept to a reasonable minimum (say, five to eight). As you can see, cohort size is one of the parameters which can be controlled. So too can the nature of the distractor voices. It would not be sensible (or fair) to seek out and select only voices which do not sound like the suspect's as it is well known that if only speakers who sound very different from the suspect are used, many false identifications will occur. Conversely, research also can be used to show that if foils with voices that sound similar to the subject's (or criminal's) are included, identification accuracy can be seriously reduced (73, 83, 86–88). At the very least, the number of false identifications will be increased (89). Note that when Rothman (73) used sound-alikes (e.g. brothers, fathers and sons), he found that identification accuracy dropped from 94% (ordinary foils) to 58% (sound-alikes). Our results were similar (87). Thus, to be fair to both the witness and the suspect, the line-up should contain a variety of voices: one or more can be somewhat similar to the target voice, one or more should be somewhat different and the rest 'in between' (42, 43, 86). Finally, the speech samples presented to the witness should be uniform in all respects. That is, the recording environment should be consistent, the text of the speech samples similar, etc. Whether the presentation is quasi-simultaneous (i.e. all voices placed on one tape and it played in its entirety) or sequential (each voice on its own tape) are under the administrator's control.

PARTLY CONTROLLABLE FACTORS

Emotional states

One of the challenges facing the person who structures an eyewitness line-up involves assessment and control of the witness's psychological state. Unfortunately, not nearly enough research has been carried out about the effects that felt emotions have on SPID, a little has been reported but the models here are incomplete (26, 36, 52, 53, 90–92). Indeed, such is the state of science that even though it is well known that psychological stress (and other emotions) will be reflected in a person's voice (42, 93–97), the magnitude of their effect has not been established. So, what impact do these emotional factors have on voice parades? First, it must be remembered that the practitioner has no control over, and, indeed, little direct knowledge of, the emotions experienced by the victim or witness during the commission of the crime. About all the examiner can do is interview the witness and, then, make some sort of an educated guess. A high level of psychological stress (especially fear and anger) would probably have been experienced by the victim if the trauma was substantial. Conversely, little stress would be expected of an agent who routinely intercepted a telephone call by a drug dealer. The primary level of stress experienced might also be complicated by varying states of arousal. Consider the discussion in Chapter 3 (90, 91) as to how these two factors can interrelate. The subjects who had been stressed and/or aroused did better at recognizing speakers than those who had not been threatened. Of course, no control is possible over the original event, however, knowing a little about what the witness had felt at the time can assist the examiner/investigator in enhancing line-up administration and better interpreting the witnesses' responses.

During the line-up

It is also important to identify the psychological states or emotions the witness is experiencing *during* the voice parade. An example here is the case of the 'Modern Marquis de Sade'. A Canadian man kidnaped a number of young women (one at a time, of course) and kept each of them captive for several days. During their captivity, he humiliated, tortured and raped them; toward the end of his spree, he killed several of them. He was eventually caught and, since he had not let his victims see him (he used blindfolds, masks, etc.) but had talked to them, earwitness line-ups were essential. Each of the surviving women, in turn, were allowed to hear tapes of his voice plus those of a number of foils; these tapes were presented 'in sequence' (see below for descriptions of sequential procedures). Several of the women could not make an identification (one said she was afraid to); others did, however. Moreover, one or two others had been so profoundly affected by the experience, they broke down when they heard the perpetrator's voice. The worst case was one where the victim had been so traumatized she could not carry out the task at all. She burst out crying the minute she heard his voice – certainly a powerful identification even if she was unable to speak. Watching the films of these women provided me with substantial insight about the various ways they coped, or did not cope, with extreme stress and the identification process. There are times when prior trauma and its effects are not so obvious, but since they can operate to degrade the speaker identification process, attempts should be made to identify and mitigate them. Obviously, they must be recognized before they can be countered.

Disguise

Finally, there is little question that any attempts at voice disguise by a suspect can reduce witness accuracy (33, 35, 41, 45, 57, 76, 84, 93, 98, 100–103). These attempts may be controlled to some extent when the exemplar is made; however, nothing can be done about the voice disguise that might have taken place during the original confrontation. Important here is collaboration with a skilled interrogator/examiner; one who is knowledgeable about speech, voice disguise and how to counteract them for purposes of a good line-up (104).

UNCONTROLLABLE ISSUES

There are some factors that simply cannot be controlled by any investigator or administrator. It can only be hoped that, if they occur, their effects will be either randomized, counter-balanced or minimal.

Training

While general training (either field training or training in general phonetics) does not always provide significant benefits to individuals conducting speaker identification evaluations, specific training in forensic phonetics will tend to upgrade performance sharply (71, 105–110). However, few, if any, witnesses can be expected to have any training at all. Hence, this factor is not subject to control by the administrator of an earwitness line-up.

Talent

A closely related issue is that of listener talent. That is, it has been shown that some listeners are simply better at identification than are others (37, 39, 58, 75, 82, 99, 105, 107, 108, 110–115). This factor constitutes another uncontrollable variable.

Memory

One of the most important of the uncontrollable variables involves the witnesses' memory (both type of memory and the ability to remember). These factors are of particular consequence because the ability of humans to remember a heard voice is fundamental to the earwitness line-up (79, 119). A complicating item is that auditory memory is rather different from visual memory. For example, it has been found that 'eyewitness memory' does not significantly affect correct identification even after delays as long as several months, whereas even shorter latencies markedly degrade memory for auditory stimuli. Thus, latencies related to earwitness identification are critically important. That is, while it would be expected that the results obtained depend a great deal on the presentation protocols (i.e. open/closed sets, length of utterance(s), number of distractors, quality of the speech samples, etc.), it is the overall factor of time which is of *prime* importance. For example, remember that McGehee (120, 121) (and others, of course) reported a considerable decay in identification after the first week. Also remember that the curve for her scores tended to resemble the Ebbinghaus 'forgetting' curve (122), i.e. a sharp but minor reduction, which occurred immediately, followed by a steady decay over time. Other data have been reported which appear to have violated this pattern (36, 58); nonetheless, overall, the decline is consistent and often sharp (26, 120, 123). To reiterate, latency is a crucial factor and significant degradation in identification accuracy can usually be expected after only a couple of weeks. The phrase 'significant degradation' is the controlling term in this instance because, even though some auditors are capable of performing well even after long periods of time have elapsed, memory for voice *will* decay and will do so even for the best of them. To summarize, it has been shown that slight delays (prior to the line-up) may not significantly impede the SPID process but those typical of the forensic situation can be quite detrimental. While sooner is better, this factor is not controllable.

Witness characteristics

You should now be aware that a rather substantial amount of research has been carried out on AP-SPID; it even can be said that a healthy segment of it has addressed earwitness identification. Yet, few projects have focused directly on those factors or characteristics which permit humans to be consistently good at this task (or, for that matter, poor at it). An exception is DeJong's work (105) a study she completed at IASCP, University of Florida. Admittedly, the 'native' talent of a witness would be subject to little, if any, control. Nevertheless, an understanding of these factors should aid the examiner in making better sense out of witness behavior. In any event, DeJong asked if a person's memory, inherent auditory capability and musical skills would affect their ability to identify speakers and, if so, just how these particular characteristics operated to influence accuracy. In order to answer these questions, she selected a group of 112 women between the ages of 18 and 35 years of age and subjected them to a SPID selection procedure. The two groups she ultimately studied consisted of 14 women who scored highest on the identification task and 13 who exhibited the lowest scores. Memory was assessed by means of a number of test vehicles; as were subjects' auditory and musical skills. The results were compared first by cohort and, subsequently, individually. DeJong reports that intelligence (as measured by cognitive processing) was the better predictor of a subject's ability to identify speakers (better, that is, than basic auditory and memory skills). She also discovered that listeners who exhibited a high degree of musical aptitude could be expected to perform somewhat better than those who did not show these capabilities. This series of experiments provides some insight about the factors which discriminate among good and poor earwitnesses. Although there is little chance that these factors can be modified in any manner by the examiner, information about them can certainly increase his or her depth of understanding about the process.

Other issues

Lastly are a number of factors which are said to influence witness sensitivity to a voice. Ordinarily, thses effects tend to be minimal; hence, they will be only briefly considered. First, it has been suggested that chronological age can affect the SPID process. If this is true, it would help in explaining some of the variance here. Some gross evidence has been presented but it seems clear that individuals are more accurate in dealing with people their own age and that, overall, children and the elderly are poorer at these tasks (24, 70, 78, 111). Further, it is often argued that listener gender must be situation specific because neither males nor females have been found to be consistently better at voice identification (4, 24, 30, 69, 116). Third, it has been reported that hearing a non-native language can reduce the level of correct identification (38), whereas various types of accents will not (117). However, I do not believe these factors to be controlling as the preponderance of the data would suggest otherwise (see the discussion in Chapter 3). Finally, it has been suggested that witnesses who have heard the subject more than once will often do better than those who have not and some reports can be used to argue this position (118). While the occurrence may be a little unusual, it does happen. An example here is the case of the 'Friendly Rapist'. A woman living in the US Virgin Islands was raped. She reported it to the police and then, later, indicated that the rapist had called her on the telephone and asked for a date. Later, she reported as having 'heard' his voice yet again but could not remember exactly where; she said that she had begun to wonder if she had only imagined these subsequent occurrences. Then, suddenly, she realized that a man who frequented the same market she did was the culprit and that having heard his voice a number of times allowed her to identify him. He was arrested and she did very well at identifying him from among the foils in a voice parade. The police also found that he had kept the jewelry he had stolen from her at the time of the rape and they returned it all to her.

PROCEDURES

There are currently three approaches to the structuring of earwitness line-ups; the first two can be identified as a type of simultaneous line-up and the form of the third is sequential. Simultaneous line-ups are where the suspect's voice, included with the foil samples, is/are heard as a set, i.e., serially one immediately after the other. Sequential presentations are where the witness listens to the tapes one at a time. These techniques parallel those developed for eyewitness identification (10, 19).

The first type of voice parade is simultaneous in nature but, in this case all samples (i.e., that of the suspect's voice, plus those of foils) are presented only *once*. The second of the three is structured in much the same manner as the first but the sets of voices are presented several times. The third approach is quite different from the first two as it is sequential in nature and the witness controls the number of times each tape is heard.

THE SIMULTANEOUS SINGLE-TRIAL LINE-UP

The procedure here is to randomly place a tape recorded sample of the suspect's voice within the set of distractor voices (or foils). The witness is only allowed to hear this tape recording once. Of course, it is difficult to understand how only a single trial could take place under any circumstance (i.e. where the witness hears the voices only that one time and never again). The question arises as to what happens if he/she asks to hear it again and a heated debate currently exists about these procedures and their consequences. Some individuals have contended that, to be valid, only a single trial can be performed, others argue that the witness(es) should have the option of hearing the tape as many times as they wish.

Moreover, the proponents of the second approach suggest that the witness must demonstrate that they can consistently identify the suspect's voice, and do so a number of times before the results can be accepted. In this case, the suspect's sample would be placed in a different position on the tape for each of several trials; the distractor voices also would remain the same but sorted into different positions.

The single trial advocates argue that these multiple presentations do not meet appropriate statistical protocols/assumptions and that rehearing the suspect's voice over and over again will cause the witness(es) to identify him even if he is not the perpetrator. In turn, the multiple trial advocates argue that repeated-measures statistical techniques will appropriately handle designs of this type and that a single trial does not permit reasonably stable judgments to be made. They will lead, potentially anyway, to false identifications and eliminations because the witness is not provided enough information to make an intelligent decision. Even more important, however, there is no reason to believe that a witness would falsely 'lock' onto the suspect; after all, why should one do so if the suspect is not the perpetrator? Since each of the distractor's samples also are repeated, there is just as much chance that the witness would lock onto one of them (if, indeed, that happens at all). The experimental data available on the issue tend to suggest that correct identification does not vary with repeated trials. That is, it has been shown (58, 99, 118) that auditors correctly identify a particular speaker with equal accuracy both early and late in a series of presentations. Finally, there currently are not enough data to establish that single trial procedures are valid in the first place. This approach probably is not a good one.

THE MULTIPLE-TRIAL, SIMULTANEOUS LINE-UP

This entity is structured almost identically to the one described above; i.e. a speech sample produced by the suspect is embedded somewhere within a sequence of samples spoken by the foils. The difference is that this tape recording is replicated a number of times. It contains the same suspect and foils but with their utterances placed in different positions each time. Speech sample content can also vary over the trials but it must be consistent for the speakers within each. The arguments cited above also apply here but, again, they favor this approach over that of a single presentation. Nonetheless, one of the principal objections to this approach is that, since eyewitness line-ups are presently carried out only once, voice parades should be similarly restricted. However, this argument is not based on fact. Eyewitness line-ups (either live or as photographic arrays) are usually presented in a single *session* but not only once. The suspect and foils are not seen a single time but rather many, many times. That is, the witnesses can look at the people in the line-up for as long as they wish and as many times as they want; they can have them step forward, turn left, turn right and so on – hardly a single trial. Moreover, consider Table 5.1. Here, you can see that very little 'locking in' on anybody (target or foil) occurred in a number of real-life situations and experimental trials. A case in point may be referred to as that of the 'Victimized Mother' (33). Several years ago a divorced woman with several children had one of her teenage daughters

Table 5.1
Summary table of mock trials conducted under laboratory and field conditions. Listeners were asked to select the speaker who 'sounded like a criminal' or 'stood out.' (A) lists the percent times the subject/suspect, and each of the foils, was chosen. (B) lists how often each of the speakers (S, F1–F5) was chosen for each of the five trials.[1]

Study	N	Listeners	Suspect	F1	F2	F3	F4	F5
(A)								
Laboratory	5	10	16	16	11	22	18	17
Field	4	4	15	25	5	15	20	20
				Trial				
				1	2	3	4	5
(B)								
Laboratory	5	10						
Suspect				8	2	20	5	5
F-1				10	15	8	10	12
Field	4	4						
Suspect				5	5	5	0	0
F-3				5	5	0	10	5

1. There always were six speakers (S, F1–F5) but only the foil with the most 'hits' is listed. Laboratory procedure: 10 listeners making five judgments for five separate trials (N = 250). Field procedure: average of four listeners making five judgments for four separate trials (*N* = 80).

kidnapped. Just about the time the police found the daughter's body, the woman received a telephone call from a man who said he was the person who had kidnapped the girl, that she was safe and well, and that he would return her if the mother paid him $6000 (a rather tacky sum, would you not agree?). Because of this call (which was recorded, of course), the police did not release the information about the discovery of the girl's body, but rather set a trap for the extortionist. An agreement was made over the telephone and the money was placed next to a dumpster in the alley he specified. Naturally, the entire area was placed under surveillance and, after several hours had elapsed, a man left one of the apartments and walked down to the dumpster carrying a container of trash. After depositing the trash, he appeared to notice the sack containing the money, picked it up, looked in it, looked both ways down and up the alley and, then, hurriedly returned to his apartment. He was arrested. During the period before his trial, he was asked to make a voice exemplar and did so. Four other speech samples were provided by two policemen, a parole officer and a social worker. Excerpts from the five tape recordings were played to the mother by the district attorney and she identified the suspect as the extortionist. Thereupon, he was brought to trial, but only for extortion as it was clear he was not involved in either the kidnapping or the murder. I was called in because the defense was unhappy with the way the prosecution had handled the earwitness line-up (they had reason to be). First, I examined the voice line-up itself and discovered that the defendant's voice was rather different from those of any of the foils. I played the tape to a class saying 'one of the men on this tape is a criminal; which one?' The students grumbled about not having enough information to do so but, 82% of them selected the defendant. Thus, I opined that the witness probably had enough cues to point him out even if he was not the extortionist. Upon hearing this, the defendant's lawyers challenged the procedure and the witness was required to repeat her evaluation in open court. Even after learning about the problems with the foils, the presiding judge still ruled that the tape had to be used 'as is' (but resorted). However, he did allow me to present a number of trials, some with the unknown caller's voice substituted for the defendant's. Since only the judge had the key, he was able to assess her performance. His reasoning apparently was that, if the witness could systematically identify the defendant, he undoubtedly was the guilty party (albeit, a pretty darn lazy guy). On the other hand, if she could not do so, the defense attorney would argue to the contrary. As it turned out, the courtroom test was only modestly conclusive. The woman was only able to identify the extortionist about 75% of the time and the defendant at a level that was slightly lower. While still a little questionable, these identifications were at a level that was well above chance and the mother completed the task under stressful conditions (on the witness stand in an open courtroom). In any event, the defendant was convicted and, perhaps, justifiably so. The point here is that the witness's patterns of correct identification showed no systematic biasing over the trials. Indeed, she did not 'lock' onto any of the speakers except, of course, the unknown talker and the defendant. And here, some of her identifications came early in the sets with her errors actually coming later. The reverse would have been true if a learning of the defendants voice had occurred. This is but one example, yet it provided further evidence that multiple trials are helpful.

The sequential procedure

The third approach is probably the most powerful of the three; it can be best understood by consideration of Figure 5.1. Note that the room is a relatively

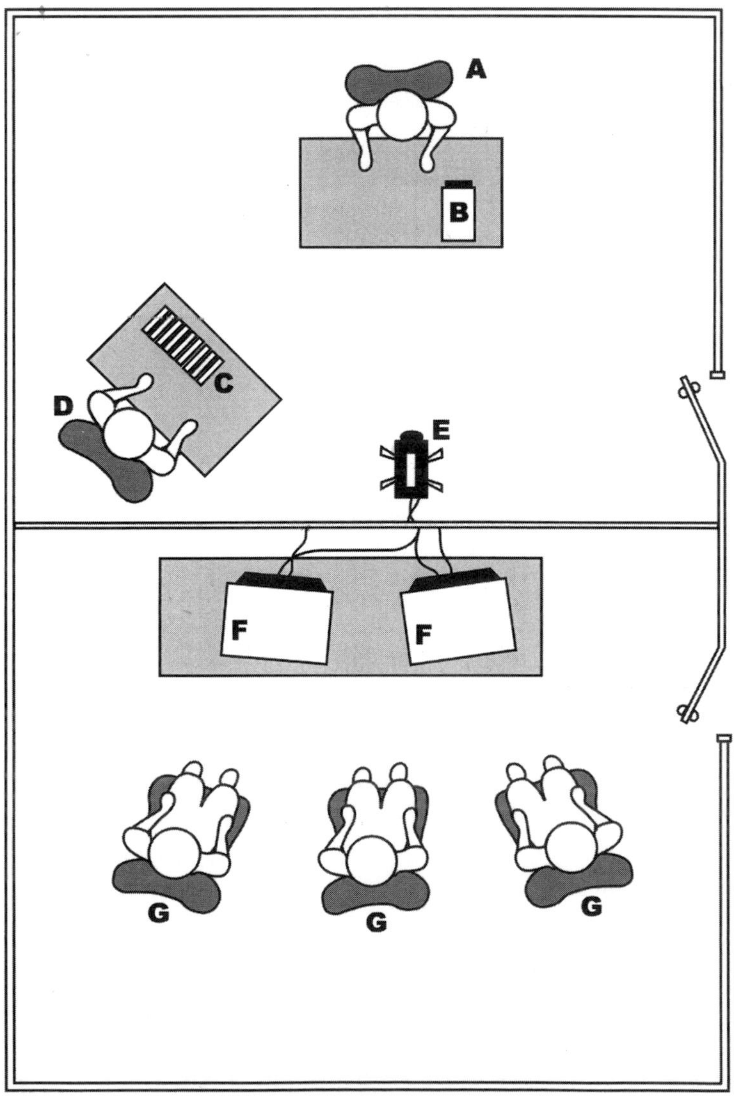

Figure 5.1

A graphic display of the 'sequential' approach to earwitness identification. A is the witness, B = a tape recorder, C = the tape recordings, D is the adminisrtator, E = the videocam, F = the TV monitors and G shows observers.

small one and contains two desks, two chairs and a mounted video camera. The witness sits at a desk with a tape recorder placed in front of her. The person at the other table provides the (numbered) tape recordings. This administrator would *not* be permitted to know which of the tapes contains the suspect's voice exemplar. The procedure is that the witness calls out a number, the administrator gives her that tape and she plays it (she is allowed to make notes if she wishes; the administrator is not permitted to do so, or to comment). The witness then hears, in turn, the rest of the tapes in any numerical order desired. Once all the tapes have been heard, the witness is permitted to request (and replay) any of them and as many times as necessary. Ultimately, they are asked if they can identify their assailant (or the suspect) and, if so, which tape contains his or her voice. They are not required to make a selection if they are unable to, or are uncomfortable in, doing so. Finally, note again the video camera seen in the drawing. It is by this means that relevant individuals can observe the behavior of the witness and, indeed, the entire procedure. The videotape of the entire session is retained for possible future use. This approach appears to incorporate virtually all of the positive features of the other two but few, if any, of their negative aspects. It also permits a permanent record to be made of the entire session. The video camera can be linked to TV sets in the other room and any number of interested parties can observe the witness's behavior without introducing any of the possible negative effects (pressure, biasing, intimidation, etc.) that could result from a more invasive procedure.

CRITERIA FOR STANDARDS

There is little question but that standards for earwitness line-ups can be difficult to establish (perhaps that is why so few people have tried). For example, note the confusions and controversies that surround eyewitness identification. Consider also the many different procedures (exact and casual, sloppy and efficient) that have been used around the world. It must be remembered also that there are many issues in AP-SPID which are not relevant (or even tangential) to earwitness identification, especially when standards are considered. For example, how a practitioner (at any level) should interface with the courts or law enforcement personnel is somewhat irrelevant, as is how suspects should be identified and/or indicted, or how basic police records should be kept. These may be of legitimate concern to practitioners but they are beyond the purview of criteria necessary for the proper conduct of earwitness line-ups. Thus, the standards found below are limited to those relationships which permit valid and efficient procedures to be established – those that will be fair to both the witness and the suspect.

So, what are they? As it turns out, a number of them are quite obvious and they provide the substrata for the guidelines to follow. Others may not be so obvious but since they enjoy support from both research and logic, they will be included also. Moreover, there are a few issues which either have to be resolved or await future research; when they are reviewed, they will be so identified. Please note that all of these three topics will be covered. To ignore what can be accomplished in order to wait for a 'full solution' is similar to the founding fathers of the United States refusing to write a Constitution because it would not cover every eventuality and probably would be subject to future amendments.

DEFINITIONS

The basic definition of an earwitness line-up can be found at the beginning of this chapter. However, further clarification probably will be useful. Simply stated, the process is one where a witness is required to identify (if possible) a suspect's voice from a field of voices. Each line-up should involve but a single witness and a single talker. The talker, then, is usually a suspect (they will be identified thus in this section). If there is more than one witness, or more than one suspect, multiple line-ups should be carried out, and they must be conducted independently of each other. The witness must have heard the suspect's voice but not have *seen* them (utterances heard over a telephone line or when the witness was blindfolded are examples). In short, a voice parade is not indicated if the witness (1) has seen the suspect, (2) is familiar with his or her speech and voice or (3) is presented the voice samples in any manner other than those specified below. In the other cases, alternative forms of identification should be carried out. The criteria for earwitness line-ups follow.

General issues

(a) **Parity.** Earwitness line-ups should be scrupulously fair to both the witness(es) and the suspect(s). Guidelines should be established for this purpose and rigorously observed.

(b) **Records.** All aspects of the process should be properly recorded. Included should be records of (1) the witness(es)' background and statements, (2) the source of the suspects and their characteristics and (3) all activities/phases related to the identification process. These records are independent of, or are in addition to, the ordinary records kept by law-enforcement personnel.

(c) **The witness.** It is important that the witness demonstrates competency in carrying out SPID tasks. They should be able to demonstrate that they attended to the perpetrators voice at a level which would permit it to be remembered. The witness also should be able to demonstrate that they have hearing adequate for the listening task and the ability to make identifications from aural-perceptual voice materials. Pretests may have to be administered in order to establish these relationships.

(d) **Instructions.** Clear instructions should be provided the witness(es); they should be told that: (1) only one suspect will be present in the line-up, (2) the suspect in the lineup may or may not be the perpetrator and (3) separate line-ups will be structured and held if there is more than one suspect. The witness should be told *not* to guess if an identification is not possible.

Procedure

(a) **Samples.** All of the exemplar samples (i.e. the utterances by the suspect and the foils) should be equal in length and of the same fidelity. They also should be long enough to provide witnesses with a reasonable repertoire of the suspect's (and foils') speech. All samples should consist of parallel texts (or approximately the same material).

(b) **Stimulus materials.** It is desirable (but not absolutely necessary) to include two types of (speech) materials among the samples. They are: neutral and text independent speech (for example, extemporaneous speech in response to neutral but structured questions) and text-dependent words, phrases and sentences (the samples here are often obtained by having the suspect and foils orally read appropriate material). Repetition of the phrases reported by the witness as having been heard in the original confrontation can also be useful. It is desirable to obtain as long an exemplar recording as possible, as any attempts by the suspect to disguise his or her voice (if they were to occur) often can be mitigated by this procedure (see Chapter 4).

(c) **Foil talkers.** Between five and eight foil or distractor speakers should be employed. They should be of approximately the same age as the suspect and generally exhibit the same dialect/accent. It also is desirable that they be of approximately the same social, economic and educational status. Care should be taken in their selection; the use of actors, or other individuals who speak quite differently from the suspect, should be avoided. The characteristics of the suspect's voice may be described to the foils but they cannot be allowed to hear it, especially because they might be able to mimic it. Finally, the witness should be provided with a reasonable repertoire of (different) voices. Hence, the foils' speech should encompass a range that extends from where, at least, one voice sounds a little like the suspect to where, at least, one is quite dissimilar.

(d) **A procedural test.** A set of mock trials or evaluations should be carried out once the earwitness line-up tape(s) is/are developed. That is, it/they should be presented to four to six dispassionate listeners who are told to either select the person who is 'different from the others' or 'who sounds like a criminal.' If these judges consistently identify either the suspect or one of the foils, the tapes cannot be considered unbiased and should be restructured.

Test administration

(a) **Use of recordings.** All speech samples should be in recorded form. The use of 'live' line-ups should be avoided.

(b) **Fidelity.** All samples should be presented on good quality audio equipment; the same system should be used to record and replay all samples.

(c) **Presentation.** Sample presentation should be carefully controlled. All sets should be administered in an identical manner, structured in the same manner (as cited above) and presented with the same ambient background with respect to noise/events (quiet is best, of course).

(d) **Feedback.** No information relative to their performance should be provided the witness(es) during or immediately after any of the trials.

(e) **Impartiality.** An earwitness line-up of any type should be presented to a witness only when he or she can be observed by neutral individuals and/or personnel representing the suspect. No person except the administrator should even speak to the witness during the trials and they (i.e. the witness) should not be able to see any of the other people. It is essential that only the administrator be in the room with the witness and all other individuals observe the process via remote links (video or one-way mirrors). Again, the person who administers the line-up should not know which of the speech samples was uttered by the suspect.

(f) **Structure.** Either the traditional (i.e. multiple presentation simultaneous) approach to earwitness line-ups or the sequential procedure are acceptable. The approach involving multiple presentations is considered preferable to the single presentation procedure for the reasons articulated above. As has been suggested, this (second) type of voice parade should be presented at least five times with the samples of the suspect and the (same) foils in different positions. On the other hand, the sequential approach permits the witness to select the order in which the samples are to be heard as each one is on a separate tape. However, just as with the traditional method, the witness must hear all the samples at least once before hearing any of the others a second time. The primary difference between the two methods is that the witness hears a repeat of the entire line-up with the simultaneous procedure whereas they can individually listen to (additional) playings of any of the speaker's voices when the sequential technique is employed.

(g) **Decisions.** A decision by the witness is sought at the end of the earwitness session. However, they should not be forced to select one of the talkers as the perpetrator if they indicate that they cannot (or are reluctant to) do so.

CONCLUSION

These guidelines, while not all-encompassing, nonetheless include most of the necessary criteria for the development of acceptable earwitness line-ups. A model such as this one can be used to signal personnel working in the field that they must start taking cognizance of good practice and rigorous procedures, as well as respond positively to new criteria as they are established. That is to say there is still room for upgrading these procedures. For example, more needs to be known about the processes a person uses to remember a voice and how to enhance presentation of voices in order to improve identification. Advances in AP-SPID techniques also should help. And, of course, some of the areas listed in the criteria section can be improved. To illustrate, research should be carried out in order to determine: (1) if actors can (or even should) be used as foils and, if so, under what conditions; (2) which classes of stimulus materials are most suitable (should the suspect's speech be text dependent and/or independent; neutral and/or stressed; extemporaneous and/or read); (3) if simultaneous or sequential line-ups, or both, should be employed and (4) how practitioners should be trained and certified. There are many other questions that also must be asked and resolved. It is sufficient to say that earwitness line-ups are a reality and they occur quite often and all over the world. As a consequence, we must be prepared to deal with them – and those individuals who wish to conduct them – both intelligently and ethically.

VOICEPRINTS

INTRODUCTION

This book should be a chapter shorter than it actually is. The 'missing' section should be this one. But, unfortunately, the problem of 'voiceprints' seemingly cannot be completely erased from the world of speaker identification. For one thing, some of the people who previously worked at one of the FBI laboratories still make noises about it from time-to-time (1). Occasionally, one hears casual references to voiceprints by attorneys and law enforcement personnel. There even seems to be a small clutch of 'voiceprint examiners' which exists in an organization called IAI (International Association of Identification). As an example, in February of 1998, a private detective gave a paper on 'voiceprints' at the annual convention of the American Academy of Forensic Sciences. Even though his background only included a degree in history from a small college and a private detective business, he somehow managed to inveigle provisional membership in the Engineering section of the Academy. His 'paper' was not very scholarly or scientific. He provided only a small amount of information about what voiceprints were all about and how you make them. He also showed slides of some of the relevant equipment plus photographs of several people who could be classed as voiceprint proponents. He did not provide any data in support of the method. As you might expect, he was badly mauled by several academy members. The point here is not that this man did a poor job (it would be pretty difficult to do a good one considering his topic), but rather that voice-prints are still around even though they have been discredited. Thus, it would appear necessary to provide you with some perspective here. You just may find them interesting both as part of SPID history and/or as an idea gone wrong.

You will remember from Chapter 1, it all started with Alexander Graham Bell. He and his family came to America (via Canada) from Scotland. More important, however, he was descended from a number of phoneticians, elocutionists and speech correctionists. He was all of these things himself, plus a teacher of the hard of hearing. This last area was one in which he was interested both professionally and because of his mother's hearing disability. (He also invented the telephone – among other things – but that is not entirely relevant here). However, you might be interested in a little-known story related to his pursuit of 'talking wires.' As you might expect, Bell had to work at a number of jobs to finance his efforts. Among them, he held a post at Boston University (BU) where he lectured on phonetics and speech. When he ran out of money and benefactors, he went to BU with a proposal. Would the University advance him his entire salary for that year (around $3500) at the beginning of the Fall semester so he could continue his work on the telephone? They could count on him fulfilling all of his obligations of course, but this was the only way he could continue his work. The BU officials were appalled. 'How would you live?' they asked. 'Family and friends' he replied. 'Not sure we can do it' they said. But somehow he talked them into it and was successful that very year. The administrators at BU are now quite proud of the contribution they made to his success Anyway, from time to time, they modestly publish accounts of the role they played in the invention of the telephone.

Once Bell had won all his law suits and otherwise fended off the many supplicants and competitors who descended on him, he grew rich. Yet, he never forgot the debt he owed all the people and institutions who made his success possible. Accordingly, he funded (among other things) what is known as the Bell Telephone Laboratories. The personnel there would carry out research and projects designed to make telephones cheaper and better. However, as a second goal, he insisted that the scientists employed there attempt to develop systems and equipment which would make speech 'visible.' His objectives were to provide ways for the deaf and severely hard of hearing to learn speech. It took years to do so but one of the teams finally succeeded in producing a device they called the Sonagraph (Figure 6.1 (top)).

This device first became available in the 1930s and when it did, it was a sensation. It proved to be one of the most sophisticated and useful inventions of its time. Indeed, this device is still in use today. In recent years, it has become easy to build, fairly inexpensive and, in some ways, quite useful. Better yet, microcomputers such as the Kay Elementric's CSL (Computer Speech Laboratory) have largely replaced the older analog machines; they allow even more sophisticated analyses to be conducted and in close to real time (Figure 6.1 (bottom)). At any rate, the 'pictures' furnished by this device can provide helpful patterns when one attempts to visualize certain sounds. Want to 'see' a tiger greeting, or a dolphin whistle? – just take a look at Figures 6.2 and 6.3; moreover, Figure 6.4 also is a t–f–a (time–frequency–amplitude) spectrogram but in this case, it is of human speech. See the differences? A discussion of how the system works, and how you can extract information from these records, will be followed by a little more about the 'voiceprint' proponents (what they claim) and, finally, a critique.

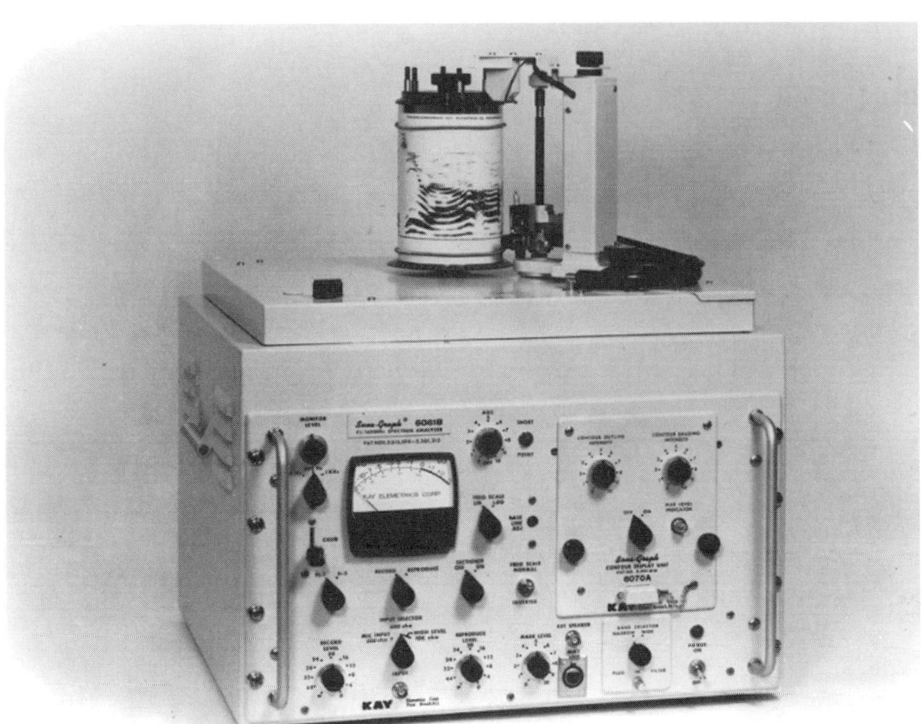

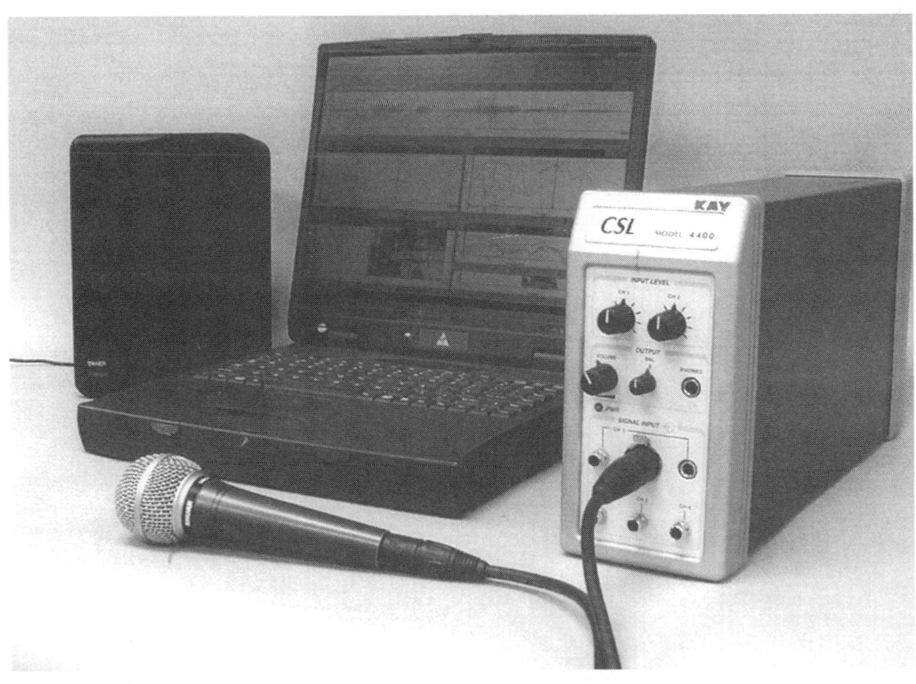

Figure 6.1

Photographs of the older (top) and newer (bottom) types of t–f–a spectrographs manufactured by Kay Elemetrics. The older unit is an analog device; nevertheless it can still be found in many relevant laboratories throughout the world. The newer approach is digital, of course, and is one of the subprograms on Kay Elemetrics CSL (Computer Speech Lab).

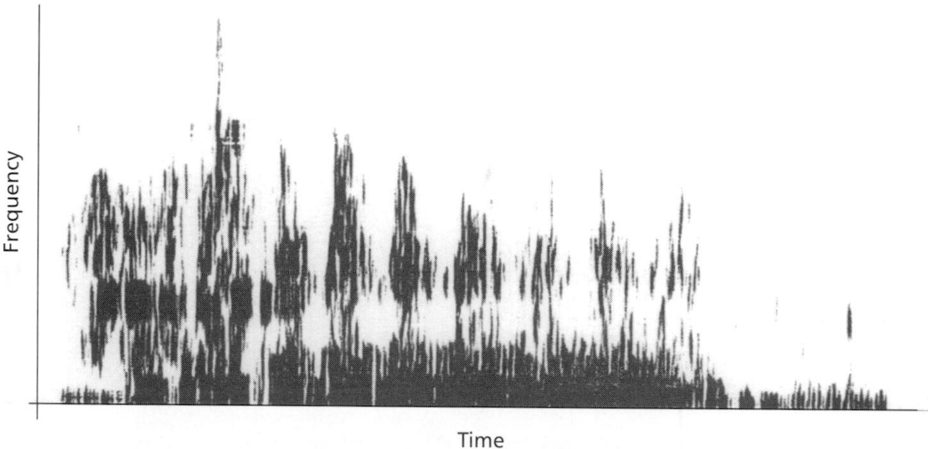

Figure 6.2

A t–f–a spectrogram of a tiger's prusten (greeting). The horizontal axis is time and the vertical axis is frequency. Energy levels are depicted by the darkness of the trace. Note the pulsing – or snorting – aspect of this young male's utterance. Sonogram ® Kay Elemetrics Co., Pine Brook, NJ.

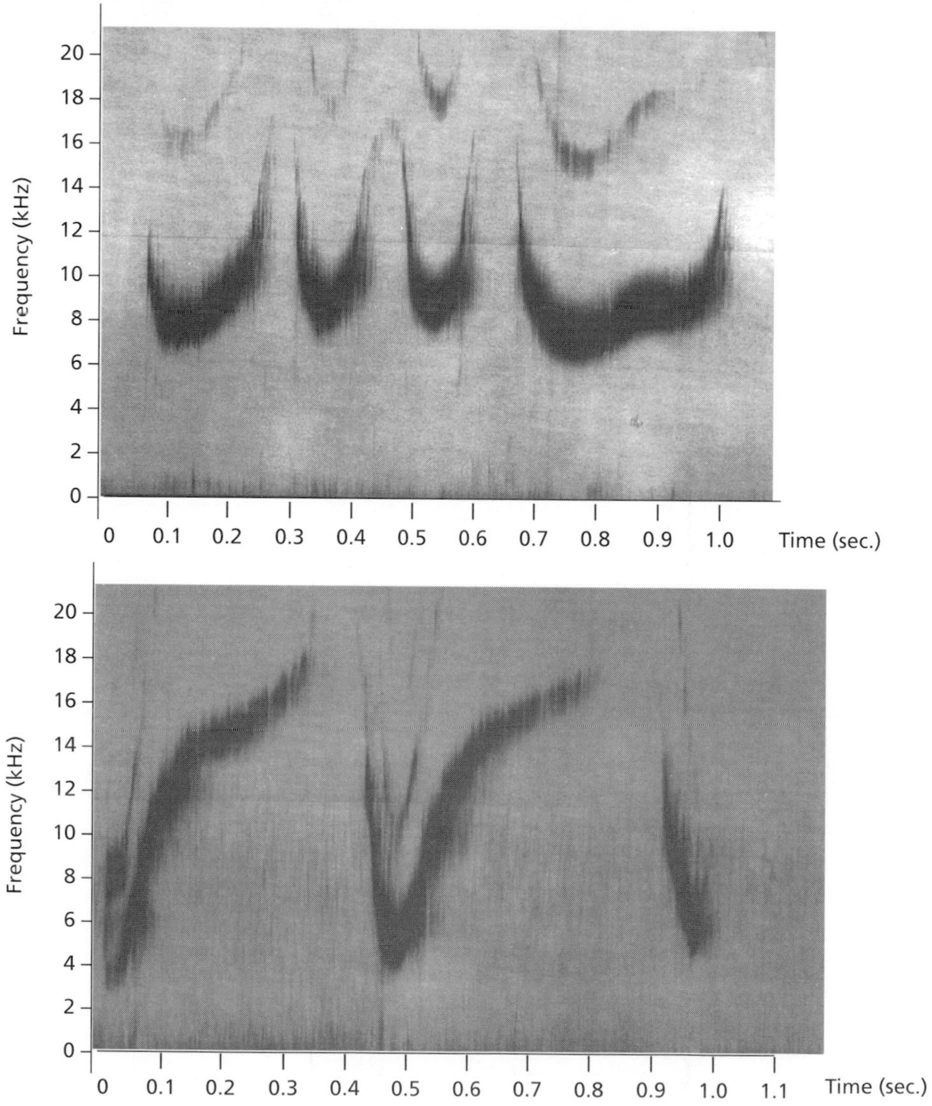

Figure 6.3

Two dolphin signature whistles. The top figure shows the signature of an adult female, the bottom that of an adolescent male.

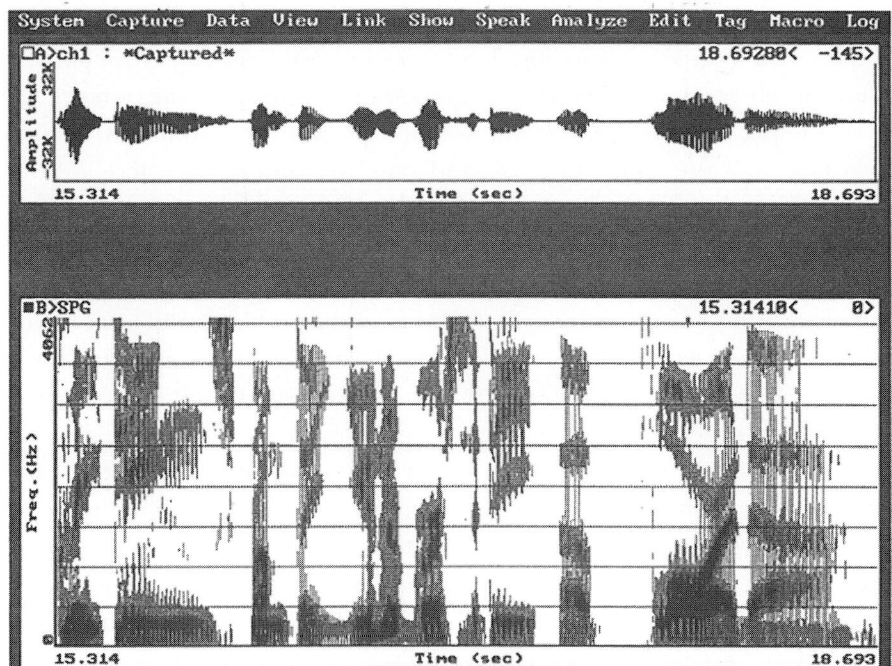

Figure 6.4

Human speech. The space between the vertical striations suggests that the speaker is a male. He is saying: 'Greetings from the University of Florida.'

THE SONOGRAPH

This device often is erroneously referred to as the 'sound spectrograph.' Actually, it is but one of many types of them. As indicated above, it is best understood as a time–frequency–amplitude system or, very simply, a sound wave analyzer. As you can see from the figures, they are *x–y* plots with the horizontal, or *x*-axis, providing the time dimension and the vertical, or *y*-axis, providing the frequency information. The darkness of the marking approximates the relative amplitude (amount) of the energy present within the channel created by the system's filter. To make a t–f–a spectrogram, a moving filter sweeps the frequency range of a speech segment of approximately 2.5 sec. duration; it does so either in a narrow band mode (i.e. a filter width of 45 Hz) or as a broad band (i.e. one with a 300 Hz band). This latter mode is the procedure of choice for 'voiceprints.' It is by this means that a rather rough approximation of the relevant acoustic events is created. Of the three dimensions, time is the most accurate. Frequency is next best; however, it tends to be somewhat distorted for two reasons. First, as indicated, most of the t–f–a sound spectrograms or programs use broadband filtering, a process which tends to remove traces of many of the actual frequencies (i.e. the harmonic partials) which make up the speech spectrum and add others where they do not exist. Thus, what you see are rough outlines of places where there are concentrations of energy. Taking vowels as an example, the relevant areas of resonance – or the vowel formants – appear as fairly well-defined black bars. Thus, these areas of energy concentration are outlined and can be seen. However, other details of the acoustic wave (i.e. the actual frequencies) are lost. It is conceded that Sonograms can portray certain speech features – ones that can be observed and even measured. In a very real sense, however, these configurations are artificial, primarily because energy is seen where it does not exist and removed from areas where it does. The patterns are yet further distorted because the frequency dimension is structured on an arithmetic basis (with equidistant 1-kHz divisions) when actually it is a geometric function based on a 2:1 ratio (i.e. the equal-tempered music scale). This error is an important one for, as a result, frequency differences can be badly distorted. For example, the difference between 4000 and 8000 Hz will be shown as four times greater than the one from 1000 Hz to 2000 Hz even though, with respect to frequency, they are equal.

The greatest weakness of this particular type of spectrography probably relates to its third feature, that of signal 'intensity.' That is, spectrographs of the t–f–a type provide rather minimal information about the energy patterns of speech sounds as they simply are not precise enough to permit accurate quantification, even when their 'sectioners' are used. Thus, as you might have guessed from the discussion above, it is relatively easy to accidentally (or deliberately) modify the patterns seen on any particular spectrogram. Moreover, and as anyone who has made a number of these records will concede, problems such as changes in calibration, variation in gain (at any stage within the process), filtering of any type, noise, internal distortion and/or any background signal can alter or bias these patterns. Indeed, individuals using spectrographs for other purposes often enhance the patterns or characteristics they wish to observe simply by manipulation of one or more of these very features. In short, this archaic approach to signal analysis is crude at best and a source of distorted patterns in any case. Little wonder that it has led to many misinterpretations when it has been used for 'voiceprints.'

'VOICEPRINT' ORIGINS

You will understand, I am sure, that the system described above has been used over the years for a large variety of purposes. They have ranged from providing the deaf with a training device (visible speech) to 'looks' at sounds other than speech. Their use also ranges from 'pictures' of vowels to those of tiger roars, from bird whistles to attempts to determine if an utterance produced by a given person is identical each time it is spoken. It all started in 1945 when Potter (32) published an article entitled 'Visible Patterns of Speech.' (Remember from Chapter 2, that he described the work initiated at the Bell Laboratories, and the operation and use of the Sonagraph.) He further described the process as a display of the changing content of a sound in visual form, i.e. the signal's component frequencies and their relative amplitudes as a function of time. Still later, attempts were made to identify speakers by analysis of the patterns on spectrograms (3, 4), but no-one at that time picked up on the suggestion that this device might be useful for SPID purposes. Indeed, it was not until nearly 15 years later that Kersta (5) published his paper on 'Voiceprint Identification.' In it he initiated the erroneous idea that a close relationship existed between fingerprints and voiceprints. For example, he wrote: 'My claim to voice pattern uniqueness then rests on the improbability that two speakers would have vocal cavity dimensions and articulator use-patterns identical enough to confound voiceprint identification methods' (p. 1253). But, as you will remember from Chapter 2, he gave no details about his research; neither did he document his claim. Hence, what he did and why he thought he was on the right track, is difficult to assess. What he may have done is to compare the ability of certain of the staff at Bell Laboratories to make identifications of known talkers using single words under both isolated and contextual speech conditions, or he may have done something else. In any event, he claimed that his error rates were very small (1%) and, from these results, he concluded that the process was a reliable one. However, since the word reliability only means repeatability, perhaps he meant that his technique was valid. The weakness of Kersta's claim was that it was not supported by anyone's research other than his own. Perhaps this naivety can be understood in that he was not one of the scientists at Bell Laboratories but rather an engineer employed to support their work. In any event, his report and claims, were eagerly picked up by a number of law enforcement agencies plus a small cadre of other individuals. He then opened a 2-week school to train 'voiceprinters' and soon there were a few dozen of them.

Before proceeding with this history, how did the 'voiceprint' practitioners ply their trade and how did they use t–f–a spectrograms when they attempted SPID?

'VOICEPRINT' ANALYSIS

It is a little difficult to describe the ways in which Sonagrams were used in attempts to identify unknown speakers by matching their speech/voice patterns with those of known speakers (or suspects). Basically, syllables, words, phrases and/or sentences uttered by both parties were processed by making traces of the type seen in the figures. However, the procedures for analyzing them have not been particularly well defined. It also appears that the techniques tended to change over time and from practitioner to practitioner. For example, if you were to review their court testimony, you would find substantial variation in the techniques they describe and their opinions. To illustrate, one of the 'voiceprinters' indicated that he attempted to crossmatch the patterns of 10 common words (6), whereas another testified that, on some occasions, he did so too but, on others, he employed the 'bars, blades, blips and bands' seen on a spectrogram (7, 8). Yet another (9) has indicated that he requires suspects to provide exemplars of the exact phrases spoken by the unknown and then makes his matches based on an unspecified number of similarities. A fourth (10), has unequivocally stated that he believes it to be unthinkable that anyone would even try to describe the pattern-matching process related to the technique and implies that it is one of such great mystery that there is no way to operationally define or quantify it. As you can see from all these 'descriptions,' the task of understanding the voiceprint method is a perplexing one.

Regardless what definitions are offered, the core of this process has to be some sort of pattern-matching procedure based on the configurations seen on t–f–a spectrograms (see again Figure 6.4). While the development of this form of spectrography was pretty exciting 65–70 years ago, modern-day technology tends to relegate it to a scientific backwater. Hence, the basis for the approach is not considered to be a sound one.

SO . . . WHAT HAPPENED NEXT?

. . . It was America . . . it was the 1960s – it is of little wonder that 'voiceprints' caught on during this period. The police needed ways to identify perpetrators from their voices alone and, now, there were a lot more perpetrators. But why were 'voiceprints' accepted at all, much less so easily? For one thing, in the beginning their use was virtually unopposed. That is, at least in the early days, the opposing attorneys were not conversant enough with the procedure to avail themselves of consultation or expert testimony by scientists and others knowledgeable about the inadequacies of the technique. In many instances, the attorneys did not have the funds to enlist appropriate aid but, in others, they simply were not aware that the great preponderance of the scientific community did not accept 'voiceprints' as a valid SPID technique. Indeed, because they were not cognizant of the many problems associated with the method, even capable trial attorneys found it difficult to impeach it. After all, it carried a kind of surface validity. Perhaps even more disquieting was the fact that, when effective opposition did appear imminent, indictments or suits very often were withdrawn, or, at least, the 'voiceprint' evidence was discarded. Worse yet, the proponents of the method tended to function pretty much as would any businessman who has a product to promote and, thus, tried to fend off people who would denounce it. However, some critics have argued that the voiceprinters actually went beyond good business practice and acted more like cultists, wherein only true believers could evaluate or criticize the art or activities of the group. They argued here that there was little need to evaluate their activities on a scientific basis, as it should be obvious that they were correct (10). They rationalized that it was this knowledge, rather than data, which should govern their behavior. The critics then countered by suggesting that, if the 'voiceprinters' were secure in their beliefs, they should not mind if others tested them in order to see if they met the criteria for validity (11–19). They (the 'voiceprint' proponents) said that they welcomed such research but if it proved negative (as so many studies did), they either attacked or ignored it.

The problem in those early days was that not very much relevant research was available; hence, it was virtually impossible to properly assess the approach. For example, little detail was available from Kersta's study and the earlier Bell Laboratory reports only amounted to suggestions. A few position papers had been written and a couple of surveys and/or reviews were carried out by the relevant scientific community (11–14), but that was about all. Thus, those interested in the approach were pretty much left in the dark. Even more important, the little research that had been reported tended to be rather negative. Even so, most scientists were reluctant to oppose the procedure in court and for several reasons. Some found that it was simply awkward to do so and others were uncomfortable with the confrontational milieu found in the courts. Yet another segment either did not care about the issue, or did not understand the societal implications of 'voiceprints.' That is, they were unaware that the method could bring harm to individuals, to society in general and/or to their professions in particular.

So began a struggle between the 'voiceprint' proponents and those few scientists who tried to establish a reasonable perspective about the issue. Early on, the 'voiceprinters' won more often than not; they usually did so when unopposed but sometimes they triumphed even when challenged. Of course, there were times when other evidence demonstrated that the defendant was guilty. Yet, there were other times when the converse was true. A few of the more flagrant errors made by the voiceprinters can be found in Chapter 10 of *The Acoustics of Crime* (16). Some were tragic, others would have been funny if only human lives had not been at stake.

The 'Rape and Poison Ivy' case illustrates such a combination of the tragic and the funny. One hot summer night some years ago, a woman was raped. Apparently, neither she nor her assailant were wearing more than shorts and a top. It was so dark that she never got a look at him but did hear his voice. He later telephoned her but, by now, the police had attached a recorder to her phone line. Then a suspect was identified, a voice exemplar taken, and a 'voiceprint' match was claimed. It was not until the trial commenced that it was discovered that the crime had taken place in a bed of poison ivy. The victim suffered from it but the suspect did not, even though it was shown that he was violently allergic to it. Did he get off? I do not know. As usual, the lawyers promised to let me know, but they did not follow through.

The 'voiceprint' problem continued to exist for years and did so even though members of the relevant scientific community finally got around to assessing the technique and speaking out. However, just as had happened when it all started, the 'voiceprint' proponents got there first. That is, they reported some research. But, what studies actually were carried out? Let us take a look. Please note, however, that the reviews to follow will not be considered chronologically but rather clustered into two main categories: (1) research by the 'voiceprinters' and (2) research by neutral investigators.

RESEARCH BY THE 'VOICEPRINTERS'

As you might expect, the voiceprint proponents made the claim that all of their research supported the validity of their method. In this regard, they cited Kersta's study plus a couple of small reports. However, the key research here involved a series of studies carried out at Michigan State University by Oscar Tosi and his associates (20). Several reports have resulted from this effort (21) but the basic publication was the one which came out in 1972. Tosi indicated that he did the research after being an early opponent of the 'voiceprint' method; he said that he wanted to check it out because of his fundamental interest in the SPID process. In any event, in the late 1960s he joined a member of the Michigan State Police (Earnest Nash) and, together, they won a grant which funded study of the technique. The resulting project was somewhat convoluted; it also was the subject of controversy as it led to some rather misleading claims. Nonetheless, a review should be useful and for three reasons; i.e. for the better understanding of: (1) the 'voiceprint' technique itself, (2) the thinking of its proponents and (3) speaker identification in general.

One thing that you should understand about this research is that the 'voiceprinters' describe its centrality to their thrust in such manner as to exclude any information generated by other investigators. In truth, the Tosi *et al.* investigation is only one of many that have used a pattern-matching process in SPID in general and t–f–a spectrograms in particular. As will be seen, there are a number of other studies that are just as relevant to the issue as is Tosi's. Further, since it was a laboratory investigation, it does not predict very well what will happen in real life. Indeed, a number of investigations exist which are far more relevant to the forensic process.

TOSI'S RESEARCH

Design

As suggested above, the structure of this project is a little difficult to unscramble. It consists of a rather large collection of substudies combined into a relatively loose presentation. Moreover, some of the experimental conditions were changed during the investigational period. For example, there appeared to be a midproject reduction in both the number of subjects used and the extent of the speech samples employed in the matches. In any event, the authors basically studied talker populations of between 10 and 40 males (drawn from a student group of 250). Their examiner teams consisted of one to three individuals drawn from a cohort of 29 students. They claimed that their 250 talkers represent a total population of 25 000 males (i.e. all the students in the area) and further argue that even a more substantial population (a quarter million) was evaluated when, in reality, the groups studied were of a size conventional for research of this type. As you might expect, the procedure employed had the talkers producing controlled utterances and the examiners comparing sonagrams of these samples with others that had been previously identified. The task, of course, was to make correct matches. The sub-issues examined were: (1) does the number of cue words used affect recognition, (2) should one, two or three utterances of a single word be employed, (3) do different types of recording conditions lead to differences in identification rates, (4) do correct identification levels vary as a result of differing cue word context, (5) does variation in speaker population affect the results, (6) does it matter if the samples are contemporary or noncontemporary and (7) does the use of open and closed trials alter identification rates?

Results

Tosi and his associates presented their results as a function of two research cycles or stages. First, the overall correct identification rate was reported as varying from a little over 86% to nearly 96%. They also presented their data as a function of the types of errors obtained (basically false identifications and false eliminations) and with respect to the number of 'firm conclusions' made by the examiners. The authors also indicate that when they replicated Kersta's original design, which they say involved essentially closed trials and contemporary spectrograms of cue words spoken in isolation, 'they were able to confirm his claim of an error rate of 1% false identifications.' Unfortunately, they repeated this particular statement extensively in the courts over the next decades. By doing so they erroneously suggest that a 'voiceprint' accuracy of 99% can be expected in a forensic context. Actually, it is virtually impossible to locate this very high level even among the laboratory data they present. Of course, the more relevant relationships are those reported above (i.e., 86% and 96% in the laboratory). Moreover, their data on contemporary and noncontemporary contrasts are more to the point as contemporary speech will almost never be found in the forensic milieu. Their trials here revealed noncontemporary error rates of about 18%. You should remember also, from a cross-reference of the SPID data found in Chapter 3, that this value (i.e., an 82% correct identification rate) is not all that different from the aural-perceptual figures (22) for the contemporary/noncontemporary relationship (for once, their data agree with those reported by someone else). Otherwise, please also remember that these results only reflect what can happen in a laboratory and not what can be expected in the field.

OTHER STUDIES BY THE 'VOICEPRINT' PROPONENTS

The 'voiceprinters' also refer to other studies they have conducted. Some of these appear to be rather casual in nature and/or quite limited in scope; others do not seem to be research at all. For example, Smrkovski testified (9) that he examined the voiceprints of twins and found that their spectrograms did not match. However, exercises such as this are not research but rather the kind of inquiry that could be carried out by any curious layman given access to certain types of equipment. On the other hand, members of this group have reported a few projects which seem to qualify as descriptive research. Most notable is the MA thesis by Hennessy (23). This study was carried out under 'businesslike' conditions; he used two examiners. First, a pilot study was conducted, involving 12 males and eight females, most of whom were Asians. This effort resulted in a 30% error rate. In the major experiment, carried out with 84 American subjects equally divided between males and females, his error level exceeded 41%. In response to those rather unmanageable error rates, Hennessy concluded ' it is the opinion of this writer that "voiceprint" identification is a reasonable identification method – the relatively low accuracy percentage rate is not discouraging.'

Another thesis was carried out by Hall (24), who investigated the ability of a comedian, Rich Little, to mimic six celebrities. Unfortunately, none of the celebrities would cooperate. Hence, the speech samples used in the comparisons were drawn from 'prerecorded interviews, telephone appearances and old movies.' Unfortunately, Hall actually did not apply the voiceprint technique but rather had 20 generally untrained students carry out an AP-SPID task in quiet and noise. The listeners were able to identify the actors as themselves 79% of the time and Little as himself 68% of the time; they also were able to identify the mimic about 74% of the time, even when he was attempting to sound like one of the actors. These values were somewhat lower when noise was present. Hall suggests that it is possible to 'discriminate spectrographically between the subjects' natural voices and their voices when mimicked by another person – even a professional.' However, his support of this statement is suspect at best because he actually appeared to conduct an investigation of speaker *verification* (not SPID) and tested aural-perceptual identification, not 'voiceprints.' Neither were the results very encouraging even if he had studied what he said he did. In any event, his data hardly supported the claim that 'voiceprint/grams' are 99% accurate.

Finally, a study of sorts has been published as a Letter to the Editor in the *Journal of the Acoustical Society of America* (1). In this letter, it was reaffirmed that the FBI would not use 'voiceprints' in court but would do so in investigations. The author went on to indicate that over a period of 15 years, FBI examiners had exhibited an error rate of only 1% for those speakers where they made a positive decision (about 35% of 2000 cases). It certainly appeared that the author was attempting to show that, while the procedure could not be used in very many cases, it was virtually error-free when it was employed. However, he did not provide very much tangible evidence in support of this position. First, his references to other studies were exceedingly sparse and tended to reflect only those that supported his particular bias; i.e. he did not include the dozens upon dozens of articles about experiments that did not support him – he also left out any reference to the extensive work carried out on AP-SPID approaches and those on machine processing. Second, and most important, he did not describe in any relevant detail just what he meant by 'voiceprints' or how this process was accomplished. For example, it could be asked if the procedures actually used were consistent among the examiners over the years of work he cites. He also appeared to confuse procedures for handling tape recordings (for other purposes) with SPID. Third, he did not describe his examiners' qualifications. Admittedly, he did list six requisites as necessary but only two appear particularly relevant (i.e. completion of a 2-week course with a 'voiceprint' examiner and formal approval by that person or some other examiner). Fourth, he did not indicate if his examiners had actually completed the 'two years of full-time experience' in voice identification before, during or after their work was included in his survey. Fifth, it is not clear if the 1000 'actual case examinations' his examiners are said to have carried out for 'certification' were also included in the 2000 cited (or were in addition to them). Finally, he did no follow-up to see if the 'voiceprinters' judgment was 'consistent with case disposition' in question. Apparently, he expected the cooperating agency to inform him if any changes occurred in the outcome of the case. As you would expect, this letter ignited controversy (16, 25–27). Nonetheless, it is a little surprising that the FBI would permit publication of an endorsement of a procedure in which it has so little faith that it will not permit its use in the courtroom. In summary, it can be seen that there is, at best, only modest support for the 'voiceprint' method and even less for its use in the forensic milieu. But what other evidence is available?

RESEARCH BY OTHER INVESTIGATORS

For a long time, the 'voiceprint' proponents succeeded (at least in court) in giving the impression that they had conducted all, or virtually all, of the research in this area. Note, for example, the following statement in the 1973 issue of the *Maryland Law Review* (28). The author wrote: 'The only challenge to Tosi available to a defendant is the testimony of theoretically skeptical scientists whose testimony is in the opinion of some courts far less persuasive than Tosi's . . . not because Tosi is right . . . but because he is the sole possessor of empirical data.' Yet, substantial work in the area already had been published by competent individuals from the appropriate scientific community. Here are some examples. In 1968, Stevens *et al.* (29), compared the ability of subjects to make speaker identifications either spectrographically or by listening to the samples. They reported that the error rates associated with the spectrographic examinations ranged from 21% to 47%; they also reported that their listeners scored somewhat better even when presented with a modestly difficult aural-perceptual task. Second, Young and Campbell (30) antedated Tosi in testing Kersta's claims; they reported far greater error rates than did either Kersta or Tosi (5, 6, 20, 21). Even more to the point, Hazen (31) used both closed and open sets as well as identifications from same and different contexts. His error rates also were substantially higher (12–57%) than were Kersta's or Tosi's. Hazen concluded that 'spectral similarities due to intraspeaker consistency are not apparent enough to outweigh the similarities due to . . . phonetic context.' In summary, none of these early investigators could achieve 'hit rates' even close to those claimed by the 'voiceprint' proponents. However, their work was generally ignored by the 'voiceprinters.'

Later investigators have addressed this problem in even a greater variety of ways. For example, Obrecht (32) tested Nash's claims about the similarity of fingerprints and 'voiceprints'; he carried out a study in which he found that examiners with experience in fingerprint analysis were no better at spectrographic speaker identification than were those who lacked that background; neither did his groups achieve the rarified levels claimed by the 'voiceprint' proponents. Even more to the point, Endress *et al.* (33) reported that the spectrographic patterns and fundamental frequency levels they studied varied substantially over time and with attempts at voice disguise. Their research has been confirmed (34, 35) and it has been discovered that, when subjects disguise their voices, very substantial changes occur in fundamental frequency, speech spectra and temporal patterning. Yet another recent study serves to further underscore the problems relating to disguise when it is faced by the 'voiceprint' proponents. In their article on the effects selected vocal disguises have on spectrographic speaker identification, Reich *et al.* (36), reported that these conditions led to identification errors varying from approximately 50% to nearly 78%. Worse yet, these investigators observed error rates of 40% and greater, even when the talkers did not disguise their voices. Finally, Rothman (37), who employed highly skilled examiners, reported a mean overall correct identification of about 20% when he used talkers that sounded similar to each other. He obtained his best identification scores (39%) when his examiners compared the same phrase and his poorest scores (6%) for the sound-alikes when the samples were noncontemporary. Other like studies have been reported also (38–40).

It is interesting to note that none of the neutral investigators were able to achieve levels even close to those reported by Kersta, Tosi and their associates. Certainly, none of them obtained a level as high as the 99% (correct) rates they claim possible, and these neutral scientists were not able to do so even under laboratory conditions. Admittedly, in some instances, the individuals they used as examiners were not as highly trained as are those the 'voiceprint' proponents suggest is necessary. However, in most cases the examiners were at least as skillful and as well trained as were those utilized in the Tosi research. In certain other instances they were experienced/educated both in the phonetic sciences and identification tasks. How, then, would you explain the extremely high levels of identification reported by Tosi (and Kersta) and the uniformly lower scores obtained by all other investigators? (I, for one, have no answer.)

ADDITION OF THE 'LISTENING' PROCEDURE

In the early 1970s, the 'voiceprinters' appeared to respond to criticism leveled at them by scientists. Or perhaps they became concerned about all of the negative results being published at that time. In any case, they added a listening procedure to their assessments. This task required that the examiner first listen to the voice of the unknown talker and then compare it with that of the suspect or suspects (i.e. the knowns). Thus, a possibly useful dimension was added to their method, one where the examiner had to judge if the two voices sounded similar or different. However, neither the exact processes employed, nor any standards upon which that processing was based, were offered by the 'voiceprint' proponents. About all that could be gleaned from their testimony in court, was that they felt this supplementary procedure added a rather important dimension to their overall method. This rather vague description makes it difficult for me to evaluate their aural-perceptual efforts. However, a reconsideration of certain studies (16, 34, 40–46) plus Chapters 3 and 4 should provide some information about the hidden dangers in the aural-perceptual approach to SPID; that is, unless it is highly structured and rigorously carried out by trained individuals. Thus, it is necessary to learn how the 'voiceprint' practitioners were trained in AP-SPID, how they structured their processes, their level of competency and just how they validated their results.

THE EXAMINERS

It also would appear useful to consider how the 'voiceprinters' train themselves. Unfortunately, only modest information is available. First, they claim that their technique is a good one because their examiners have developed 'exceptional skills' in the identification process. However, they provide very little, if any, evidence to support this claim. They do list a few requisites for examiners and a general processes by which they should operate (5, 6, 10, 20, 21, 47). Perhaps these criteria are best iterated by Black *et al.* (47) who indicate (my paraphrase) that a trainee must: (1) possess academic training in audiology and speech sciences; (2) complete at least 2 years of supervised apprenticeship dealing with field cases; (3) (when certified) be entitled to five alternate decisions after each examination (namely, positive identification, positive elimination, probable identification, probable elimination and no opinion); (4) be entitled to use as much time and as many voice samples as deemed necessary and (5) be held responsible for the positive decisions reached as a result of these examinations.

Truby (10) has argued that being a 'speech scientist' does not qualify an individual in the area of 'voiceprinting.' He would reject anyone who had not 'accumulated personal mileage pouring over sound spectrograms' and 'who had not scrutinized thousands of voiceprints.' Truby wrote further, 'I contend that *constant immersion in voice identification exercise* is the only criterion for acquiring the indicated expertise. NO AMOUNT of substitute intelligence or professional intellect can approximate the experience of DOING' (the emphasis is Truby's). Unfortunately, he does not suggest how the person is to determine if they are correctly carrying out the process and making accurate judgments. Truby further contends that 'anyone capable of leveling *truly valid* criticisms at voiceprinting should seek certification and if capable of attaining same; either withdraw his/her criticism or thus *appropriately qualify* his/her objections' (again, his emphasis). He did not indicate if all of the 'qualified voiceprint/gram examiners' had scrutinized thousands upon thousands of 'voiceprints' or who the supervisors were that evaluated their work (or who evaluated the supervisors in the first place). Nor did he provide details as to how one would go about learning the process or determining his or her level of success. Thus, the proponents of 'voiceprinting' stressed that one of the major strengths of their technique (Truby, calls it an infallible one) is that they use only 'highly trained' professionals who presumably adhere to some set of regulations. Unsupported as they are, these arguments appear both weak and self-serving. What is missing is scientific evidence demonstrating that the procedure actually is a valid one and that its 'certified examiners' can (successfully) carry it out.

EXAMINER OBJECTIVITY

There is no question that the 'voiceprint examiners' were serious about their craft. As to whether they were (and are, if any of them are left) objective in their judgments is quite another matter. First it must be remembered that these examiners are primarily law-enforcement agents (not scientists) and, hence, are emotionally tied to the technique. While it is doubtful that any of them have ever engaged in misconduct, it is difficult to discount their biases. Moreover, some of the statements they make in court are disquieting. For example, in 1976 Smrkovski (9) testified that he had been using the 'voiceprint' method of speaker identification for about five years and that, during that period, he had examined nearly 30 000 spectrograms. That many surely is a lot. To carry out each of these tasks, he would have had to: (a) become familiar with the specific case or task in question, (b) listen to the relevant tape recordings, (c) establish records, (d) find the sections to be analyzed, (e) record the samples on the spectrograph, (f) make the spectrograms, (g) log/identify them, (h) study them, (i) make his judgments (presumably concerning matches between them), (j) record these judgments, (k) write his report and (l) communicate his findings. Could he have done all this at an average rate of 20 min. per case? Unlikely, but if he did and worked a 40-h week for 50 weeks per year, it would appear that the processing of this many spectrograms would have required the entire five years he cited. No trips anywhere, no coffee breaks, no aural-perceptual analyses, no telephone calls, no conferences, no testimony, just spectrographic analysis. Perhaps the worst case was when Nash testified that he had analyzed over 100 000 spectrograms (48, 49). Even on the incredibly unrealistic basis that each of these complete analyses took only 10 min. each (please reconsider the 12 steps above), it appears that he would have had to have crowded about 15 years of full-time work into the nine years he had been active in the field. Finally, there is no question but that the pressure of 'doing voiceprints' and having to defend their results in court tended to distort their judgments and behavior. For example, please consider 'The Case of the Union Steward' (50). In this instance, bomb threats were received at a telephone company over a line dedicated to its workers. Worse yet, the speech was partly machine processed (a kind of vocoder) before it was heard. All relevant workers were asked to provide a sample of their voice and all complied except the union steward who cited the union rules against doing so. Naturally, he immediately became the prime suspect and, ultimately, was forced to provide a sample. As would be suspected, a 'voiceprinter' selected him as the culprit and he was brought to trial. After a while, the case against him began to unravel. Witnesses challenged the 'voiceprint' method, and even its results and the operator who received the calls said that she knew the steward's voice and he was not the person she had heard. The judge became suspicious and had the 'voiceprinter' tested. Unfortunately for him, he picked one of the foils (an assistant district attorney) not the defendant as the culprit and the judge threw out the case. Further, he reprimanded the 'voiceprinter' who was (you guessed it) Lt. Earnest Nash.

What is perhaps a more telling series of events occurred less than a year later. I refer to this case (51) as that of 'The Fancy-stepping Con Artist.' Oddly enough, it occurred in Tosi's and Nash's backyards as their respective institutions are both located in East Lansing. Odder still, the crime took place at Michigan State University (Tosi's employer). First off, the 'artist' who set it all up and then carried it out, had to have known a great deal about the University' s financial holdings and the day-to-day workings of its administration. Second, he (it was a man or a small gang of men) carried out almost the entire operation by means of a series of telephone calls. In his first call, he spoke to a fairly low-ranking administrator but one who nonetheless had the authority to access the University's holdings of bearer bonds and draw a large number of them for 'internal' transfer. He (the con man) followed the original call with a series of others consisting of(1) requests that the package of bonds be transferred from office to office and (2) assurances that he would soon arrive (with proper identification, of course) and exchange appropriate written authorization for them. While these personal appearances were unfulfilled, they did lead to the transfers. Ultimately, the package containing the bonds was deposited with a secretary who was led to believe that it only contained student IBM cards. The exercise, as carried out, was an impressive one indeed. It culminated when the package was (finally) picked up by a 'courier' and delivered, by taxi, to another pickup site located downtown East Lansing. From there, it – and the small fortune in bearer bonds it contained – simply disappeared.

As you might expect, the ensuing furor led to an extensive investigation by the Michigan State Police. Even from the first, there was a good chance that 'voiceprints' would play a major role in the case since (1) nearly all telephone calls (these included) directed to the University administrative offices were recorded and (2) Lt. Earnest Nash's 'voiceprint' laboratory was situated nearby. In any event, a young MSU graduate student was included in the suspect pool (just why he was, I am not sure). When Nash conducted a 'voiceprint' analysis comparing his speech with that on the evidence tapes, he concluded that both were produced by a single speaker. Sayeth Nash (at the trial), 'it could have been no other person in the world.' I was called to testify *against* 'voiceprints' but not asked to conduct any kind of speaker identification procedure.

Nash was being subjected to a vigorous cross examination about the time I arrived. Then, something rather unusual happened. He was asked if he had his work checked by another 'expert.' He was rather offended by this question. In reply, he essentially said that he always worked alone and did so because he was the 'authority' in the area and there simply was no one in the field who was competent to evaluate him. He also complained that, even if there were, the 'other side' would use the analyses to pit one 'voiceprinter' against the other. At this point, the judge had had enough. He recessed the trial and called in Tosi to replicate Nash's work (after all, Tosi had done the 'relevant science' on 'voiceprints' and worked nearby). Tosi acceded and, when the smoke cleared, he was in the witness box testifying that the defendant was not the person who had made all those clever telephone calls. And that was that! After all, it would be expected that two disasters in a row (plus others elsewhere) would doom the 'voiceprint method.' Or, so it seemed at the time. Moreover, Nash soon retired and Tosi became ill. Thus, what was left of 'voiceprints' was passed on to others, who simply could not provide the fireworks of the Tosi-Nash team. Tosi with his elegant accent and assurances that 'voiceprints' were 99% accurate; Nash with his imposing stance and promises that his competency could not be questioned. Yet, while the excitement was pretty much gone, the method was not quite dead. It lingers on to the present.

This short description of voiceprints – their nature, failings and general demise – has been rather brief. If you want to read more about them, you can consult the reference list. Please note, however, that I simply could not leave them out of this book. They play an important role in the development of SPID in both the USA and Europe. Moreover, their use (some would say abuse) stimulated a good deal of important research. So, how can we sum up what has been presented? Perhaps the following will provide insight.

CONCLUSION

Confusion still exists to this very day about the nature and merit of the 'voiceprint/gram' technique of SPID. Among the major criticisms that can be leveled at the procedure are that (1) it uses archaic equipment and procedures, (2) its validity has not been established and, indeed, is in serious question, (3) it appears to permit decisions to be made only about one-third of the time and (4) the training and competencies of its operators are largely a mystery (14–18, 27, 48). Its effectiveness in the field is so uneven that the only conclusion which can be drawn is that it lacks merit. What then are its contributions to SPID? Primarily that it assisted in raising the level of consciousness about speaker identification and has stimulated research on the question.

It is amusing to write about this controversy and there is lots to tell. Unfortunately, failed procedures such as this one do not rate a lot of space. So, what are our hopes for effective and valid SPID? Since the aural-perceptual approaches cited appear to be more of a stop-gap – no matter what Hecker (41) says – the best and most reasonable solution to the problem appears to be the development of some sort of human-controlled but computer-aided, procedure. The next two chapters provide historical information about these approaches plus a review as to how these techniques are structured and tested. The actual development of a method of this type will be used as an example and is the focus of Chapter 8.

CHAPTER 7

MACHINE APPROACHES

INTRODUCTION

The nature of speaker recognition changes radically when attempts are made to apply modern technology to the problem (see Jiang (1) for a useful review). Indeed, it would appear that solutions are but a step away – that is, with the seemingly limitless power of electronic hardware and computers now available. Unfortunately, this may not yet be the case as quantifying human behavior is not all that simple. For example, many, many years have passed since the first efforts were made to develop machines that would type letters dictated by voice, automatically translate the speech of one language into another and understand spoken speech. Yet no matter what the claim, none of these goals has been fully met (nor have ours). Indeed, some authors in our area (see Hecker, 2) insist that there are no machines which are both as sensitive and as powerful (for our purposes) as is the human ear. What Hecker means by ear is, of course, the entire auditory sensory system (including the brain) with all its sophisticated memory and cognitive functions. He may once have been correct in his assumptions but I do not believe he is now. All that has happened in this area, plus what currently is being accomplished, would ague against him. Accordingly, the question about SPID to be addressed in this chapter is: can machines/ computers be made to operate as efficiently for SPID purposes as does the human auditory system. That is, can they be made to mimic those processes or, if not mimic them, at least, effectively parallel the recognition task? I think that you will find that we are fast approaching these goals.

Please be aware that it is not my intent to list or review *all* of the efforts that have been made to develop machine-based SPID methods. Indeed, while some approaches have shown promise, most have not. Moreover, we also will see that very few groups have persevered in their efforts to solve the problem and/or develop a system that operates reasonably well under forensic or field conditions.

A PERSPECTIVE

It is a little difficult to separate what has been accomplished in machine-supported speaker identification (SPID) area from that which has been carried out on speaker verification (SV). This problem results (in part, at least) from the fact that the two concepts have not always been properly structured and/or differentiated. Some engineers have confused or interchanged them (3); other investigators have simply used the terms improperly.

Moreover, since this book is on 'identification,' I intend to focus on that area exclusively; that is, I will try to sort SPID from SV and not include the latter. However, I recognize that some of you may be interested in verification anyway and have tried to respond appropriately. A list of roughly 70 SV references are included as part of the Chapter 1 bibliography section. While the list is not exhaustive it includes a number of the articles and books which should be helpful.

EARLY HISTORY

Research into machine/computer assisted SPID has only been going on for a little over 45 years. It is ironic, but some of the earliest attempts were as promising as are many of those currently being developed. However, few of those projects were sustained. Some of the problems encountered by the early investigators resulted from the SPID–SV confusions, others from the fact that the projects were tangential to the primary mission of the sponsoring agency and, finally, some occurred because of the relatively crude processing devices (including computers) being used at the time. However, two of these many problems proved controlling. The first was that the objectives of the sponsoring agencies (or the investigators themselves) were actually in the verification area. (The commercial value of SV was recognized from the very beginning.) Indeed, the need to be able to determine if the speaker is a member of a known and finite population and/or if he or she actually is who they claim to be was the driving purpose behind many of the projects. The second problem appears to have been even more critical. It resulted from the erroneous concept that a solution to the speaker recognition problem could be achieved within a finite period of time (one that sometimes was as short as 2 years). Thus, when the specified goals were not reached, a 1–2 year extension was reluctantly provided and, when that period too proved insufficient, the entire project would be scrapped. Several rather promising programs were developed during this early period (4–13). I am not sure as to why they were terminated or downgraded as even reviews of the work carried out during that period (14, 15) shed little light on the issue.

One of the more interesting of these projects (6) was based on SRI's IMMSAS program (Interactive Man–Machine Speech Analysis System). With it, the

Becker group (6) could process speech samples of up to 6 sec. In turn, these samples were segmented and analyzed so as to produce speaker-dependent representations of the relevant parameters. The investigators subsequently used these data to discriminate among speakers. Once they had established the system, they submitted it to experimental evaluation. A database consisting of 200 utterances produced by 100 male speakers was used for this purpose. From their report, it appeared that this team had made a pretty good start. One wonders if a sustained research program here would not have led to a usable SPID system.

Certain of the other reports also described systems with the potential for success. However, several were structurally limited; i.e. they either used very short samples, restricted utterances (such as digits) or were text-dependent. Others focused on the verification problem rather than on identification and virtually all of the relevant experiments were carried out under laboratory conditions. Thus, forensic application of any resulting system would have been problematical. Even the best of them needed further investigation both with respect to their basic power and potential forensic applications.

SUBSEQUENT APPROACHES

First, regardless of what you think of voiceprints, we must concede that they were among the earliest of the machine-based approaches. Of course, they involved visual pattern matching by humans so you also can argue thatthey were unlike any system where computers do the processing. Moreover, it also must be conceded that this approach is about the crudest of all and that it hardly can be listed as a valid method. In any case, these relationships were covered in the previous chapter. It is only mentioned here to complete the historical perspective.

Work went on at a number of laboratories during the next several decades (16–20). A sampling of a few of these studies will follow. Please be advised, however, that those selected are merely representative of many which were conducted throughout the world.

Several SPID–SV programs originated at the Bolt, Beranek and Newman (BBN) Laboratories, and as early as 1972 (21). One of their earliest approaches consisted of comparing speakers on the basis of as many as 17-parameter sets; they included fundamental frequency, vowel and nasal consonant spectra, glottal source spectrum slope and word duration. A SPID algorithm was tested using these specific parameters and no errors were found for a set of 21 adult males. However, a replication of the study, under the same conditions, resulted in a 2% error rate. Later, the BBN group worked on text-independent SPID under various other conditions (22–25). In the latter case, the vectors employed were based on short-term spectra obtained from linear prediction coefficients

(LPC), log-area-ratio coefficients, cepstral coefficients and spectral-band amplitudes. The speech samples used by these investigators were drawn from a variety of sources and included high-fidelity utterances, speech degraded by noise and samples recorded over a radio channel. Ultimately, reasonably good system performance was established (i.e. their correct speaker identification rates ranged from 68% to 76%).

A little later, research on an automatic speaker recognition system was initiated at the Joint Speech Research Unit in England (26). The system developed there employed statistical analyses of fundamental frequency and spectral shape patterns as produced by a real-time cepstral processor. Subjects for a key experiment were 20 males and two females who produced 154 speech samples, each being 20 sec. long. These materials consisted primarily of weather forecasts read by professional meteorologists and recorded from FM radio receivers. Two experiments were carried out with system performance very similar for both. That is, correct identification levels ranged from 75% to 89%, depending on the specific procedure.

By the mid-1980s SPID experiments were being conducted at a number of laboratories throughout the world; most were based on signal processing techniques. The procedures employed here included vector quantization (VQ), Hidden Markov Models (HMM) and neural networks (NN). As you might expect, most were developed by electrical engineers (27–31) and, hence, the focus was on signal analysis with the relationships involving human behavior regulated to a secondary status. For example, the work conducted by Soong *et al.* (29) at the Bell Telephone Laboratory involved a VQ approach. Basically, a VQ codebook was established as a means of characterizing the speaker's spectral features. A set of these codebooks was used to permit recognition of an unknown speaker from their spoken utterances on the basis of a minimum distance (distortion) classification rule. Once structured, the system was evaluated by means of a series of traditional speaker recognition experiments. The data base employed consisted of telephone recordings of 10 isolated utterances (digits) produced by 50 males and 50 females. An accuracy rate of better that 98% was achieved. But, again, the approach here seems to have been slanted more toward SV than SPID.

A number of newer programs have been introduced during the past decade or so. For example, Tseng *et al.* (30) have developed an approach to the problem which they labeled CPAM (Continuous Probabilistic Acoustic Map). The speech input they employ consists of a parameterized mixture of a universal probability density functions (pdf) with either a CPAM model alone for text-independent operation or a CPAM-based HMM for text-dependent processing. This particular group used a continuously spoken database of digit strings, uttered by 20 speakers to evaluate the technique for *both* SPID and SV purposes. According to their reports, it performed better than did a VQ-based method. It did so for both text-independent SPID and for text-dependent SV. It also exhibited as good a performance as did a text-dependent, conventional HMM approach. Moreover, the CPAM-based HMM exhibited an identification error rate of less than 1.7% and a verification equal error rate of 4.0% with only a 128 pdf CPAM. In contrast, the conventional, (continuous mixture) HMM approach needed 400 pdf to achieve error rates that were roughly comparable (1.9% and 4.0% respectively) when the same cepstral features and three-digit test utterances were used as experimental tokens. The thrust of this project also was one designed more for use in SV than in SPID. For example, the investigators confined their sample to spoken digits; thus, speech sample duration was very short. While the method appears intriguing, it would need further evaluation in a forensic context before it could be considered for use in speaker identification.

The neural network approach has not been neglected. It was also in 1992 that Hattori (27) reported on a text-independent speaker recognition system which was based on the NN approach. His model allowed transitions to any other state, including self-transitions, as well as the creation of a predictive neural network for each state. The robustness of Hattori's method was evaluated using 24 female speakers; he employed distortion-based methods, HMM-based methods and discriminative NNs for this purpose. His recognition rates ranged from 95.7% to 100.0%. He also observed that performance levels varied depending on the number of training iterations carried out. Both approaches (i.e. predictive neural networks and discriminative neural networks) shared in these difficulties. Of course, it is not known if approaches such as these would be useful in the SPID area as they closely parallel SV procedures, especially with respect to laboratory, rather than field, conditions (i.e. they involve closed speaker sets, top-flight computing power, high fidelity audio equipment, high subject/speech sample control, and so on).

Finally, Webb and associates (31) have researched a SPID approach using HMMs. To do so, they carried out experiments, in a text-dependent mode, for the purpose of determining if SPID accuracy would decline as a function of increases in the number of speakers. This goal would serve to explain why they used an amazing total of 963 speakers (all women). These investigators had their subjects utter digit strings which, in turn were recorded over a telephone link and used in the identification paradigm. However, the general approach they followed was patterned after SV (all sets were 'closed'). An overall mean accuracy of 98.7% was obtained and the minimum of the means was 95.2%. The Webb *et al.* project can be seen to provide useful information about the effects of varying population size on speaker recognition. As would be expected, they found that identification accuracy decreased as the number of their speakers increased. However, this team tested their algorithm only with short samples and (as stated) closed sets. Before forensic applications can be considered, a great number of additional experiments would have to be completed.

As has been pointed out, most of the cited approaches are *said* to be focused on SPID. Yet many of them show distinct signs of being strongly influenced by typical verification philosophies. For example, nearly all were carried out under pristine laboratory conditions; most either used very short speech samples, limited utterances (such as digits) or were text-dependent. Thus, even though their identification scores were high to very high, they cannot be treated as being forensically realistic. Why? Because the investigators in question did not take the distortions, vagaries and confusions associated with forensic reality into account. Most importantly, they seemed not to be aware that they were dealing with human behavior and not just the machine processing of acoustic signals.

As can be seen, even from this short review, many of the approaches were elegant; certainly, they were insightful. But, just how well would they perform if the recording of the 'unknown' talker was actually that of a stressed-out woman, with a cold, speaking over a telephone? How about the speech of an aggressive male which had been picked up by a body bug (i.e., a listening device) in a busy restaurant? Accordingly, you should be aware of the need for research teams made up of a mix of phoneticians, engineers and forensic specialists. Such groups tend to work out pretty well; for one thing, they directly address the forensic issues. A practical demonstration about just how much they can accomplish will be found in Chapter 8.

MORE RECENT DEVELOPMENTS

As you might expect, progress continues in semi-automatic SPID (32–36). Of course, some of these programs were initiated before (often much before) the 1990s. So many of them are now in existence, a selection process must be instituted again. Our SAUSI program will be considered, not just because of its success but also because it was collaboratively developed by phoneticians and engineers. It will be reviewed in the next chapter.

For my review of other people's work, I have selected just two programs. They nicely illustrate the wide range that can be expected among extant SPID efforts; especially so because one of them draws from SV and the other stresses the use of multiple evaluation modalities. Further both (1) have been sustained over time, (2) involve strong research programs plus application in the forensic milieu and (3) are peopled by mixed teams. The first is headed by a computer specialist with a background in phonetics and the other by a pair of engineers, one of whom has dual status as a phonetician. They also reflect the social customs and forensic contexts of two different countries.

A PROGRAM FROM THE USA

Dr Robert Rodman is a professor of computer science at the North Carolina State University. His research programs are quite varied but a key thrust is in computer-supported forensic SPID (37–47). This program should serve to illustrate how a team of computer specialists, who are competent in the behavioral sciences, can develop a semiautomatic 'machine' approach to SPID. The identification procedure the Rodman team has developed is based on U–K comparisons (i.e. of the unknown vs. the known speaker) of the same phonemic sequences (they call them isophonemic sequences) drawn from available speech samples. As it is currently structured, a human analyst selects the isophonemic sequences to be processed and compared. Consider an example he provided (R. Rodman, personal communication). Three speakers are to be contrasted; one has uttered the phrase 'In the heat of the night,' a second has said 'By the seat of your pants,' and the third 'On my own two feet'. As you can see, the vowels from the words heat, seat and feet are isophonemic and, hence, can be used to provide material for the comparisons (a number of samples will be contrasted).

It is a strength of this method that it obviates the loss of discriminatory power when masses of speech from each speaker are treated statistically. While there obviously will be intraspeaker variation even when a single person says 'heat, seat and feet' in different sentences, these differences tend to be of lesser magnitude than are those for interspeaker variation under the same circumstances. In other words, acoustic differences among the words as spoken by three different speakers will largely reflect individual differences in pronunciation. For another thing, the Rodman technique trivializes the variation in vowel transitions which result from the effects of their (differing) consonantal environment. Rather, the totality of such differences, as measured over *many* sequences, individualizes the speakers.

How do members of the Rodman group process the relevant speech samples so as to permit quantification of the acoustic differences among and between the isophonemic sequences? First, the speech segments are digitized at a 22.046 kHz, 16-bit quantization and, then, Discrete Fourier Transforms (DFT) are computed for each of the isophonemic sequences. Where the speech is voiced, the glottal pulse period (GPP) is chosen as the window size for the DFT; where the speech is not voiced, a window size of 100 samples (= 4.54 ms) is employed. Isophonemic sequences that are purely voiced or purely unvoiced are usually chosen for these assessments and sequences with stops and affricates are avoided.

An algorithm is then structured as follows (from Rodman, personal communication):

1. Compute the discrete Fourier transform (DFT) using a window width of N samples.
2. Take the absolute value of the result (so it is a real number).
3. Shift over 1 sample.
4. Repeat steps 1–3, N times.
5. Average the N transforms and scale (them) by taking the cube root (to reduce the influence of the first formant), drop the DC term and interpolate it with a cubic spline to produce a continuous spectrum.
6. Convert the spectrum to a probability density function by dividing it by its mass, then calculate the first moment m_1 (mean) and the second central moment about the mean m_2 (variance) of that function in the range of 0 to 400 Hz. and put them in two lists. Let S(f) be the spectrum. The following formulae are then applied; they are appropriately modified for the discrete signal (i.e. the glottal pulse period or GPP).

$$\text{mass} = \int_0^{4000} S(f)\,df$$

$$P(f) = S(f) \div \text{mass}$$

$$\text{mean} = m_1 = \int_0^{4000} f * P(f)\,df$$

$$\text{variance} = m_2 \int_0^{4000} = (f - m_1)^2 * P(f)\,df$$

7. Repeat steps 1 through 6 until less than $3N$ samples remain.
8. Scale each moment: m_1 by 10^{-3} and m_2 by 10^{-6}.

As you can see, the result is a sequence of points in two-dimensional m_1–m_2 space; it is one which can be interpolated to provide a *track*. In turn, the tracks are smoothed by a three-stage cascading filter: median-5, average-3, median-3. That is, each value (except the endpoints) is replaced on the first pass with the median of itself and the four surrounding values. The second pass takes that median-5 output and replaces each point with the average of itself and the two surrounding values. Subsequently, that output is subjected to the median-3 filter to provide the final (smoothed) track.

A visual impression of intra- and inter-speaker variation may be seen in Figure 7.1. The first two tracks in the figure are created by a single speaker saying */owie/* on two different occasions. The third and fourth tracks are of two different speakers also saying */owie/*.

Several factors must be considered in order to compare these tracks; they include (1) the region of moment space occupied by the track, (2) the shape of the track, (3) the center of gravity of the track and (4) the orientation of the track. Each of these characteristics will display larger interspeaker than

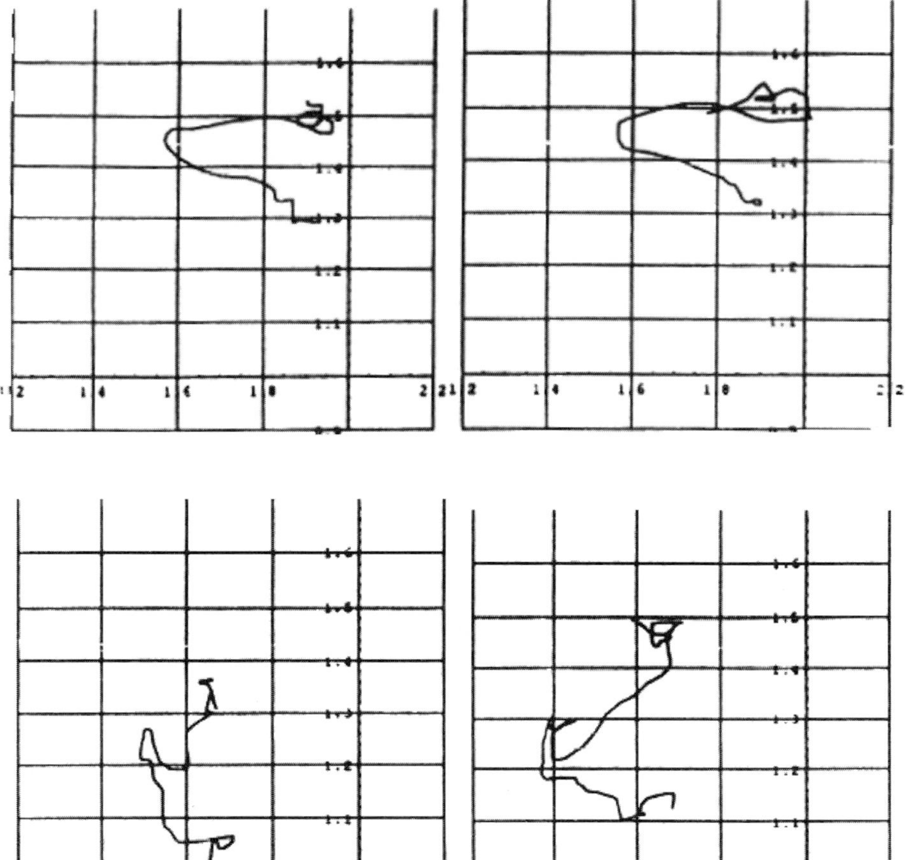

Figure 7.1
The two left-hand blocks show a single speaker producing the same word twice; those to the right, two different talkers saying the same word. Provided by R. D. Rodman.

intraspeaker variation (at least when they are reduced to statistical variables). Rodman suggests that the way to extract these variables is to surround the track with a minimal enclosing rectangle (MER), which is that for the minimal area containing the entire track. The MER, in turn, is computed by rotating the track about an endpoint one degree at a time and computing the area of a bounding rectangle whose sides are parallel to the axes each time. The minimum is then taken; it will be found within 90° of rotation. These relationships are illustrated by Figure 7.2.

Four of the 10 variables used to characterize the tracks are then extracted from the MER of the curve in its original orientation, namely the x-value of the midpoint, the y-value of the midpoint, the length of the long side (L) and the angle of orientation (α). Four additional variables (relative to the track) also can be identified; these are the minimal x-coordinate, the minimal y-coordinate, the maximal x-coordinate, and the maximal y-coordinate. These values are

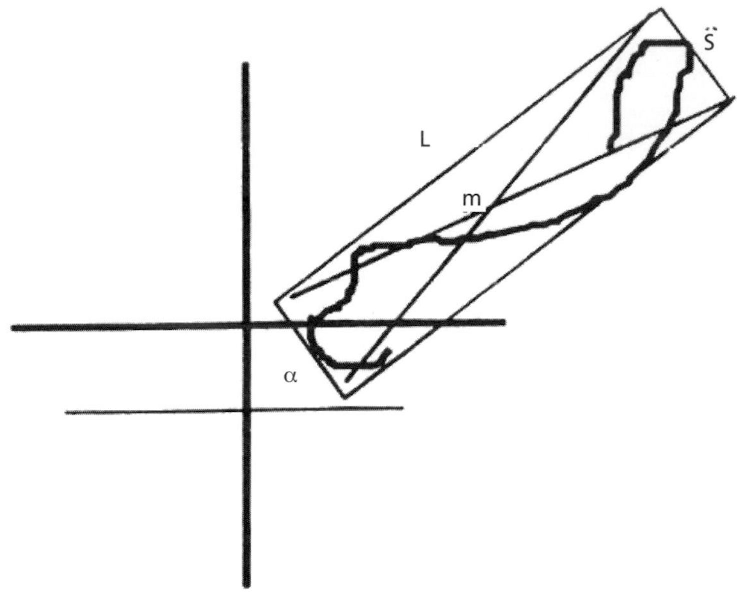

Figure 7.2
An illustration of the minimum.
Provided by R. D. Rodman.

derived by surrounding the track, in its original orientation, with a minimal rectangle parallel to the axes and taking in the four corner points. These eight parameters provide measurement of the track's location and orientation in moment space.

The final two variables are applied to reflect the shape of the track. That is, they (i.e., the tracks in m_1–m_2 space) are parameterized into integrable curves by plotting the m_1-value of the point *p* against the distance in m_1–m_2 space to point *p*-1 (providing, of course, that the distance exceeds a prespecified threshold). If it does not, point *p*-1 is discarded and the next point taken. This process continues until the threshold is exceeded. The abscissa is then normalized to [0,1] and the points interpolated into a smooth curve by a cubic spline. This is defined as a *normalized arc length* parameterization. A second curve is then produced by application of the same process but by using the m_2-value of the point *p*. The two quadrature-based variables are then calculated by integrating each curve over the interval [0,1].

Figures 7.3–7.5 illustrate the discriminatory power of these variables. Figures 7.3 and 7.4 represent two different utterances of /*ayo*/ (extracted from 'we *may owe* money') by speaker X. The first plot in each figure is the track in moment space. The second and third plots are the normalized arc length parameterization for m_1 and m_2 with the actual variable used being the quadrature of the curves. As you can see, similarities are evident in the shape of corresponding plots for the same-speaker utterances. Figure 7.5 then is the set of plots of that same utterance by speaker Y. The different curve shapes in the figure confirm that the syllable was uttered by a different person.

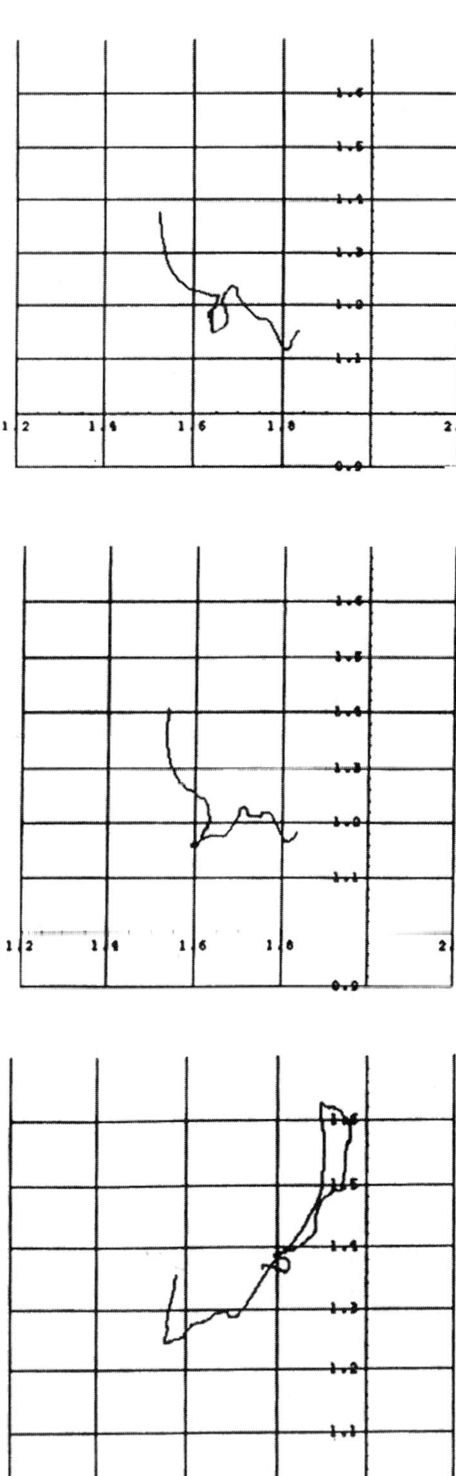

Figure 7.3

A speaker produces a word.
Provided by R. D. Rodman.

Figure 7.4

The same speaker repeats the word.
Provided by R. D. Rodman.

Figure 7.5

A second speaker produces the word.
Provided by R. D. Rodman.

Once the Rodman group had successfully completed several methodological studies, they proceeded to carry out a number of experiments designed to assess the method. One involved a scenario wherein 10 speakers spoke *owie*, *eya*, and *ayo* four times each. These utterances were used to create a training database. Later, 10 unknown speakers uttered these same words a single time each and the resulting materials were used as the test database. All of the speech signals were then processed to create the *tracks* described above. The 10 cited parameters (again, see above) were used for the comparisons between the utterances. Both closed- and open-set SPID procedures of each of the 10 unknowns were then carried out. When the unknowns were chosen from among the 10 speakers (closed set), the error rate was 0%. For open-set identifications, the error rate varied between 10% and 20% depending on the level of the thresholds employed. In short, Rodman found that it was not possible to establish a single threshold to produce error-free open set identifications; hence, he has provided a critique. He wrote (paraphrased) 'I employed discriminate analysis in 30-dimensional space (10 variables for each of three sounds) for this research; the squared Mahalanobis distance (as a measure of similarity) was processed in a similar way. I then chose a threshold to determine whether a speaker resided or did not reside within the particular set being tested. When a speaker was not in the set, all the distances were expected to exceed the threshold. Thus, a single threshold, one which would correctly identify both the three outsiders and the seven insiders was not established in this experiment. Further, a manual procedure (one which resulted in a single miss) simply was not considered appropriate. On the other hand, the "reasonable" algorithm (established to determine the threshold value) resulted in two misses. Thus, we are assessing new threshold determination for our next series of experiments.' He then indicates that characterizing each speaker by '10 or more isphonemic sequences improved discriminatory power considerably.' The research program described is being continued with the current focus on both upgraded thresholds and with samples drawn from criminal investigations.

A PROGRAM BASED IN POLAND

The philosophy expressed by the leaders of this group is simply that, when faced with a problem of forensic identification, it is important to gather and apply any and all of the SPID procedures that might permit success. The program is headed by an engineer, Prof. Dr Wojciech Majewski; the other principals are Dr Czeslaw Basztura and Dr Janusz Zalenski (43–51). The term engineering may be a little misleading as Majewski in particular is cross-trained (and experienced) in the phonetic sciences. Moreover, the efforts of this group have not been entirely confined to Poland as Majewski initiated some of his SPID research at my laboratory in the 1960s; he also spent time at Michigan State University with Oscar Tosi (of 'voiceprint' fame). Basztura too has a primary understanding of human behavior. Accordingly, it should not be surprising that this team uses both machine and human processing. And, as stated, their philosophy relative to the forensic situation is one where they use every procedure and parameter they can develop or adapt. Thus, the review to follow includes descriptions of their entire approach, even if it is only their machine procedures which are consistent with this chapter's theme.

Let us start with the computer-based procedures. When our consideration is restricted only to them, their efforts would appear to stem from SV (after all, they are engineers first). For one thing, they argue that there is a need for *automatic* SPID and do so on the basis of the practitioner's easy access to computers. They insist that adding superior decision rules to the computer's program, and objectively measuring the features of speech, will permit them to determine if a particular utterance was produced by a given speaker. They further suggest that the number of algorithms which can be used for these purposes is quite large and list some they use; included are: spectra, cepstrum, linear prediction coefficients (LPC), fundamental frequency, formant frequencies, zero crossing ratios (ZCR), temporal features. They adapted these algorithms for use with SPID tasks, suggesting that a variety of them should be applied in association with the decision criteria and classification rules they have adopted (48, 53). Subsequently, they established a number of approaches which involve application of the nonparametrical algorithms of NM (nearest mean), NN (nearest neighbor) and/or K-NN. These entities are applied to the speech parameters which either have been averaged over time or established for particular time windows. For forensic purposes, this team indicates that they prefer the NN algorithm with dynamic time warping (DTW). That is, they compare the parametric representation of an unknown speech sample with the parametric representations of all known speakers. To speed up calculations, the simplest possible distance measure (i.e. the Hamming distance) is used. Basically it can be expressed as:

$$d(X,Y) = \sum_{P=1}^{P} [X(p) - Y(p)]$$

Since forensic applications involve the recognition of speakers in open sets, these investigators have worked out a parametrical, probabilistic algorithm based on Basztura's work (44, 47); indeed, his metric was found to be especially useful for SPID purposes. The procedure (i.e. a statistical algorithm of speaker recognition in open sets, or OSA) generally combines two classical tasks. The first consists of a speaker identification procedure which assigns the utterance of an unknown speaker to one of the known speakers; it is followed by a verification procedure which either confirms or rejects the preliminary identification decision.

To be more specific, these investigators assume that their set consists of *M* known classes (i.e. known speakers who belong to a closed set) plus a one multi-object class (one which corresponds to all the voices that do not belong to set M). These latter voices constitute the 'ground' or unknown voice class (m = 0) where conditional distribution of the ground Q(x/0) is generally a multi-model distribution with a large number of modes (they approach infinity). For the known voices (m = 1, 2, . . . M), it is assumed that the conditional distributions of Q(x/m) are normal. Examples of them, for one-dimensional parameter space (*P* = 1), are presented in Figure 7.6.

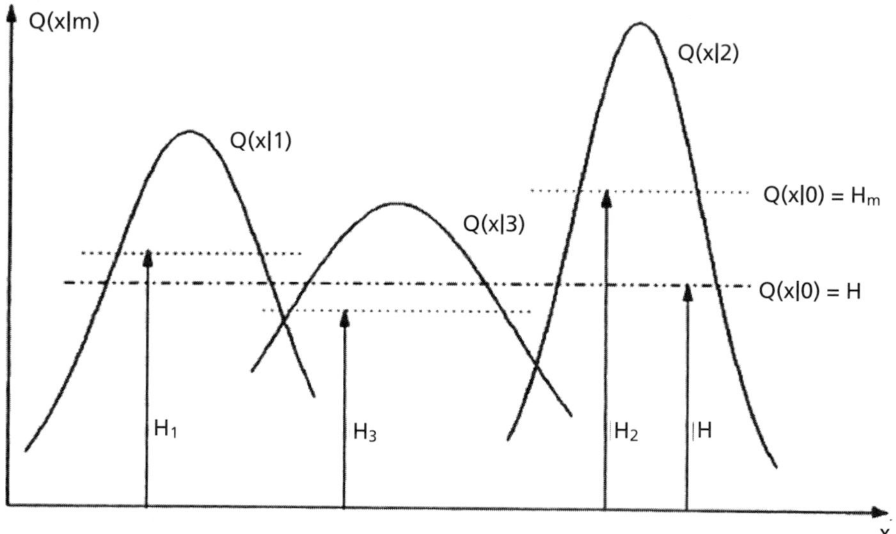

Figure 7.6
Examples of distributions of the conditional probabilities X (x/m) and Q (x/0). From Majewski and Basztura (34).

The algorithm employed by the Majewski–Basztura group is based on Bayes's decision criterion. However, a more general term is substituted for the distance measures used in the nonparametrical (heuristic) algorithms (see again the equation). Indeed, they indicate that 'a mean risk Rm (Xn) connected with the assignation of pattern (Xn) to class m is established.' As the basis of these assumptions, they present the recognition procedure for open sets in two stages:

1. Identification in the closed set; i.e., the finding of m* which means the temporary assignment of recognition pattern Xn to class m*.

$$Rm^* = \min_{n} Rm\ (X_n)$$

2. Verification; i.e., the checking of condition 2.

$$Rm^* = (X_n) < Ro\ (X_n)$$

If the condition found directly above is fulfilled, pattern Xn belongs to class m*. In the opposite case, it belongs to class m 0; i.e., the ground.

The selection of boundaries for the unknown voice class (m = 0) may be limited to two simple cases (see again Figure 7.6):

1. Q(x/0) = H, where H = a constant threshold,
2. Q(x/0) = Hm, where Hm = a relative threshold.

In the closed set, an incorrect identification may occur. The verification procedure diminishes this error to its own cases. However, the procedure also introduces an error (α) of incorrect rejection; it is related to the cases initially recognized correctly but then rejected in the verification process. In relation to the open set, the identification procedure introduces the error of false acceptance (β); this error is related to the patterns from outside the closed set which are accepted.

The procedure cited is applied to different parametric representations of speech; i.e. fast Fourier transforms (FFT), LPC, fundamental frequency (F0) and temporal features (ZCR). It has demonstrated a usefulness at least under laboratory conditions (43, 44); it does so even for unfavorable signal-to-noise ratios (SNR) (49). More importantly, it also is useful for forensic applications since it results in a relatively small false-acceptance error – a consideration very important to the legal consequences of false accusations.

As you would expect, these authors have carried out a number of experiments to assess the sensitivity of their techniques. They also provide a practical example (see below) as to both how, and how well, it works. However, please note that when they apply their method in the forensic sector, they employ their 'triple' approach; that is, they add-on their structured AP-SPID techniques and a 'visual' pattern matching method reminiscent of 'voiceprints.' However, this approach includes fairly sophisticated spectrographic displays (50) (one of them can be seen in Figure 7.7). Examiners trained in both AP-SPID and their type of visual analysis organize the data for use with the computer-based procedures described above. The way in which all three methods of speaker recognition are applied and correlated can be found in the operational plan presented in Table 7.1. In order to minimize any subjectivism by the examiners, each of the three procedures are carried out by different sets of individuals.

Consider Table 7.1; you will note that the first task (item A-1) involves an auditory analysis of the evidence and exemplar tapes; it is carried out by three or four experienced examiners. Their major goal here is to make a transcript of the dialogue and compare it with the protocols provided by the police. The second and third tasks simply are routine; i.e., they check the tape for authenticity and record a group of foil or distractor speakers (see items A-2 and A-3).

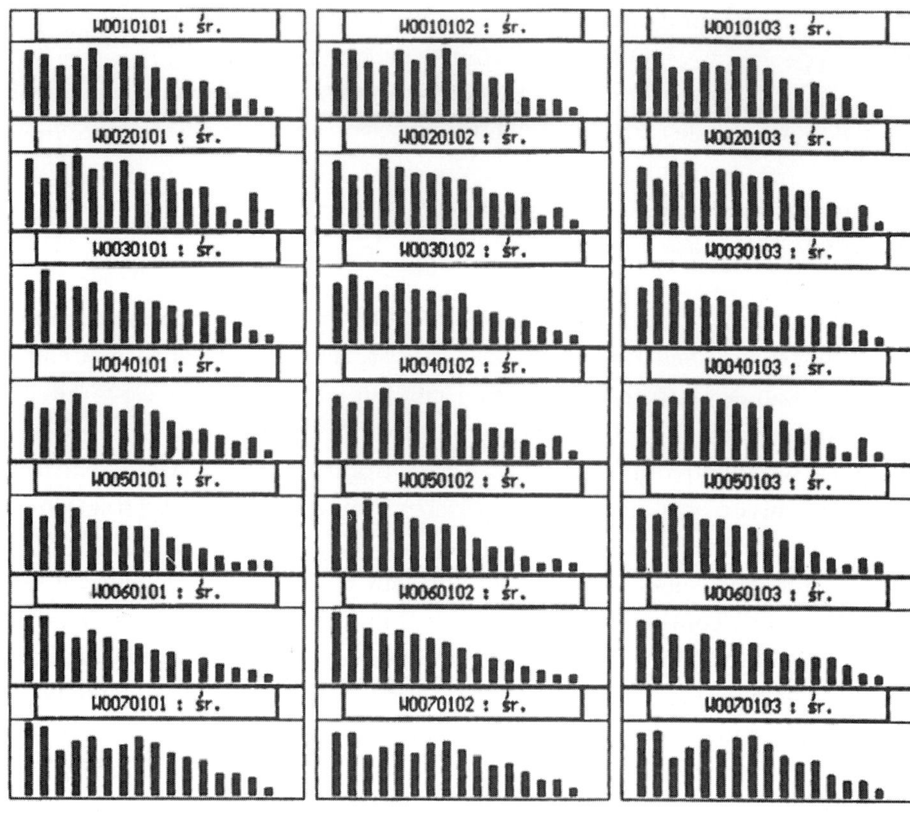

Figure 7.7

Examples of one-third octave spectra of the word /awek/ produced three times by seven speakers. From Majewski and Basztura (34).

Table 7.1

Operational plan of investigation. From Majewski and Basztura (50).

	Procedures
A. Preliminary steps	1 Auditory analysis of the recorded speech 2 Tape authentication 3 Recording the foil speakers 4 Selection of key utterances and labeling the utterances, speakers, samples and repetitions 5 Extraction and A/D conversion of the key utterances
B. Evaluation for SPID	1 Listening tests 2 Visual examination of: a. t–f–a spectrograms b. one-third octave spectra c. distributions of time intervals 3 Automatic learning and classification procedures: a. The NN-DTW algorithm b. The OSA algorithm

The fourth task (A-4) is to select key utterances for the SPID procedures and label them. These selections are based on the frequency of occurrence, capability to convey individual voice features, neutral content, etc. All speakers produce six (key) utterances (the same ones). Subsequently (A-5), extraction and A/D conversion of the cited utterances, is carried out. That is, the utterances are digitized, transferred to computer memory and used in the comparative analyses.

As can be seen from consideration of the lower half of Table 7.1, the second phase of the SPID effort is to apply the three types of SPID procedures. As stated, they are AP-SPID, visual examinations of three types of spectrographic materials and at least two computer-based approaches.

The authors provide an example, it is one drawn from their forensic database. In this instance, an unknown speaker (U) was recorded when attempting extortion. A group was examined; it included five suspects and foils. The examination proceeded as follows. First, the listening tasks (paired comparisons or ABX) were carried out; speaker No. 2 appeared most likely to be the extortionist. These tests also demonstrated that a striking similarity existed among voices 1, 2 and 4 and did so despite the fact that speakers 2 and 4 appeared to be attempting voice disguise. The similarities apparently were caused by the fact that all three were members of a single family. At this juncture, the visual and quantitative procedures were carried out. These comparisons were performed on both t–f–a spectrograms and parametric representations of the utterances (i.e. by means of FFT and ZCR displays). The assessment of the speakers temporal features (ZCR results) could be quantified

Speaker	Inter[1] ZCR	Intra[2] ZCR	Procedure [3] OSA	NN[3] DTW
1	47.2	18.5	53.4	51.0
2	41.1	31.2	54.7	54.0
3	48.9	16.8	23.6	21.8
4	57.6	24.6	52.9	51.9
5	112.8	–	6.9	6.9

1. Interspeaker distance; the lower the score, the more that speaker is like the target.
2. Intraspeaker distance; the higher the score, the more the speaker resembles the target.
3. In percent; the higher the score, the closer is the know–unknown match.

Table 7.2

A composite table extracted from the Majewski–Basztura data. It appears that speakers 1, 2, 4 have voices similar to the unknown (all are members of the same family) but speaker 2 is consistently most like him

and, hence, they are included in Table 7.2 along with the results from computer processing (OSA and NN-DTW). In any event, the ZCR values for both inter- and intra-speaker distance can be seen in the first two columns (note that No. 2 is again most like the unknown). At this point, the investigators activated the computer programs described above. First, steady-state segments of several samples of the vowels /a/ and /o/ were identified; subsequently, nine randomly chosen segments, each lasting 50 ms, were extracted for each of the vowel-speaker combinations. These samples were chosen because this group considers the vowels cited to be relatively good carriers of individual voice features; they also exhibit a reasonably high frequency of occurrence in Polish. The specific computer programs applied in this case included OSA (i.e. the previously described algorithms for speaker recognition in open sets) and the heuristic NN algorithm with DTW (NN-DTW). In turn, two sets of parameters were used: one-third octave amplitude spectra (P = 16) and distributions of time intervals between zero crossings in time channels (also P = 16). The averages resulting from these procedures also can be found in Table 7.2. Comparisons among the ZCR data indicated that the intraspeaker distances were smaller than those for the interspeaker measurements. In this case, a known speaker is considered more like the unknown if the distances between the ZCR scores are large; smaller ZCR ratios also indicate great similarity. In short, the ZCR data supported the postulate that the three related suspects were most like the unknown and, while the differences were again small, it appeared that speaker No. 2 quite possibly was the same person as U. This conclusion was in agreement with the aural-perceptual results and the visual analyses of the several types of spectrograms.

Finally, the statistics for correct identification, based on the NN-DTW and OSA analyses, also may be found in Table 7.2. These values are the percent probabilities that any of the known speakers actually is the unknown; (they result from composite values of the means for all vowels produced by that speaker). As can be seen, the judgments here are consistent with the previous ones. Even more important, one particular speaker was consistently found to be most like the extortionist. Of course, the fact that his individual values were not markedly different from the others on any given test does not constitute particularly robust evidence of a voice match. On the other hand, that he is closest on test after test is quite a different matter.

This real-life case should provide insight as to how Majewski and Basztura approach the problem of forensic SPID. They believe that it is important to combine aural-perceptual assessments with several pattern matching spectrographic techniques *and* multiple computer-based algorithms. In my judgment, their approach is a sensible one and it should serve them, and the relevant law enforcement and judicial organizations of their region, quite well at least until more sophisticated approaches are developed.

SAUSI

Finally, a speaker identification program was initiated at IASCP, University of Florida in the mid-1960s. Our motivation was partly based on scientific curiosity, partly on my personal interest in 'identification' (how old did the person sound, how well can we localize acoustic signals underwater, etc.) and partly because we recognized the need for a procedure that could be used to mitigate a steadily growing social problem. However, an additional motivation on my part was simply one of guilt. I had joined the group of scientists opposed to the use of 'voiceprints' (I did so simply because they were not valid). That both research and logic strongly supported my decision was of little consolation. Law enforcement and other relevant groups needed help. Someone simply had to provide them with a valid and effective SPID system. Thus, both our SAUSI and the AP-SPID research programs were initiated (in part anyway) to assist in meeting this problem. The description and history of our AP-SPID program was included in Chapter 4; that for SAUSI follows.

CHAPTER 8

SAUSI

INTRODUCTION

While my semi-automatic speaker identification system (SAUSI) has been referenced throughout this book, its full description (plus some discussion) has been deferred to this chapter. First, the questions. Where did it come from, how was it developed and why did we do what we did?

MOTIVATION

As was indicated in the last chapter, the SAUSI research program developed naturally. For one thing, my students, colleagues and I were already into 'identification' in a big way – we just did not realize it. Neither did we realize (in the beginning anyway) that some of what we were doing actually was 'speaker' identification. A short review should provide some perspective here. It may be especially useful in allowing you to understand just how a program such as SAUSI actually develops. We had already established a number of cohesive research programs; ones that were either directly focused on 'identification' or were complementary to it. For example, one of them involved determining a person's *age* by means of perceptual and/or acoustical speech analysis (1–6). This research program was rather well received and has been continued (7–13). In any event, these projects paralleled our efforts in SPID.

Another of our early thrusts involved the study of speaker *intelligibility* (14–18). Research in this domain also has continued in parallel with that on the SAUSI system (19–25). As a matter of fact, many of the concepts and procedures developed for these projects also were adapted for the SPID program.

Several of our (later) research programs had their roots in speaker identification (remember, we also studied AP-SPID). To illustrate, we developed research programs designed to discover the effects of stress on voice (26–33); others focused on the acoustic identification of gunfire (34, 35) and on the effects of intoxication on speech (36–40). As indicated, these particular projects did not originate prior to, or even at the same time as, our SPID programs. However, a great deal of interaction and cross-fertilization took place between them, especially during the later stages of SAUSI development. After all, acoustically identifying a gunshot, or the age of a speaker, present challenges quite similar to personal identification.

Motivation of a somewhat different type resulted from the arrival of two of my early postdoctoral students; both were interested in 'identification procedures.' These students were Wojciech Majewski (he later became Professor and Dean of the Institute of Acoustics and Telecommunications, Wroclaw Technical University, Wroclaw, Poland) and the late Thomas Shipp (who, for many years, headed the Speech Research Laboratory at the San Francisco Veteran's Administration Medical Center). Wojciech had won his doctorate primarily in engineering but was interested in the acoustic processing of speech. While at our university, he continued his study of experimental phonetics and initiated several relevant research programs. Our collaboration ultimately led to the examination of power spectra as a possible SPID cue (41, 42); it also led to the testing of other (somewhat less successful) techniques. Tom Shipp was not as interested in SPID *per se* as was Majewski. Rather, his focus was on the recognition of human behavioral states by the analysis of subjects' vocal output. Nonetheless, he contributed much to the early methodologies and our initial planning in the speaker identification area.

The third impetus to the SAUSI program resulted from the growth of the 'voiceprint' controversy. My observations of what was going on, plus requests that I 'analyze the problem,' put me in contact with a number of groups (especially law enforcement agencies) that had an interest in, or a need for, valid and reliable SPID procedures. It did not take long to discover just how desperate certain members of these groups were for assistance, or how lacking was any solution based on 'voiceprints.' It would have been difficult to ignore this problem even if the SPID topic was not one in which I was developing a fundamental interest.

STRUCTURING AN APPROACH

It is a little difficult to describe just how we organized our thinking, philosophies, methods and operations. This is due primarily to the realities associated with large and complex research projects. Only rarely do they develop in an orderly manner. So, rather than confusing you by sorting things into a strict chronological order, let me cluster the discussions around the SAUSI-linked events and/or 'breakthroughs' (to us anyway) which have occurred over the past 35–40 years. This discussion should give you, at least, some insight into how we operated and roughly how we achieved a modicum of success.

The first excitement came from our early realization that there would be no simple solution to the problem. There just did not appear to be any single factor, parameter or vector which was at once sensitive enough to permit discrimination among the many talkers who would populate even a modest-sized group and yet be robust enough to resist the degrading effects of the various types of distortion. Moreover, the available processing equipment (even our laboratory computers) was/were initially pretty crude. I vividly remember the data reduction problems associated with our early research. In those days, it took a half dozen research assistants upwards of two weeks to complete a SAUSI experiment. Later, a single computer operator would need only about half that time to process even larger experiments. These same procedures now take less than a day to complete. But back to our initial problem. We soon realized (along with others, of course) that it would be necessary to dissect the acoustic signal in some way if we were to tease out those parameters that would support identification. On the other hand, we also discovered that we could cluster a number of them together in order to create useful *vectors*. We postulated that, if we were successful, we could then study how they operated both individually and collectively, and, having got that far, we could initiate an integrated research program.

At this juncture, I realized that traditional research approaches might not be robust enough for our purposes. Typically, a scientific project is developed by asking a question (or series of questions), structuring a theoretical framework and then carrying out appropriate experiments. As you might expect, the process also involves specifying a precise research design, the equipment to be used, the population to be studied, the utterances to be generated, the experimental protocols, the statistical analyses, the procedures for data interpretation, and so on. (Research is a complex business, is it not?) In any event, the plan cited appeared lacking. While it was both rigorous and extensive enough to support research focused on some sort of limited relationship, it just did not exhibit sufficient cohesion, organization and depth to permit our long-term project to be properly conducted. Moreover, we had already obtained evidence that supported this postulation. That is, we had noted that even some of the more elegant SPID and SV research programs being carried out at that time (see Chapter 7) seemed not to be producing very much in the way of results; still others had withered and/or had met with an early demise. The fact that most of these projects were a little limited in their scope probably had something to do with it. Finally, we took no succor from what was happening in the 'voiceprint' area. Clearly, chaos reigned there (probably the result of poor structuring, lack of cohesion and little to no research). In short, we opined that, to be successful, we should organize our efforts differently than did most of the others. That is exactly what we did.

STRUCTURING SAUSI

BASIC ORGANIZATION

The approach we developed can best be understood by consideration of Figure 8.1. This flow chart was among the very first we structured as a basis for the SAUSI program. As you can see, it is reasonably comprehensive, yet flexible enough to be adapted for use with any set of features or vectors (a vector is a complex entity made up of a number of related elements or parameters). Note that this model first requires that the vectors be tested relative to their ability to

Figure 8.1
Model providing the basis for comprehensive development of a semi-automatic speaker identification system (SAUSI).

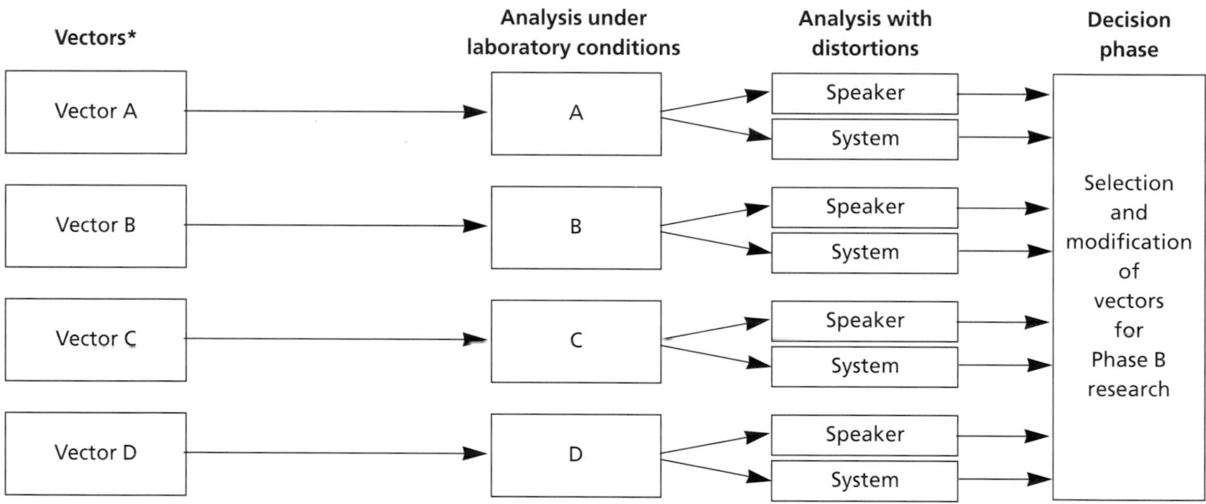

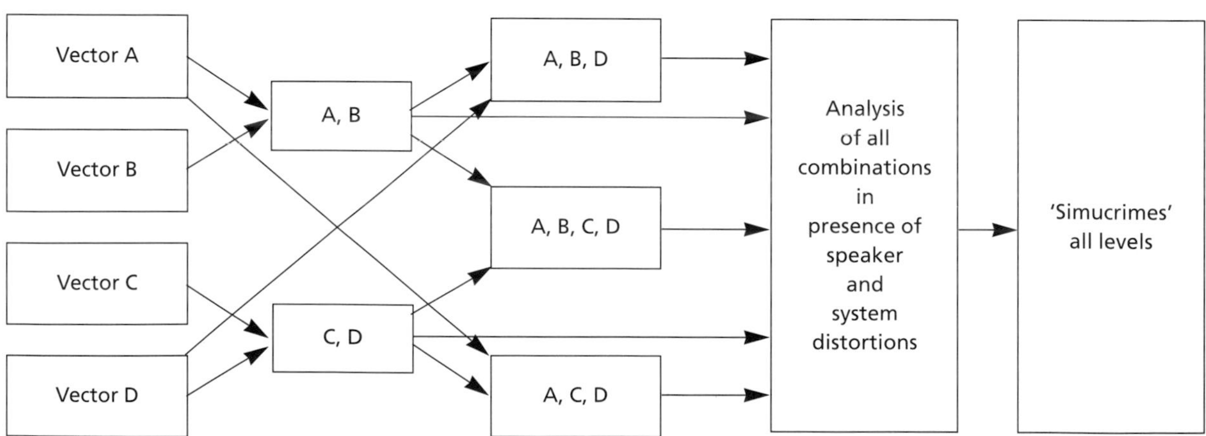

discriminate among talkers drawn from fairly large groups of subjects. The basic strength of each vector can then be assessed experimentally and changes made as needed. Moreover, the process can be repeated and as often as necessary. Once a vector begins to show promise, it can be evaluated in situations where distortions are present. You will note from earlier chapters that channel distortions include such things as telephone (frequency) bandpass, noise, and so on, whereas subject distortions involve speech which is produced when the talker is stressed, sick, intoxicated, attempting disguise, etc. The purpose of this second phase, then, would be to test (and modify if necessary) the vectors for use with the more severe challenges occurring in the field. This servomechanistic process could then be continued until those conditions which serve to enhance or degrade the vectors are identified and their effects integrated or mitigated. An alternative result would be to find that the vector is simply not sensitive enough to provide useful information about a speaker's identity. Indeed, we discovered that several of those we proposed and tested fell into this category. They were discarded, of course. As you might suspect by now, these (several) initial stages took a long time to complete.

The next phase of virtually any SPID program is to attempt to increase *system* effectiveness by combining the constituent vectors into sets of various size. The specific process we used was to first test the strength of all possible pairings and then to go on to more complex combinations. Ultimately, we assessed all the vectors at once. As may be seen in the lower part of Figure 8.1, these procedures are even more complex than are the initial ones. For example, 11 separate research programs were required to test the set of four SPID vectors we eventually developed. Each involved several experiments focused on normal conditions and then replications with various distortions present. Many experiments were repeated further because of changes designed to upgrade the process. As suggested, when the procedures seen in Figure 8.1 were carried out, some of the early vectors had to be eliminated.

More advanced phases of system development may be best understood by consideration of Figure 8.2, which is but a modification of Figure 8.1. However, this structure is different enough from the original to permit experiments to be conducted under 'real life' (or close to 'real life') conditions. Better yet, it provides the basis for structuring field tests. We have found two different approaches useful for that purpose. The first involves attempted solutions of *simulated* crimes (ones which are generated under field-like conditions). The second involves application of the method to *actual* investigations (usually criminal). Either can provide helpful information about system validity and/or efficiency when used in the field; however, both have limitations. For example, even well-designed 'simucrimes' are somewhat artificial and only roughly parallel real-life situations. In contrast, the use of criminal cases permits only nonscien-

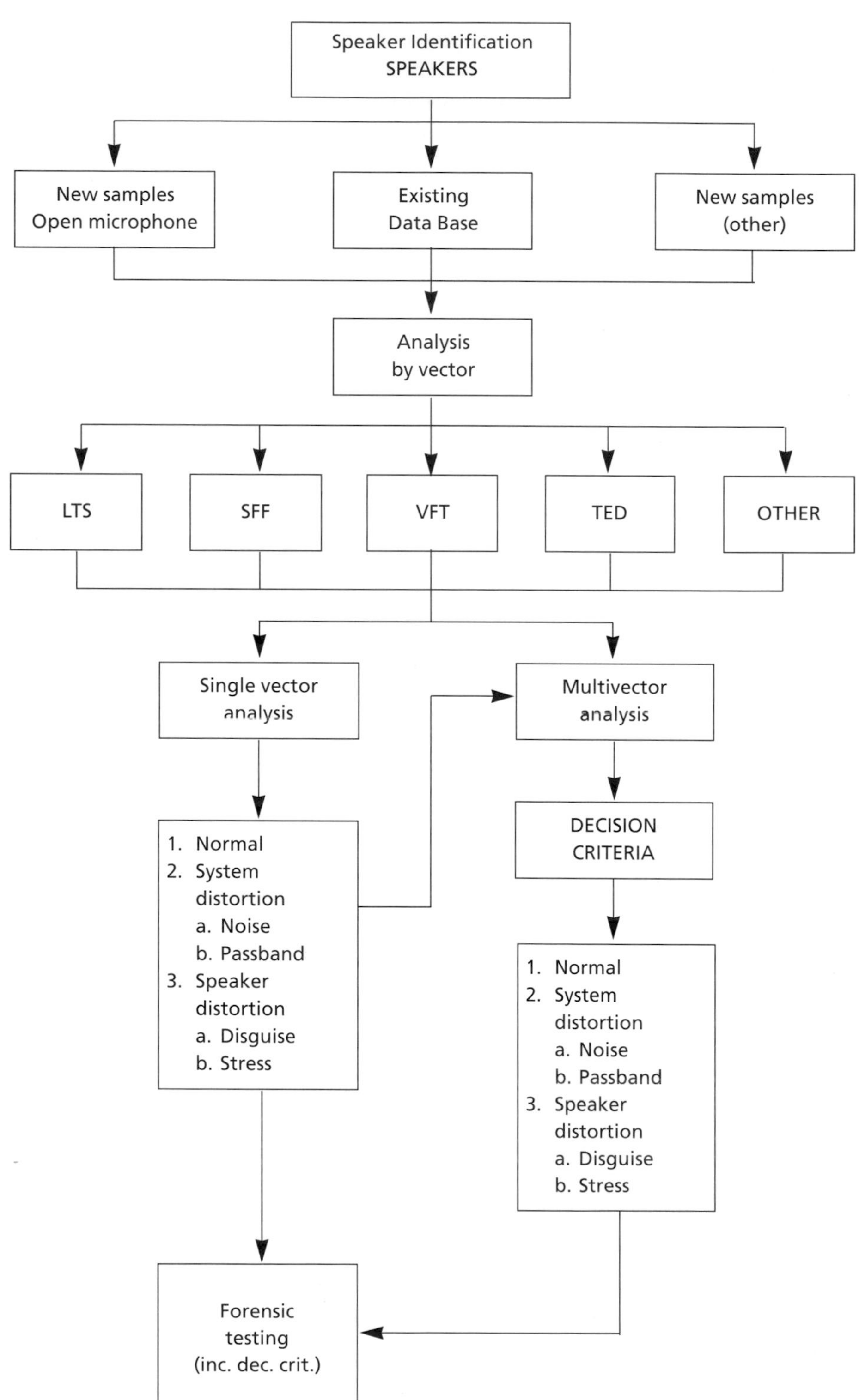

Figure 8.2

Modification of the SAUSI developmental flow chart. Its purpose was to extend the scope of the program to include field research.

tific verification (i.e. that based on confessions, convictions, etc.) and results of this type simply cannot be substituted for experimental data. Yet, field research often can demonstrate, to some extent anyway, if the SPID procedure being developed actually is of merit or is inadequate. Indeed, this final step proved valuable in the development of SAUSI. It led to the two-dimensional profile approach we use, as well as to our procedure involving 'rotations.' Both of these techniques are now counted among the strengths of the SAUSI approach.

To summarize, the development of an efficient SPID system is not a trivial endeavor. As we discovered, a successful outcome takes years of research and careful application. Moreover, the research conducted must be highly organized, extensive and, yet, flexible (see again, Figures 8.1 and 8.2).

THE VECTORS

In the beginning, we studied all sorts of speech elements and relationships. We also assessed certain parameters within the signal itself (i.e. traditional signal analysis). In these latter cases, little regard was paid to human motivation or behavior. However, some of our techniques also involved signal processing but wherein the process was modified by direct observations of speech behavior and consideration of relevant theoretical constructs. Certain of the approaches we tried were very simple in scope (so simple they involved but a single feature or parameter), others were quite complex. Slowly (actually, *very* slowly) we came to the realization that the factors which appeared to have the greatest SPID potential were those that reflected the processes employed by humans of course. People – ordinary people – carry out all kinds of SPID. It was at this point in time that we began to closely observe what individuals actually did. We discovered that they made their identifications quite rapidly and they did so without external assistance. Indeed, I realized that I personally carried out these very activities; I did then and I do now. For example, I recently listened to an actor (who I could hear but not see) narrating a program about the Founding Fathers of the United States; his voice sounded familiar. Then I realized who he was. I could not remember his name but I knew that he often had played the role of a detective on a television program entitled 'Law and Order.' Sure enough, he was identified at the end of the program as Paul Sorvino. While he does not exhibit a particularly unique voice, I recognized it and did so quite casually. So, which of his speaking attributes had I (unconsciously) processed and stored? We now know that it is not the way the signal is constructed but rather the elements (voice quality, pitch level/patterns, prosody, dialect, and so on) it carries that are important. List them and you will see that they resemble the AP-SPID checklists found in Chapter 4. To reiterate, what I had *not* done was to subject Mr Sorvino's speech to some sort of machine-based analytical method. Rather, all I did was tune in on those 'natural' speaking attributes embedded in his utterances.

These insights first occurred to us many years ago. No light bulb flashed; nevertheless, the idea quickly took root at our laboratory and we began to apply it to our SAUSI program. Specifically, we postulated that humans (unconsciously) identify speakers by listening to their 'natural speech features,' storing away the idiosyncratic elements they hear and then recalling them. Thus, all we had to do was teach machines to carry out this very same process.

This shift in focus occurred at an opportune time for us as we had been experimenting with traditional signal processing techniques and found them less than exciting. Indeed, we had discovered that many of the factors we were attempted to employ were rendered functionally inoperable when impacted by the distortions associated with criminal activity. Thus, we had even more of an impetus to shift our focus from the traditional (with an associated search for a single omnipotent factor) to a multifeature approach involving natural speaking characteristics. It was at this point that we also began the process of profiling speakers.

Our new approach made a great deal of sense to us (43–46). But, identifying and generating the actual vectors was not all that easy. How did we do it? Well, for one thing, we sat down and reviewed our personal experiences; we also reread all the AP-SPID literature that was available at that time (see Chapter 3). We then made a list of potential vectors. It was about this time that I listened to a paper on this subject presented by Kenneth N. Stevens (47). He too had listed a series of features which he believed were particularly important to speaker identification. We put his list together with ours and found a number of commonalities. We then began to experiment with various clusters of parameters – either those that grouped themselves around a central theme or others that resided in some identifiable domain. Those that we selected all appeared potentially useful but, as expected, only some of them proved to be so. Of course, many of the analysis techniques we had to use at that time were a little crude and, hence, may not have been sophisticated enough to provide fair evaluations. However, any procedure devised would ultimately have had to perform in negative (i.e. forensic) environments. That is, it would, at once, have to be sensitive to small differences among talkers and yet resistant to forensic distortions. Moreover, the end product (i.e. the method or system) would have to be easy to understand and interpret.

Some of the (natural) vectors that were of little use included vocal intensity, consonantal structure, nasality and vocal jitter. There appears to be little reason to review them here (at length anyway) since they did not exhibit even marginal potential. Thus, a sentence or two should suffice. Vocal intensity was simply too difficult to assess accurately. Since absolute intensity level can be varied by a number of factors external to the speaker's behavior, the rise and decay times of the speech (energy) pulse often are changed by events that have little to do with vocal intensity itself. A similar problem was encountered when we attempted to use consonant characteristics as identification cues. We were hopeful that we could do so as Ingeman (48), Schwartz (49) and others had suggested that phoneme analysis should provide a rich source of speaker specific information. Yet, reliable quantification of consonantal structure (and, especially, consonant clusters) proved difficult. Indeed, so many allophones occurred (within each speaker's productions) that intraspeaker variability was usually high. It is one thing for a modest relationship of the sort noted by Ingeman and Schwartz to exist; it is yet another for it to permit extraction of accurate information about a person's identity. Finally, the same kinds of problems occurred when nasality (50, 51) and vocal jitter were assessed. In all fairness, however, it must be said that these elements/clusters were assessed and discarded when the available processing equipment was not as sophisticated as it is today. Nor did we know as much about speech and speaking as we do now. It is just possible that, if one or more of these old vectors were restructured, it/they would prove useful for SPID purposes.

THE FOUR VECTORS

Which of our vectors have proved useful? It might appear to be getting ahead of the story were I to describe them at this juncture. However, it would seem necessary to do so, especially if you are to keep them in mind as we discuss how they were structured and how they work.

Each of the vectors was originally chosen on the basis of deductive logic, subjective observation and a little research. The formation of their constituent parts and assessment of their strength resulted from inductive logic and experimentation. SAUSI currently consists of four vectors; they are: (1) Long-Term Spectra (LTS), (2) Speaking Fundamental Frequency (SFF), (3) Time–Energy Distribution (TED) and (4) Vowel Formant Tracking (VFT).

The Long-Term Spectra vector

This vector reflects that elusive but very important attribute of voice quality. Vocal timbre, or tone, is fairly easy to understand (remember my example?). If a violin is played by one person and a clarinet by another, you will be able to differentiate between the two even if the musicians playing them do so at the same fundamental frequency and intensity level. The way you do so is by listening to their overall tone quality. The same relationship holds for human voices (at least, to a great extent). More importantly, power spectra provide good information about this characteristic.

Long-term spectra are among the most extensively investigated of any of the entities we have considered and/or researched. Indeed, a rather large number of reports have been published in the area (52–62); those provided by our group are particularly prominent (41, 63–72). In any event, we have found LTS to be one of the more stable of those vectors we have tried. It is sensitive to a speaker's identity even when noise, limited passband and speaker stress are present. It is not as resistant to the effects of disguise but still functions reasonably well under those conditions.

Please turn to Figure 8.3; as you will see, it provides two curves. Both are graphic representations of long term, or power, spectra. That is, they consist of frequency information about all the acoustic events which have taken place during the unit of time to which this analysis was applied (20 s for example). Note also that these frequency–energy patterns have resulted in line spectra. In turn, they provide information about the person's overall voice/speech quality and do so irrespective of the actual phonemes being produced. SAUSI's LTS vector uses up to 40 individual parameters to generate the curves seen in the figure; they cover a frequency range of about 60–10 000 Hz (less if the signal being analyzed is bandpassed). The decision as to whether these curves were produced by one speaker or by two is made by comparing them on the basis of their absolute differences. The (mathematical) measures we employed include both Euclidean and Hamming distances. Since there are about 88 semitones between the lowest and the highest frequencies associated with this procedure, measurements are made at approximately two-semitone intervals. The resulting 40 (or fewer) distances are then used to compare the patterns between and among the target speakers. This process can be carried out for as many individuals as required.

Previously, the LTS curves were generated by means of a Fast Fourier Transform (FFT); i.e., a Real Time Spectrum Analyzer coupled to a computer. However, in 1995 Jiang (66) carried out research on several procedures in order

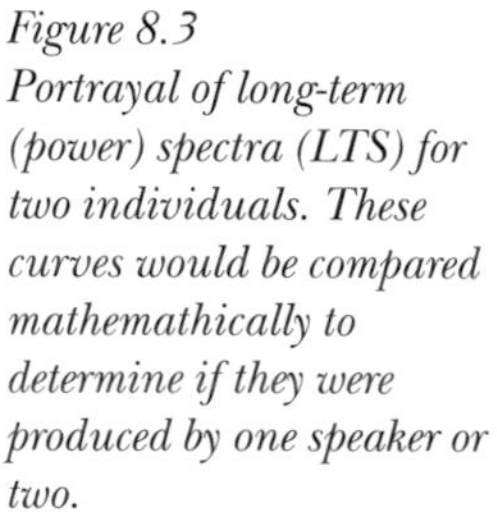

Figure 8.3
Portrayal of long-term (power) spectra (LTS) for two individuals. These curves would be compared mathemathically to determine if they were produced by one speaker or two.

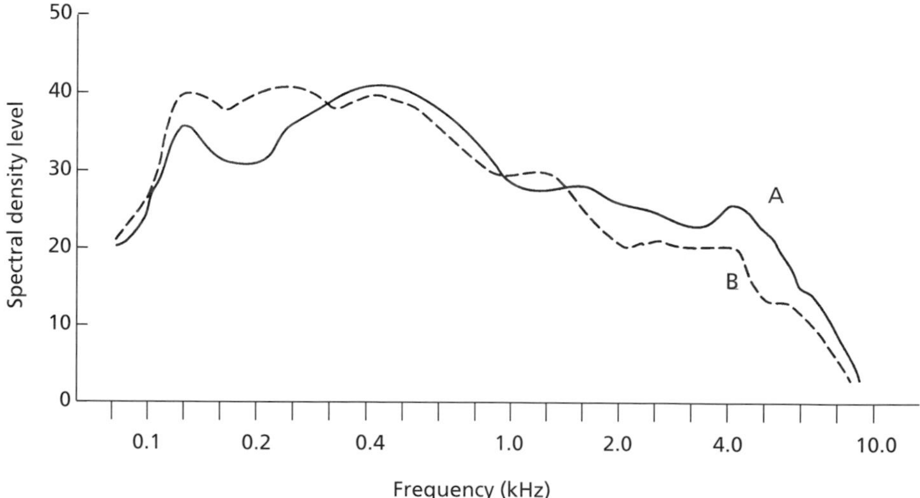

to determine which of them would provide the most powerful data. He was aided in this endeavor by the fact that a number of robust power spectrum analysis methods had become available. He considered three of them to be particularly attractive and assessed them experimentally by means of available software approaches. They were: (1) the FFT method, (2) a cepstrum method and (3) a linear prediction coefficent (LPC) approach. The FFT technique proved to be the most robust.

To generate data by this method, Jiang first preprocessed input for frame length and identified the speech signal; he then applied the formula

$$[\hat{PS}(k) = \frac{1}{k} \sum_{m=0}^{K-1} 10 \log / PS_m(k) /^2]$$

to yield the power spectrum of a particular speech signal within a frame (K is the number of speech frames). Note also that he used 1024-point FFTs in order to obtain high resolution and that the vector could employ 512 points of the average power spectrum for the Euclidean distance calculations. The process was repeated for each frame and a Hamming window (200 points) was applied to permit evaluation. As will be seen, the power spectra vector (LTS) is usually the most powerful and stable of the four vectors now employed. It even has been suggested that, under favorable conditions, it could be used as a standalone procedure.

The Speaking Fundamental Frequency vector

Speaking fundamental frequency (F0 or SFF) has been shown to be a reasonably good indicator of speaker identity (63, 64, 73–89). While early computer-based results were not as encouraging as those from perceptual research (73, 81, 87), it now seems possible that (if properly processed) SFF will provide a rather robust vector (78, 83). That is, while we too were disappointed in early SFF performance, we later realized that its problems resulted from a lack of a sufficient number of constituent parameters. The situation changed markedly once we used an approach involving measurement of up to 32 of them; indeed, contemporary results show that SFF is a reasonably sensitive identity cue (66, 78, 79, 83). The parameters which make up our SFF vector include F0 geometric mean, phonation-time ratio (PTR), the standard deviation of all the fundamental frequencies produced plus semitone intervals (or 'bins' of semitone width) containing information about the number of times each frequency was produced.

Over the years, our fundamental frequency data were obtained primarily, and automatically, by means of the IASCP Fundamental Frequency Indicator (Models 8 through 12). This system always has operated in such a manner that its output could be fed directly to one of our computers (for processing of any kind). In short, the fundamental frequency indicator (FFI) is a digital readout F0 tracking system which consists of a series of successive low-pass filters with cut-offs at half octave intervals; in turn, they are coupled to high-speed switching circuits controlled by a logic system (78, 79). FFI measures each wave (it does not sample) by producing a string of pulses, each of which marks the boundary of a fundamental period as extracted from the speech wave. These data, in turn, are delivered to the computer in the form of a series of square waves. The computer's internal pulses are then used to measure the intervals of the waves and the results processed to obtain the statistical data.

Recently Jiang (66) assessed this technique and compared it with two others. That is, he evaluated and contrasted: (1) the IASCP FFI, (2) the F0 extraction function of the Kay Elemetrics, Computerized Speech Laboratory (CSL) and (3) a cepstrum F0 extraction algorithm. It was found that FFI proved to be the most robust of the three procedures and hence continues to be the one used to provide the F0 material for the SFF vector. As will be remembered, these parameters include the geometric mean, the standard deviation, PTR and the number of waves in each of the semitone intervals. (Figure 8.4 is a FFI printout showing these values, plus some others.) These data are stored digitally in the computer; the SFF comparisons are subsequently made among and between the individuals being assessed.

The Time-Energy Distribution vector

Prosody or speech timing appears to be one of the more important aids to successful SPID, especially if listeners are involved (63, 64, 78, 90–93). As you will remember from Chapters 3 and 4, attributes such as rate of speaking, speech bursts, pauses, and so on, can provide idiosyncratic information about an individual speaker. Thus, there is strong logic that these talker-related prosodic speech elements can be extracted and used for speaker recognition purposes. Given the hypothesis that talkers do differ in the durational characteristics of speech (i.e. syllables, words, phrases and sentences), the time a person uses to produce a specific amount of such discourse should constitute a cue for identification. Morever, individual speakers should vary in their production of silent intervals (pauses). In any case, we believe that a *substantial* number of temporal speech features will provide useful speaker-specific information. In response, we developed and tested a large body of prosody-related factors. Some have proven useful, others have not. While TED has always performed at well above chance levels, it has not been as robust an identity predictor as have LTS and VFT. Nevertheless, it upgrades the SAUSI process when it is combined with them.

The time–energy distribution vector consists of a number of parameter clusters. Those found to be acceptable include: (1) total speech time (TST),

FFI reference freqency is 16.35159 Hz. Cast limit = 6 semitones.
4157 FFI cycles were validated in joellen.DAT collected on 4/14/1993
Time: Start 12:31:45.52 Stop 12:32:11.83 Total 26.31 Seconds
Mean Frequency : 43.80 (St), 205.25 (Hz)
S. D. (ST): 3.287 Phonation Time Ratio : 0.742

	LOW RUN(%)	HIGH RUN(%)	CAST (%)	GOOD (%)	TOTAL(%)
Cycles	52(1.1%)	57(1.2%)	442(9.4%)	4157(88.3%)	4708(100%)
Seconds	1.25(4.8%)	2.07(7.9%)	2.87(10.9%)	19.52(74.2%)	26.31(100%)

DISTRIBUTION TABLE

ST	HZ	#	SECS	%	ST	HZ	#	SECS	%
27	77.8	0	0.000	0.000	40	164.8	148	0.900	4.613
28	82.4	1	0.012	0.064	41	174.6	257	1.470	7.533
29	87.3	1	0.011	0.059	42	185.0	338	1.822	9.335
30	92.5	2	0.021	0.110	43	196.0	467	2.378	12.185
31	98.0	6	0.060	0.309	44	207.7	557	2.684	13.753
32	103.8	8	0.077	0.396	45	220.0	536	2.437	12.484
33	110.0	19	0.172	0.883	46	233.1	494	2.121	10.868
34	116.5	29	0.248	1.269	47	246.9	330	1.338	6.857
35	123.5	34	0.275	1.411	48	261.6	242	0.927	4.747
36	130.8	39	0.296	1.518	49	277.2	156	0.564	2.891
37	138.6	53	0.383	1.964	50	293.7	65	0.225	1.153
38	146.8	76	0.519	2.657	51	311.1	0	0.000	0.000
39	155.6	90	0.574	2.941	52	329.6	0	0.000	0.000

```
% TIME          HISTOGRAM
    14                            *
    13                            *
    12                           ***
    11                           ****
    10                           ****
     9                          *****
     8                         ******
     7                         *******
     6                         *******
     5                        *********
     4                        *********
     3                      ************
     2                    **************
     1                 ******************
       +----+----+----+----+----+----+----+----+----+----+----+
ST     15   20   25   30   35   40   45   50   55   60   65   70
Hz     39   52   69   92  123  165  220  294  392  523  698  932
```

Figure 8.4

The fundamental frequency data for a single female speaker as provided by FFI-10. The values used in the SFF comparisons are found in lines (rows) 3–5 and the distribution table.

defined as the period (in ms) it takes a speaker to produce an utterance of a set number of syllables; (2) number of silent intervals (NSI); (3) length of the silent intervals (LSI); (4) the speech–pause ratio (SPR); (5) speech time/total time ratio (ST/TT); (6) the speaking time ratio (S/T), defined as a measure of the total time for which acoustic energy is present during a specific utterance; and (7) speech rate (a measure of the syllable rate – not word rate – per unit of time). Each of these primary features is, in turn, constructed from several parameters (see Figure 8.5 for a theoretical illustration) and data for each of these sets calculated at 10 interval levels (above a predetermined base) for the entire sample. For example, there will be a TST-10, TST-20, TST-30, and so on.

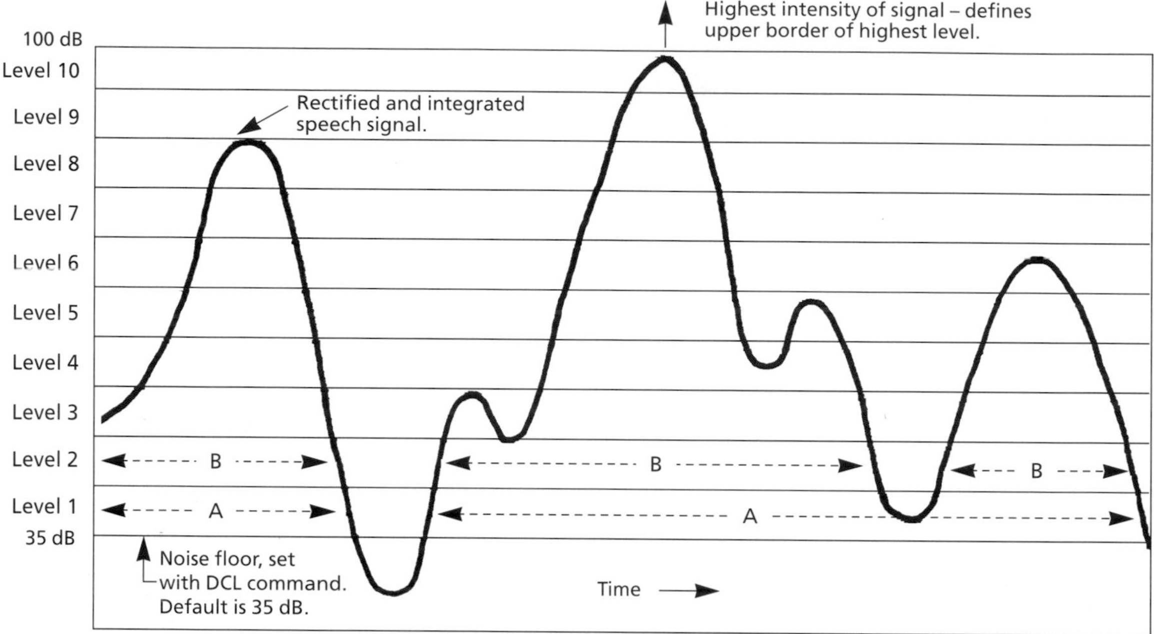

Figure 8.5
Display from Hollien (78) illustrating how the TED data are collected. All parameters are measured at 10 equidistant levels from the calculated noise 'floor' to the greatest peak.

Over the years, a number of analysis techniques have been employed to generate the TED data. They were recently upgraded (94) but still were found to be marginal. Accordingly, Ming Jiang (66) conducted a series of studies in which he attempted to determine which of three proposed measurement approaches would be most suitable. He defined them as the (1) traditional TED, (2) short-time energy and (3) short-time magnitude procedures. The third proved superior and is now the basis for TED extraction. It can be described as follows. The short-time magnitude of the *i*th frame of the signal is defined as:

$$M(i) = \frac{1}{L} \sum_{m=0}^{L-1} | x_i(m) | \quad i = 0, 1, \ldots, N-1$$

where N is the number of the frames and L is the frame length. The absolute values of the signal are summed (rather than squared as would be the case for a short-time energy procedure). The short-time magnitude function is then calculated as follows: (1) frame length is selected, (2) the summation of the absolute values for each signal point of each frame is calculated, (3) energy is averaged by dividing these summations by the number of signal points and (4) averaged energy is then converted into decibels (dB). Short time magnitude data for the entire passage are obtained by repeating steps 2 to 4 for each frame in the sample. The temporal parameters are then calculated by determining the means of the noise floors for speech and 'silence.' This level ordinarily relates to the particular energy level of an individual speech signal. Thus, if the samples are recorded under similar conditions, they all should have the same noise floor and, hence, a single level can be applied in most circumstances. It is at this juncture that an energy file is created for each sample and the basic elements of the TED vector developed as a function of (1) the mean levels and length of the segments, (2) the number of occurrences and (3) the standard deviation. Included are calculations of SPR, sample length, the ST/TT and so on. Note that the total time for the passage is measured prior to sample trimming. Hence, this value provides additional parameters, i.e. those which reflect the speaker's utterance speed. The TED vector now consists of 33 parameters calculated from the relationships cited.

The Vowel Formant Tracking vector

This vector is a powerful one. It competes with LTS as most sensitive to speaker-specific differences; it also is quite resistant to distortions of all types. Indeed, studies in both the aural-perceptual and the computer-related domains suggest that elements residing within vowel formant structure can create very important speaker identity cues (88, 91, 95–108). A second rationale for including this vector is based on individual differences in the size and shape of the vocal tract. While they can be modified somewhat by articulatory movements, speakers cannot significantly alter their dimensions. Hence, they are thought to provide a substantial number of measurable traits. Accordingly, we have included the VFT vector; its parameters are based on the vowel formant frequency distributions of voiced speech.

Construction of the VFT vector is carried out at the same time as the power-spectra calculations. That is, after the power spectrum of each speech frame is obtained, a vowel formant frequency search program is applied. Its purpose is to identify and extract the three major formant frequencies associated with any vowel residing in that portion of the signal (see Figure 8.6). The data are then stored in a formant file to permit tracking.

Again, Jiang (66) experimentally upgraded the measurement procedures associated with this vector. He selected and assessed three analysis methods; they included several linear prediction coefficient techniques and a cepstrum method. Since the LPC order 10 proved to be the most robust, it has been adopted as the basis for VFT processing. It is described as follows.

Because of the logarithmic nature of sound and the simplicity of histograms, the frequency bins displayed in Table 8.1 can be used to organize the VFT data. That is, a range of frequency bins for each vowel formant frequency were selected and are now used. Specifically, the 200–1000 Hz range (i.e. from bin 8 to bin 20) was selected for F1, the 500–3000 Hz range (or bin 15 to bin 30) for F2 and the range of 1000–5000 Hz (bin 21 to bin 34) for F3. These boundaries

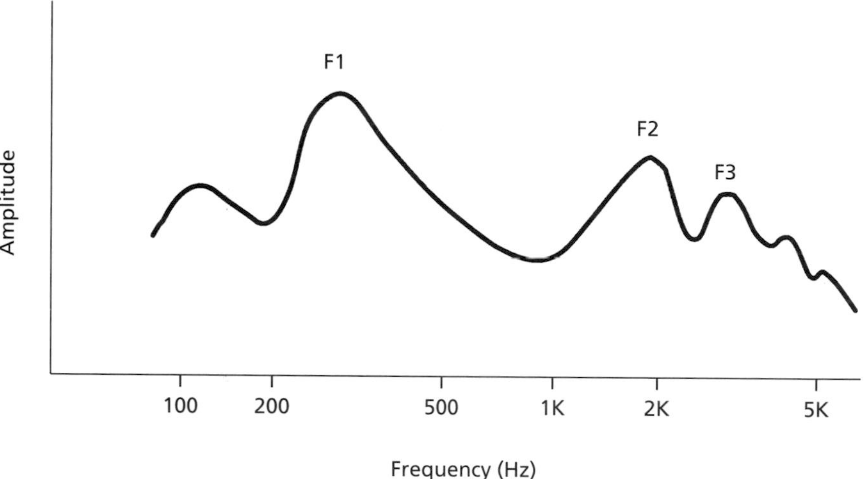

Figure 8.6
Line spectrogram of a speaker producing the vowel /i/. VFT comparisons are based on the format data as described in the text.

proved substantial enough to encompass the frequency range of the target formants. The histograms were then formed by counting the presence of each formant frequency found in the bins. Thus, the parameters for VFT include: (1) 13 values representing the distribution of the first formant (i.e. a histogram for F1); (2) 16 values representing the distribution of the second formant (a histogram for F2); (3) 14 values representing the distribution of the third formant frequency (a histogram for F3); and (4) six values of the geometrical means and standard deviations for F1, F2, and F3. Therefore, a total of 49 values are employed to form the VFT vector. As with the others, both VFT sensitivity and resistance to distortion have been assessed experimentally.

Table 8.1
Frequency bin distributions (in Hz) for the VFT vector (66).

No.	Frequency (Hz)	No.	Frequency (Hz)	No.	Frequency (Hz)
1	60–80	13	381–440	24	1421–1660
2	81–100	14	441–500	25	1661–1800
3	101–120	15	501–560	26	1801–2020
4	121–140	16	561–620	27	2021–2260
5	141–160	17	621–700	28	2261–2540
6	161–180	18	701–780	29	2541–2860
7	181–200	19	781–880	30	2861–3200
8	201–220	20	881–1000	31	3201–3600
9	221–260	21	1001–1120	32	3601–4040
10	261–300	22	1121–1260	33	4041–4540
11	301–340	23	1261–1420	34	4541–5000
12	341–380				

PROBLEMS ENCOUNTERED IN GENERATING PROFILES

As we trundled our way down through the years, we attempted to use the vectors described above (and others too) in profiling our speaker-subjects. We did so in order to contrast each with all the others and thereby develop a structure that permitted us to discriminate among them. As might be expected, we carried out many experiments in order to achieve these goals, we also learned from others (109–114). In doing so, we ran into some problems.

THE DIMINISHING RETURNS PROBLEM

In the early days, we simply tried to add up the values by parameter set in order to obtain some sort of a 'personal' score for each subject. We then realized that the serial adding of scores (parameter by parameter) might permit us to achieve even better levels of correct identification. We did so and kept on adding them until we ran into the law of diminishing returns. The best way to understand what this means is to consider the hypothetical relationship found in Figure 8.7. As you can see, adding parameters will tend to increase the success rate (i.e., the per cent level) and this improvement will continue until the process is

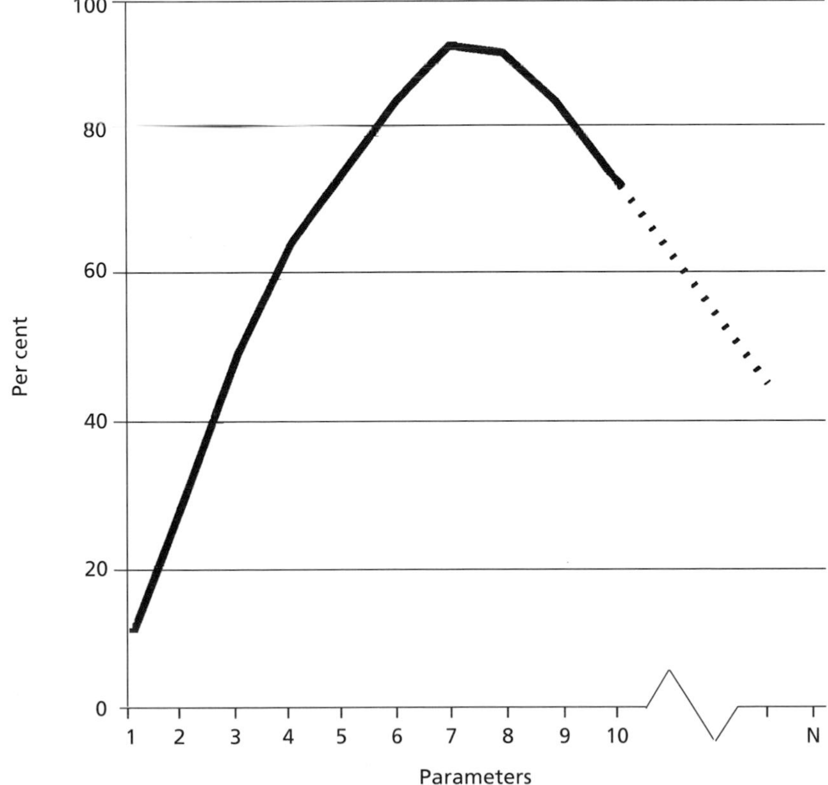

Figure 8.7
Hypothetical curve illustrating the Law of Diminishing Returns.

saturated. At that point, the asymptote (i.e. the peak) will be reached and then, if you keep on adding elements, system performance will begin to deteriorate. That is just what happened to us. So, at this juncture we began to examine the strengths and weaknesses of each of the parameters we were using. We then selected only the best and clustered them into vectors. Not 'overloading' the system helped a lot.

THE 'MIGHT MAKES RIGHT' PROBLEM

We then ran into another 'law' – 'bigger things will overwhelm smaller ones.' Our problem in this case was created by the fact that we were using the raw data values (from the parameter measurements) when developing the vectors. It turned out that the values for one of the parameters were naturally three times greater than those for the second, 11 times larger than those for the third and 40 times greater than those for the fourth. Thus, the SPID comparisons ended up being almost totally dominated by one of the vectors simply because its 'numbers' were very large. As a response, we tried different statistical procedures. First, we shifted to the three nearest-neighbor procedure and then to discriminant analysis. Nothing seemed to help. And why should it? After all, the values from one set of measurements simply were larger than those for all three of the others combined.

We then organized a new approach and the results were something of a breakthrough. What we did was normalize the data by converting them into proportions of a 10-point scale. This technique worked rather nicely. To understand just how it does, please consider the following example. If the magnitude and range for Vector A is 6000–22 000 units (of some type) and the magnitude and range for Vector B is 14–88 units (of a different type, of course), the difference between the extremes will be 16 000 and 74, respectively. Thus, a 10% shift in A will amount to 1600 whereas a 50% shift in B will be only 37 – or a 10% shift in A will have a 43 times greater effect on the process than a 50% one in B. However, if the 6000 is converted to a 1, the 22 000 to a 10 and the intervening values into proportions of 10, we have normalized these data. Then (in the second instance), if the 14 is similarly converted to 1, the 88 to 10 and the 74 values in between them into proportions, a parallel continuum is created. In this case, the data for Vector B will carry just as much weight as will those for Vector A. Since the vectors now are equal in their impact, either (or both) can be placed on a continuum like the one seen in Figure 8.8 and their effect on SAUSI will no longer be biased by the size of their calculated values.

Figure 8.8
A continuum providing normalized data for the unknown, known and eight foil speakers.

THE INTERNAL VALIDATION PROBLEM

A third problem then occurred, and it was just as wearisome as the first two. That is, when we ran a SAUSI trial, we simply had no way of determining if the process was stable and/or operating properly. Our response here was to experiment with various types of trials. After a few, it occurred to us that we might be able to establish an internal validation procedure if we placed a second sample of the unknown speaker's voice among the targets (i.e. those of the suspect and foils). To be valid then, the procedure would have to first 'select' the unknown as himself. Indeed, if the known speaker's speech sample also was produced by the unknown talker, the two should vie for 'first place.' The strength of this particular subprocedure is that it provides an internal checkup on the validity of the process. That is, the method will be functioning properly if the 'unknown-test' sample is selected as being produced by the same person as was the 'unknown-reference.'

This procedure can be understood by consideration of the values provided by a SAUSI printout (see Figure 8.9). As can be seen, it has two parts. The top section identifies both the process employed and the individuals who people the several categories. There is an 'unknown-reference' (U_r), which is the sample to be identified (if possible). Then, there is an 'unknown-test' (U_t), or a second sample of the unknown's speech. This sample provides the control as to whether or not the system is working properly as it is compared to the reference and all others. It goes without saying that if the unknown is not selected correctly, the system is not efficient enough to be used for SPID purposes. The third listed category is that for the known speaker. He is the person being compared to the unknown in order to determine if he is, or is not, the same individual. Next in Figure 8.9 are the 11 foils; ordinarily we use 8–12. They are chosen in much the same manner as are the 'distractor' voices for earwitness line-ups (see Chapter 5).

The lower portion of Figure 8.9 provides the data from the SAUSI run. As you would expect, all are normalized. That is, no value is less than 1.0 and none is greater than 10.0 and all those between these boundaries are proportions of the whole. In this instance, the unknown was selected as themself by three of the four vectors and the known (as the unknown) by the fourth; both came second with the others. These individual vector assessments are quite important when

Figure 8.9

Printout of a single SAUSI trial (with F = 11). Note that the unknown vs. unknown comparison validated the run and that K = U.

```
Unknown Reference   C:\SAUSI\E3
Unknown Test        C:\SAUSI\E3
Known               C:\SAUSI\E3
Foil  1             C:\SAUSI\E3
Foil  2             C:\SAUSI\E3
Foil  3             C:\SAUSI\E3
Foil  4             C:\SAUSI\E3
Foil  5             C:\SAUSI\E3
Foil  6             C:\SAUSI\E3
Foil  7             C:\SAUSI\E3
Foil  8             C:\SAUSI\E3
Foil  9             C:\SAUSI\E3
Foil 10             C:\SAUSI\E3
Foil 11             C:\SAUSI\E3
```

	LTS	TED	SFF	VFT	SUM
Unknown test	1.0000	1.4818	1.0000	1.0000	1.0000
Known	1.5323	1.0000	1.2836	1.2292	1.1686
Foil 1	3.8862	7.8851	3.9469	2.6166	5.1448
Foil 2	6.1144	4.4177	9.5805	3.1202	6.6102
Foil 3	9.1714	5.4474	5.2633	3.4391	6.6367
Foil 4	9.0549	5.5074	10.0000	10.0000	10.0000
Foil 5	5.9006	3.4713	7.0671	2.0996	5.2058
Foil 6	6.1824	10.0000	9.5805	4.6620	8.7621
Foil 7	9.7969	3.5349	9.5805	3.6224	7.5982
Foil 8	7.6665	8.2456	7.4505	4.4635	7.9845
Foil 9	10.0000	5.4801	9.5805	4.7024	8.5640
Foil 10	8.6318	7.4416	5.8762	4.4418	7.5553
Foil 11	4.0598	4.7911	6.3774	2.7540	5.0393

SAUSI is either being evaluated or used in controlled experiments. However, it is the fifth or Sum column which is the most important for SPID purposes. It is created by summing the normalized scores across vectors; this process is followed by new rankings. That is, even though all data are normalized, a simple vector mean is not calculated. Rather, the scores are combined to place each speaker on a group continuum; each is then re-ranked. As can be seen from the 'Sum' column in Figure 8.9, the unknown is selected as most like himself and foil F4 as least like him. The known speaker is positioned at a point very close to the unknown and a substantial distance from the nearest foil (i.e. F11). A decision now can be made. In this instance, there is little doubt that the system is operative and the known speaker is the same person as the unknown.

What happens if SAUSI is applied to a SPID task under different circumstances (e.g. where distortion is present)? Ordinarily, the vectors will tend to compensate for each other. Note Figure 8.10; it also is a printout of a single trial

```
Unknown         C:\SausiFca\T-MING\Bk_hc.vec
Unknown2        C:\SausiFca\T-MING\Bk_hb.vec
Known           C:\SausiFca\T-MING\Bk_ha.vec
Foil 1          C:\SausiFca\T-MING\cj_hb.vec
Foil 2          C:\SausiFca\T-MING\dd_hb.vec
Foil 3          C:\SausiFca\T-MING\dm_hb.vec
Foil 4          C:\SausiFca\T-MING\hc_hb.vec
Foil 5          C:\SausiFca\T-MING\hr_hb.vec
Foil 6          C:\SausiFca\T-MING\jh_hb.vec
Foil 7          C:\SausiFca\T-MING\jw_hb.vec
Foil 8          C:\SausiFca\T-MING\ng_hb.vec
```

	LTS	TED	SFF	VFT	SUM
Unknown	1.000	1.000	1.000	1.000	1.000
Known	2.523*	2.126	1.035*	1.868*	2.062*
Foil 1	5.019	1.392*	1.258	6.694	4.097
Foil 2	4.519	9.900	10.000	4.989	8.594
Foil 3	9.597	7.385	7.554	6.659	9.128
Foil 4	10.000	7.658	6.562	9.779	9.966
Foil 5	6.596	7.562	2.051	2.520	5.402
Foil 6	9.544	10.000	4.570	10.000	10.000
Foil 7	4.064	5.054	4.170	2.914	4.647
Foil 8	5.466	4.376	1.406	4.070	4.383

Figure 8.10

Printout of a SAUSI trial where the samples were somewhat contaminated by thermal noise. Note that while $U_{ref} = U_{test} = K$ overall, F1 scored closest to the unknown on TED.

drawn from an experiment involving a large number of comparisons made under noisy conditions. As can be seen, the unknown always is picked as himself (i.e. U_t is always at 1.000 when compared with U_r). This is not so for the known (K). A review of his data on a vector-by-vector basis will reveal some inconsistencies. First, his LTS score is 2.523 (the asterisk indicates a secondary placement) whereas the value for Foil 7 (the next best) was 4.064. However, with a TED score of 2.126, the 'known' talker was not second best for that vector; rather Foil 1 had a better score (i.e. 1.392). Foil 1 and K were close for SFF but when VFT is considered, the competition came from foil talkers F5 and F7. Thus, when the vectors are assessed individually, the positioning of K is a little uneven. On the other hand, once the normalized scores for the four vectors are combined, the known talker is found to be closer to U than any of the foils. Indeed, the values for even the closest competitors placed them at some distance from either U or K. Moreover, this effect was enhanced (not shown) when additional runs were carried out with the same talkers but with different samples. Finally, the procedure also polarizes the values, but in the opposite direction, when the unknown and known speakers are not the same person.

As stated, these two examples were drawn from laboratory projects and, hence, the neat relationships they provide do not always hold in the field. The forensic reality is such that all kinds of distortions occur and, when they are severe or combined, they can challenge the process. The lower part of Figure 8.11 (i.e., examples C and D) illustrates what can happen if these less desirable outcomes occur. As you can see, the continua range from acceptable (top) to marginal or worse. Of course, (except for the 'non-match' B, that is) these displays illustrate mostly positive matches. It should not be forgotten, however, that the known and unknown speakers could be two different people. If they are, SAUSI should place the unknown in the first position and the known mixed in with the foils somewhere between 4.0 and 10.0 (as seen in Figure 8.11, example B).

Finally, it is my unalterable position that human beings – not computers – should make all decisions about speaker identity. Indeed, determinations of this magnitude are simply too important to be left to machines. The issues/behaviors with which we are working are so complex that only the highly trained human mind should be permitted to resolve them. Only humans should judge humans! The specialist can use the data generated plus good decision criteria for these purposes (for example, a match would occur if $U/K \leq 3$ and the lowest $F \geq 2K$). However, neither he nor she should abdicate responsibility here.

A. Acceptable match

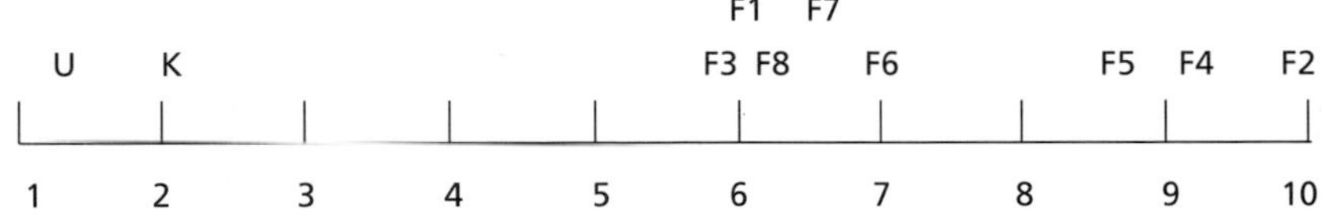

B. Acceptable non-match

C. Marginal match

D. Unacceptable

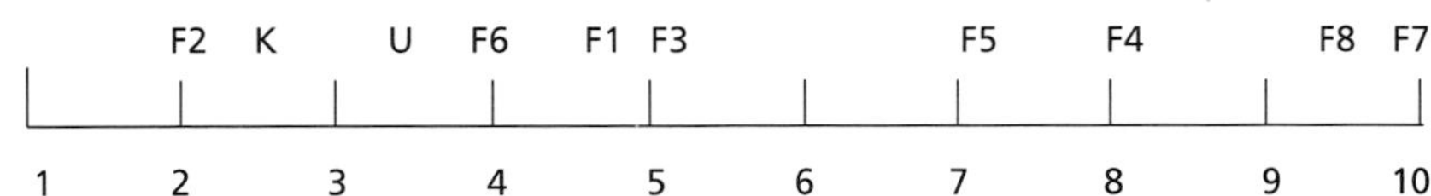

Figure 8.11

Four continua resulting from different SAUSI trials. Validations are provided by the unknowns comparison with himself for A and B, possibly for C but not for D. The outcomes are specified in the headings.

THE ROTATIONS

While the next step in SAUSI development occurred only 10–12 years ago, its roots extend back to formation of the scientific method. That is, good scientific practice requires that all experiments be replicated and that, when they are, the results be consistent. What this means is that, if you do not repeat an experiment and/or obtain the same results, what you found out (or think you found out) is simply not valid. To establish a relationship, you must be able to demonstrate it, validate it with external evidence and then repeat what you did with the same results.

The insight to be described occurred when we were carrying out multiple experiments for reliability purposes. That is, most of our projects are routinely replicated two or more times in order to determine if the original findings are stable and accurate. During the period cited, we began to realize that formalization of that approach might enhance SAUSI and do so especially when it was used in the forensic environment. At this point in time, a 'rotational' system was structured and tested. Its characteristics are as follows.

First, three 20–30 s speech samples are obtained from all the relevant talker-subjects. Regular SAUSI processing is then carried out (see Figures 8.8 and 8.9). Subsequently, the entire process is replicated two more times using different samples each time. The overall summation rankings are then calculated. They are based on the 'sum' means, as drawn from each of the three rotations (each of these, in turn, is based on data from the four vectors). Thus, any decision about identity would be based on three complete projects. Better yet, they would result from comparisons which would number in the millions – specifically, the number of rotations, factored by the number of speakers, factored by the number of vectors, factored by the number of parameters within each vector, factored by the number of comparisons within each parameter. In any event, we found that the rotations both enhanced the results and stabilized them.

Unfortunately, the procedure introduced a number of new problems. First, the operator had to be certain to place each foil speaker in the same position for each of the rotations. Not to do so would tend to artificially shift their position away from the unknown and hence lead to errors. Second, while speech samples of sufficient length can easily be obtained from the known speaker and the foils, the same is not always true for the unknown. Indeed, the worst-case scenario is where the evidence tape contains only enough of the unknown's speech (say 15–20 s) to permit but a single SAUSI run. However, it is sometimes possible to mitigate this particular problem by reversing the roles of the known and unknown. In such instances, the known speaker becomes the target (contributing both reference and test samples) and unknown is compared to him. While this approach will often provide acceptable data, when it does not, the practitioner must either rely on AP-SPID techniques or decline to carry out any type of speaker identification at all. In summary, it can be said that the technique of conducting several SAUSI runs has been found to enhance its accuracy. Just as the vectors tend to compensate for each other, the rotations tend to smooth out and polarize the relationships which occur among the speakers (115–117).

ASSESSMENT OF SAUSI

As you now know, many SAUSI-related experiments have been carried out over the years. A number of them have been presented in the articles cited in the reference list, others were sent off to the various granting agencies (in report form). We also have been able to provide other materials in our presentations to scientific groups and societies. Of course, we did not and do not, feature those projects where the outcome was 'negative', or where the data seemed confusing. Rather, we used those (negative) studies to learn about SPID in general and SAUSI in particular. These studies often led to perceptions which permitted improvement. In any case, the following should provide some insight as to how our procedures and techniques were developed. First, it should be useful to describe our data base; then the structure of our experiments. Finally, some of our results can be discussed.

THE SAUSI DATA BASE

As might be expected, a rather extensive data base is associated with the many research programs being carried out at IASCP. Indeed, several-thousand highly controlled speech utterances were already in existence by the time the SAUSI research program was initiated. Since then, a further 20 000 (plus) samples (also strictly controlled) have found their way into this corpus of speech material. While many of these samples were generated for other projects, some of them were collected expressly for the SAUSI research. Not all of the other sets were useful; for example, we have not used any of the speech samples produced by singers, cheerleaders, mongoloid children, children between birth and adolescence, divers underwater, divers in HeO_2 environments, the elderly, people with voice or speech disorders, psychotics, subjects wearing gas masks, and so on. In most of these cases (plus those to follow), the carefully selected speaker/subject uttered speech such as a standardized passages ('Rainbow,' 'Apology for Idlers,' 'My Grandfather,' 'Arthur the Rat'), standardized sentences, extemporaneous speech (i.e. responses to neutral questions) and/or lists of phonetically balanced words. Ordinarily, subject selection criteria included freedom from speech and voice disorders, normal hearing and the ability to read at the 8th grade level (age approximately 14 years). Social status, race, education, etc., often were controlled also (depending on the nature of the study). In any event, some of the cohorts we were able to use include the following.

- American males (four studies): $N = 375$; age range 17–33 years.
- Laboratory males (seven studies): $N = 653$; age range 18–38 years.
- Aging males (three studies): $N = 410$; age range 21–85 years (in sets).
- American females (four studies): $N = 285$; age range 17–37 years.
- Aging females (two studies): $N = 192$ (in sets); age range 25–91 years.
- Texas Instrument data-base: $N = 107$ (56 males; 51 females); subjects, drawn from six sites around the USA, read digits (in random sequence).

Nearly all of the men and about 80% of the women from these sources have been used in SAUSI experiments. All equipment and the recording environments were of laboratory quality.

The telephone data base

This data base was created expressly for the SAUSI projects; support for it was provided by the US Army Research Office (ARO). My associate on this particular project (and the 'on-scene' supervisor) was Dr Gerard Chollet, then serving as one of my post-doctoral researchers (now of ENST/CNRS, France). This set of materials is referred to as the 'Telephone' data base; it consists of 5040 samples as follows.

- Subjects: 30 males: age range 19–58 (mean 31) years; 30 females; age range 18–38 (mean 26) years.
- Passage: 'My Grandfather.'
- Protocols: (N = 14 repetitions): (1) normal speech (N = 5), (2) whisper, (3) slow rate, (4) falsetto, (5) hoarse voice, (6) pencil in mouth, (7) pinched nose, (8) hyper-nasal, (9) muffled by hand, (10) free disguise.
- Procedures: six readings were recorded *simultaneously*; they were made using (1) a laboratory quality microphone (in front of subject) (2) a hidden (laboratory) microphone, (3) a suction cup microphone (adhered to the telephone), (4) a line tap, (5) a remote line tap and (6) an acoustic coupler. The last two recordings were made at a second site, one 3 miles (4.8 km) from the laboratory.

The speech samples thus generated can be used in all sorts of experiments. Any of the nine disguise passages plus five 'normal' readings by the 30 men and 30 women (over two high fidelity systems and four telephone taps) can have noise added. Small wonder that we have used this particular data base in over half of our studies.

Specialized data bases

We also have organized five other data bases which target speakers who are producing controlled utterances of specific types. They involve samples of speech produced (1) under psychological stress, (2) with disguise, (3) during real-life criminal activity, (4) with dialect and (5) during alcohol intoxication. They are as follows:

- Psychological stress (four studies). N = 231 (140 males; 91 females); age range: 18–48 years. Materials: read passage. Stress condition: electric shock, first public speech, threatening video. Stress level assessed by standardized tests, self reports, etc.
- Disguise (in addition to the Telephone Data Base) (two studies). N = 110 males, age

range: 20–33 years. Speech: standard passage, sentences, extemporaneous. Subjects chose the type of disguise.

- Speech during criminal activity (drawn from real life cases). $N = 63$ (as of 1998), 54 males, nine females. Free speech with about 65% over the telephone and 30% resulting from the use of 'body bugs'.
- Dialect (three studies plus samples of student's speech). $N = 80$ (45 males; 35 females). Dialects: Southern American, Spanish.
- Effects of Intoxication (three data sets for 17 studies). $N = 104$ (66 males, 38 females). Speech materials (all conditions): read passage, extemporaneous speech, sentences. Conditions: (a) sober, (b) BrAC 0.04–0.05, (c) BrAC 0.08–0.09, (d) BrAC 0.12–0.13, (e) BrAC 0.09–0.08 plus some conditions of greater intoxication and others of simulated inebriation.

RESEARCH DESIGN

We have applied a number of different research designs to the assessment of SAUSI; some were experimental, others were descriptive in nature. One particular design has been most useful for our purposes. Indeed, we have used it in around half of the SPID projects where the focus was on SAUSI. It is described briefly below.

The key to this design is the use of large groups of rigorously selected subjects; they can be either men or women but both sexes are rarely included in a specific experiment. Ordinarily, a 1-min read (or extemporaneously spoken) passage is used as the speech sample. As such, it can provide the three 20-sec. samples for the required rotations, (sometimes 30-sec. overlapping samples are extracted). If the Telephone data base is used, the research can focus on normal (high-fidelity) speech, or speaker disguise (of several types, or in combinations), speech in noise, various types of telephone or surveillance passbands, or many combinations of these elements. Ordinarily, the protocols call for a 'closed sets' design.

Once the combinations are selected, the speech samples for each of the subjects are digitized and stored in the computer. The vector programs are then applied. The performance of a single vector (or multiple vectors) may be studied or all vectors can be run with the decisions made on the basis of the summed normalized values. Since our protocols demand that we normalize all scores, this factor is not one we subject to experimentation. However, we often compare our single trial results with those from three or more rotations.

Assessments are usually made on the basis of percent identification for the various conditions imposed by the protocols. Statistical analyses are not ordinarily necessary. However, when they are, we do not use discriminate analysis or nearest-neighbor approaches (as in the past). Rather, a bioequivalance approach is employed (118,119); an example of its use can be found in Hollien and Jiang (120). Basically, it is used when firm decisions are not possible but the data suggest that a relationship does exist. That is, when the unknown and known speakers appear to be the same person and the nearest foil is not also the unknown, the bioequivalence technique will reject the null hypothesis for the U–K combination but not for U–F. Conversely, if the unknown and known talkers are different people, the null hypothesis will not be rejected.

Now, back to research design. As you would expect, other research protocols have been applied when special questions have been asked. However, the one reviewed briefly above is so flexible, it permits a great number of critical relationships to be studied under highly controlled conditions. The size and nature of the population to be investigated can be varied easily, as can the type and source of the speech material. The kind of speech and speaking environment also can be varied for research purposes, as can the manner in which the vectors are investigated. Hundreds (perhaps thousands) of different studies can be designed and carried out when the relevant elements are factored – so many so, that we have only been able to carry out a limited portion of them. Now for some results and, more importantly, what they might mean.

SOME SAUSI RESULTS

In my estimation, it would not be very helpful to attempt to describe all the results we have generated over the years. Presentation of that number of tables and graphs would be stultifying in and of itself. Moreover, many would look pretty much alike, only the numbers' would be different. Accordingly, only a summary overview (plus illustrations) will be presented. Nevertheless, these materials should provide some insight about (1) the way we generated our data, (2) what we found out and (3) how we interpreted the results.

First, please note Figure 8.12. This graph portrays the results of a series of vector modifications (nine experiments in all) carried out in the late 1970s. Note that just three vectors – SFF, TED and INT (or vocal intensity) – were included. We started each at its own performance level, and called it zero. We then modified each vector by stages and carried out experiments of the type described in the last section. Note that all three improved (TED most of all) when the first set of upgrades was affected. Convinced that we were on the right track, we applied a second set of modifications. Shifts of a different type resulted from this second set of 'improvements.' Here, TED appeared to level off, SFF continued to improve and INT got worse. We then decided that SFF had been improved about as much as possible (i.e., no additional modifications were practical) and so terminated this part of the program. However, additional ones were possible for TED and INT. It was especially important to continue

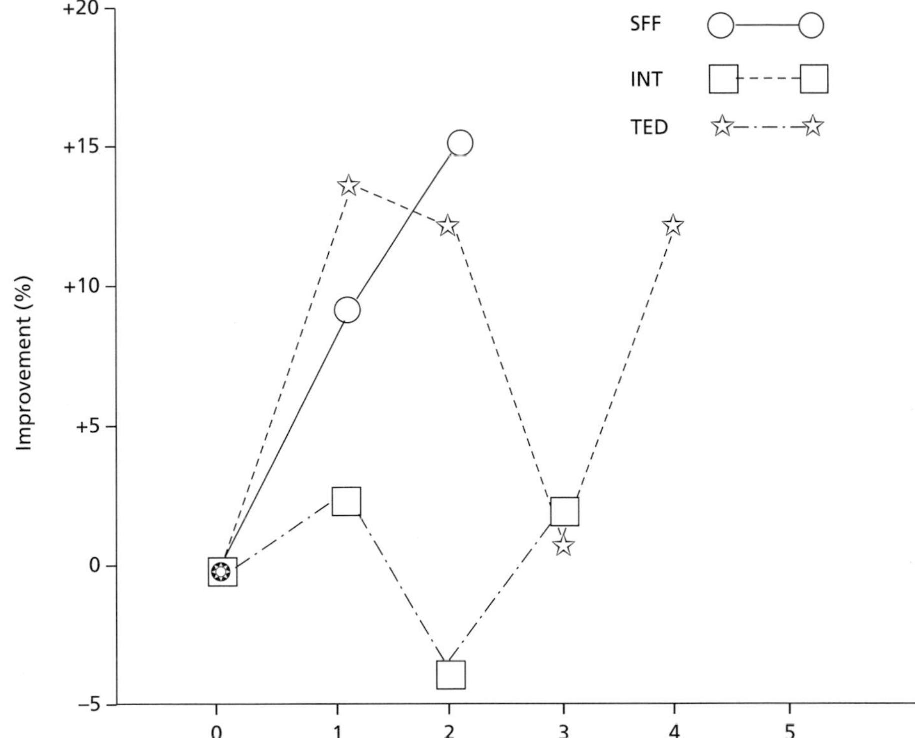

Figure 8.12
A graph of improvement in vector performance resulting from modifications to SFF, TED and INT.

with the INT vector because the second set of changes resulted in a reduction in its ability to identify speakers. The third set of experiments demonstrated that INT was just not going to improve; hence, we terminated that series. In fact, while we continued to struggle along with INT for a while, our results were so poor overall, we ultimately gave up on it. TED also proved a disappointment when this third series of modifications was applied. However, it was not clear whether the observed decay was due to the law of diminishing returns or some error in our attempts to restructure. Anyway, additional (and planned) changes were made and a fourth experiment carried out. It resulted in the desired level of efficiency being re-established. We now have a number of graphs that are similar to Figure 8.12. Some document the shifts in just these vectors; others focus on LTS, VFT, etc. Few in the series extend much beyond four or five sets of modifications.

Experiments were carried out to assess the reliability (or repeatability) of our results. One set can be seen in Figure 8.13; it provides data for SFF, LTS plus five vectors combined. These experiments were run in the early 1980s. Reliability for LTS and SFF was rather good; it varied little over the five sets of experiments; i.e. the results showed only 2–3% change, at worst. The same was not true for the multiple vector approach. Here, the level of correct identifications began to climb. There appeared to be no reason for it to do so as all the experiments

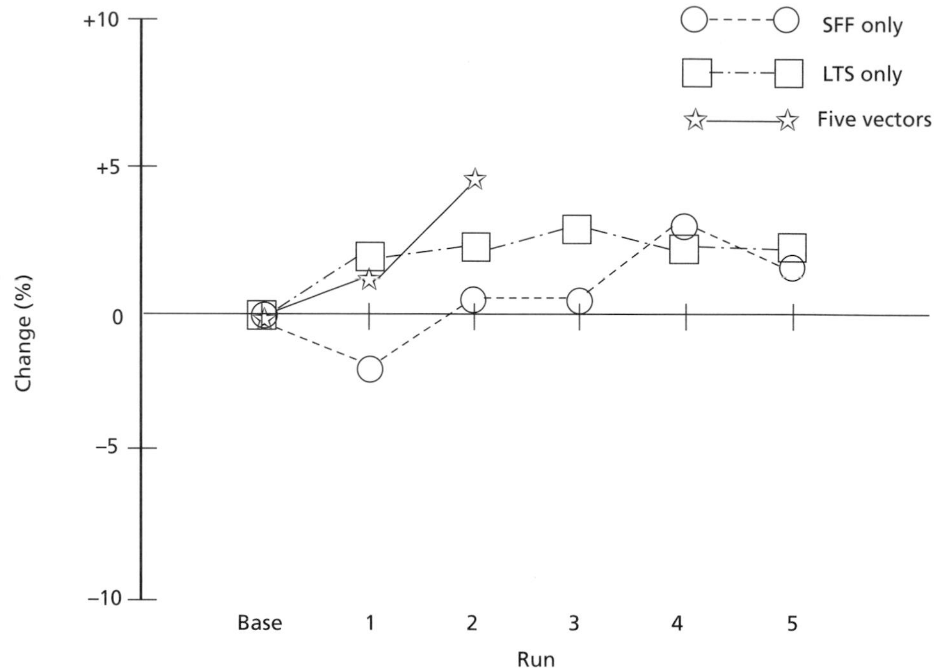

Figure 8.13
Reliability trials for the LTS and SFF vectors plus a combination of five vectors.

were virtually identical to the base study (only the talkers were different). We later found out (from additional experiments) that the statistical procedure used to combine the vectors was systematically biasing the outcome; sometimes the observed levels improved, sometimes they were poorer. What was important was that the approach created a multivector instability. Thus, it was the statistical procedure that was modified.

Figures are helpful in determining just how various factors relate to each other in space. What is even more important, however, is being able to understand how well a procedure is performing or how the various sets of results may actually relate to each other. Data tables provide this type of information. Two of the many types we have produced can be seen in Tables 8.2 (from the 1970s) and 8.3 (the 1980s). First, Table 8.2 (78). Here, the strength of four vectors is tested in various combinations for good-quality normal speech when contrasted with itself (i.e. normal–normal) and to samples bandpassed (telephone) or with noise added. The bandpassed and noisy speech were also compared with themselves (for SPID purposes) but not with each other. Subjects were 26 men drawn from our American male data base; two (parallel) experiments, involving the three nearest-neighbor approach, were carried out. Note that this summary table provides data on thousands of SPID comparisons. Note also that the LTS and SFF vectors, when combined, provide the highest correct identifications under virtually all circumstances. Indeed, only this two-vector combination was able to achieve a 81–85% correct identification level (it did so in three

Table 8.2
Percent correct classification when individual vectors are paired. Data are from an early (1972) set of experiments. Subjects were 26 young, healthy males. The three nearest-neighbor statistical approach was employed. From Hollien (78).

Vector and condition	Talkers					
	Run A			Run B		
	1	2	3	1	2	3
Normal/Normal						
SFF/LTS	58	64	75	62	73	81
INT/LTS	46	54	58	42	50	54
TED/LTS	42	64	73	58	58	65
SFF/INT	30	35	59	42	50	62
SFF/TED	46	62	62	54	58	73
INT/TED	27	31	39	27	27	42
Noise/Normal						
SFF/LTS	31	35	50	42	50	62
INT/LTS	27	42	46	35	46	59
TED/LTS	30	36	62	35	50	65
SFF/INT	27	27	50	27	35	42
SFF/TED	35	50	62	31	42	54
INT/TED	19	27	31	27	31	36
Bandpass/Normal						
SFF/LTS	46	50	65	39	62	62
INT/LTS	27	42	46	23	27	35
TED/LTS	42	42	50	35	42	46
SFF/INT	27	31	46	27	35	35
SFF/TED	31	46	58	31	42	54
INT/TED	15	23	31	12	15	19
Noise/Noise						
SFF/LTS	54	69	81	46	73	73
INT/LTS	46	46	62	42	54	59
TED/LTS	27	46	62	31	39	46
SFF/INT	36	39	46	35	42	54
SFF/TED	27	31	54	31	50	58
INT/TED	27	31	36	27	27	36
Bandpass/Bandpass						
SFF/LTS	50	65	73	73	73	85
INT/LTS	23	27	42	27	39	42
TED/LTS	46	59	65	46	50	62
SFF/INT	39	46	59	35	39	58
SFF/TED	42	50	59	35	46	54
INT/TED	19	27	31	23	31	35

Table 8.3
Rankings (%) for 32 closed set trials (18 for the SFF vector). The nearest neighbor approach was used; foils were 9–11 similar sounding speakers.

Vector	*N*	Unknown[1]		Known[1]	
		1–2	3 (or more)	1–2	3 (or more)
LTS					
Trials	32	25	7	25	7
Percent		78	22	78	22
SFF					
Trials	18	17	1	14	4
Percent		94	6	78	22
VFT					
Trials	32	29	3	28	4
Percent		90	10	88	12
TED					
Trials	32	27	5	19	13
Percent		85	15	60	40
Summation					
Trials	32	31	1	32	0
Percent		97	3	100	0

1. The unknown talker's test sample should appear in the first or second position; a U = K match exists if the known talker's sample also appears in one of those positions.

instances). An 85% level means that 21 of the 26 men were correctly identified for that procedure – in this case, the third for Run B passband.

A more typical data display may be seen in Table 8.3. In this case, the LTS, SFF, VFT and TED vectors are assessed first singly and then in combination. The procedure involved the typical paradigm seen in most SAUSI printouts (i.e. U, K and 8–11 foils all compared with U). Note that, at 94%, SFF performed best and, at 78%, LTS was worst in system validation. This was a little surprising as LTS and VFT usually score best (and did so even then). However, VFT did indeed provide the best score (88%) for the U–K comparisons (please remember that these experiments involved closed sets). Finally, the best overall results were obtained when the vectors were combined and a fifth set of values calculated. As can be seen, only one error occurred in 64 contrasts. Conversely, only one foil was picked as the unknown out of 662 comparisons. Progress appeared to be occurring (and it was).

Figure 8.14 is one that I cannot resist including. Note that the figure provides results for 14 talkers when the LTS, SFF and TED vectors were calculated (not for identification purposes but rather to create a profile of each subject). The patterns seen here are quite important as they provided the first set of results for the normalized scoring procedure. We were, of course, most pleased to discover that the (combination) score for each subject was different from any of the others.

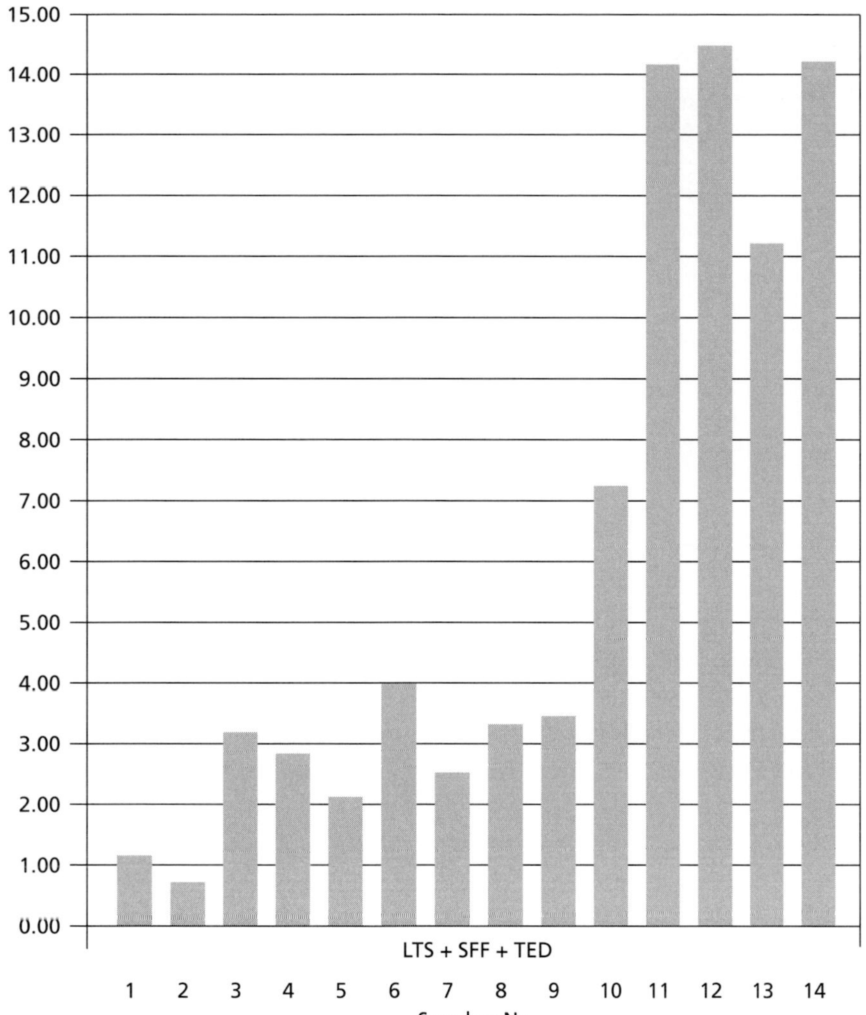

Figure 8.14
Summated three-vector scores for 14 male speakers. The success of this normalization process led to our current one which involves 10-point scaling.

Incidentally, the illusion of a lesser-to-greater trend in score magnitude was due only to chance and subsequent studies showed no such tendency. While not all of the many follow-up studies exhibited relationships that were quite as clear-cut as this one, most did. In any event, we found the profile approach to be more effective than any of the other procedures we tried before or since its adoption.

Table 8.4 provides data from one of the earliest of our successful field experiments. In this instance, a relatively challenging set of protocols was employed. That is, the tabled scores are based on all comparisons among 37 talkers with speech samples distorted by telephone passband, noise and the acoustics of several speaking environments. Note that even under these rather difficult circumstances, the identifications provided by the LTS, VFT and SFF vectors reached the 80% range. Only TED was minimally effective. This vector has since been upgraded twice (66, 94) and, as will be seen, it is now somewhat more

Table 8.4

Summary table of field research procedures based on trials with 37 male speakers. Conditions included limited frequency response, noise and varying acoustic environments. The first column provides validity assessment (i.e., U = U or U ≠ U), the second identifications (i.e., K = U or K ≠ U)[1]

Vector		Unknown (U) Match	Non-match	Known (K) Match	Non-match	U = K Total Match	Non-match
LTS	*N*	32	5	33	4	65	9
	%	86	14	89	11	88	12
TED	*N*	26	11	22	15	48	26
	%	70	30	59	41	65	35
SFF	*N*	32	5	30	7	62	12
	%	86	14	81	19	84	16
VFT	*N*	33	4	31	6	64	10
	%	89	11	84	16	86	14
All	*N*	36	1	35	2	71	3
	%	97	3	95	5	96	4

1. *N* = 37. Field recordings.

robust. Although it is the 'weakest' of the vectors, TED contributes materially to the overall efficiency of the SAUSI process. Finally, please note that an overall (i.e. all-vector) level of 96% correct identification was achieved even under the onerous circumstances cited. In all fairness, however, it should be pointed out that (1) we were able to rigorously control our procedures, (2) the speech samples were appropriately long and (3) a closed-set paradigm was employed. Hence, while these robust results could not be expected to occur under all real-life conditions, the SAUSI system is often just as effective in the field as it is in the laboratory. Consider the following example.

While real-life cases admittedly do not provide firm evidence about a system (i.e. if it is operating effectively or not), sometimes the circumstances are such that one will provide insight of a practical nature. The case I have in mind is titled 'The Old Man Didn't Do It.' It happened right here in Florida just before the leaders of our great and benign state decided that it would be desirable to go into the gambling business. They called their first game 'LOTTO.' What they actually did was establish a legalized version of the 'numbers' game. Of course, this game had been around for centuries but now Florida decided it wanted some of the loot generated so, the illegal became legal.

Back to the 'Old Man' case. One day 'bF' (before LOTTO), a middle-aged man brought his father to see me. He claimed that the old fellow could not speak English but had been indicted for making a telephone call in that language. The case unfolded rather slowly (partly because I rarely work directly for a client), so please permit me to summarize it. As you must have guessed by now, this case was all about the numbers game. The old man apparently was the leader of a 'group' engaged in this illegal activity. Their operations would be threatened if he was convicted of making a sale over the telephone (the call had been intercepted by means of a telephone tap). The son was adamant; his father had *not* made that call even though a 'voiceprint expert' said that he had. It quickly became apparent that the reason the son was so sure it was not his father's voice was because they both knew who actually *had* made the call. Moreover, they had heard about SAUSI (where? I wondered) and wanted me to prove that the father was innocent. First, I told them that I never, ever, attempt to exonerate or convict anyone, but, rather, go with my data no matter how it comes out. But, right about then, I had an idea. 'Find a competent audio-engineer,' I said to them, 'and have him make good recordings of six to eight of your "colleagues". And, you might consider including the man who actually made the call (if you know who he is, of course). If you do so, do not tell me which one he is.' Soon thereafter, I received eight fairly long speech samples, numbered (you will never guess) 1 to 8. They were of good quality and since I already had recordings of both the telephone call and the old fellow who was said to have made it, I was able to set up a SPID analysis using SAUSI.

A single SAUSI run resulted in foil-speaker F-6 being chosen as the telephone caller. The values for the old gentleman, and for the other seven foils, were fairly remote from his. When I called the son to tell him about these results, I heard an uproar at the other end of the line. 'Your method works' shouted the son and all the background cheering seemed to confirm his statement. That the father ran a large numbers operation is immaterial. He (apparently anyway) did not make the telephone call. You will recall from Chapter 4 that the job of the forensic phonetician is simply to be *right.* The police, attorneys, courts and juries have their own jobs to do; ours is to give them information which will permit them to operate appropriately. Back to the example; when the prosecutor received a copy of my report, he took the 'voiceprinter' to task. The poor fellow admitted that he might have been a little hasty and the case was dropped. Again, not real scientific evidence but useful nonetheless (see also Hollien, 78, for other examples).

Finally, please consider Table 8.5. It provides a summary of three (only partly published) major projects conducted first in 1988 (44), in 1993 (94, 120, 121) and in 1995 (66, 120). The first of these experiments involved a large number of subjects but only high-fidelity recordings. Note that, at the time it was carried out, none of the vectors provided 100% correct identification. However, a related study (not shown) also was conducted; it was designed to test the SAUSI procedure to see if it would eliminate talkers if they were not the unknown. A correct elimination level of 100% was found for that investigation. Thus, even in the late 1980s, it could be stated that, while the SAUSI procedure was only about 90% effective overall, false positives would not be expected.

Table 8.5

Data are summarized from three large projects wherein the SAUSI vectors are evaluated under the cited conditions. Values are the percent correct identifications for 25 male speakers. Data were normalized and replicated (i.e., rotated) three times.

Conditions and study	Vectors				
	TED	LTS	SFF	VFT	SUM
A. High fidelity					
Hollien (44)	62	88	68	85	90
Hollien and co-workers (94, 120, 121)	63	100	100	100	100
Jiang (60)	82	100	80	100	100
B. Noise					
Hollien and co-workers (94, 120, 121)	64	90	77	92	100
Jiang (60)	76	94	76	96	100
C. Telephone passband					
Hollien and co-workers (94, 120, 121)	55	92	90	88	98
Jiang (60)	58	100	90	96	100

The second set of experiments also included a large group of subjects but this time separate replications were carried out for high fidelity, noise and telephone passband. As has been stated, only part of this large project has been published. However, the upgrading of the vectors (which occurred prior to its initiation) resulted in a marked improvement for the high-fidelity procedure; it also was effective for the two conditions involving distortions.

The third of these projects was carried out only recently. Its primary objectives were to further upgrade the vectors and test them for possible improvement (66, 83). Re-examination of the relevant part of the table will reveal that, after this stage of vector enhancement, correct identifications were strikingly higher than previously for nearly all conditions and that the correct identification levels for the SUM rotations reached 100% in all cases. Note also that only two reductions (out of the 15 major ones) occurred when these results are compared with those of our studies. The progress cited is judged to be due to (1) improvements in vector design, (2) the use of better equipment, (3) upgraded vector processing, (4) insights based on completed research and (5) experience in the field.

Finally, some of our early (and late) attempts to organize SAUSI operations (66, 78, 115, 116, 120–122) have led to sets of structured procedures. One such set of step-by-step instructions has been developed recently. It can be found in Table 8.6.

EPILOGUE

So ends the description of our semi-automatic speaker identification system. There seems to be no question now but that it is a useful, if not a definitive, system. One of its features is that a great deal is known about it (i.e. a substantial

Table 8.6

Model of the steps which must be taken for SAUSI-based speaker identification.

A. Selection of samples

B. Digitize signals

C. Vector analyses

D. Normalize values

E. Compare with unknown
    1. Unknown
    2. Known
    3. Foils

F. Sum vector data

G. Rotational replications

H. Evaluations
    1. Continuum
    2. Statistical

I. Decision

amount of research data about SAUSI are available). A second feature is that its product has been shown to be consistent with the results of good aural perceptual speaker identification procedures; third, it has exceeded the '80% correct' identification rule-of-thumb minimum and has done so for years. Fourth, it employs an internal validation procedure (i.e. a sample of the unknown talker is compared with his own reference). Fifth, its application procedures (i.e. data normalization, the continua, the rotations) permit stable results to be obtained. Sixth, the process and results are easily understood. Finally, another possible advantage for a potential user is that no fees or royalties are charged for its use. No doubt better systems, perhaps even infallible ones, will be created in the future. Until then . . . !

REFERENCES AND FURTHER READING

CHAPTER 1

References

1. Muller, E., Hollien, H. and Murry, T. (1974) Perceptual Responses to Infant Crying: Identification of Cry Types, *J. Child Lang.* 1: 89–95.
2. Murry, T. Hollien, H. and Muller, E. (1975) Perceptual Responses to Infant Crying: Maternal Recognition, *J. Child Lang.* 2: 199–204.
3. Hollien, H. (1990) *The Acoustics of Crime*, New York: Plenum.
4. Scherer, K. (1986) Voice, Stress and Emotion, *Dynamics of Stress: Physiological, Psychological and Social Perspectives*, (H. Appley and R. Trumbull, eds.) New York: Plenum, 157–179.
5. Compton, A. (1963) Effects of Filtering and Vocal Duration Upon the Identification of Speaker Aurally, *J. Acoust. Soc. Am.*, 35: 1748–1752.
6. LaRiviere, C. (1975) Contributions of Fundamental Frequency and Formant Frequencies to Speaker Identification, *Phonetica*, 31: 185–197.
7. Meltzer, D. and Lehiste, I. (1972) Vowel and Speaker Identification in Natural and Synthetic Speech, *J. Acoust. Soc. Am.*, 51: S131(A).
8. Stevens, K.N. (1971) Sources of Inter- and Intra-Speaker Variability in the Acoustic Properties of Speech Sounds, *Proc. Seventh Int. Congr. Phonetic Sci.*, Montreal, 206–232.
9. Bunge, E. (1979) Automatic Forensic Speaker Recognition, *Proc. Carnahan Conf. Crime Countermeasures*, Lexington, KY, 41–45.
10. Doddington, G. and Schalk, T.B. (1981) Speech Recognition: Turning Theory to Practice, *IEEE Spectrum*, 18: 26–33.
11. Hecker, M.H.L. (1971) *Speaker Recognition: An Interpretive Survey of the Literature*, ASHA, Monograph 16, Washington D.C.
12. Jassem, W. (1983) Vowel Format Frequencies as Linguistic and Speaker-Specific Features of the Speech Signal, *Lang. Global Perspective*, (B.F. Elson, ed), Summer Inst. of Ling., 303–312.
13. Fry vs. United States (1923) 293 Fed. 1013–1014, Circuit Court, District of Columbia.
14. Daubert vs. Merrell Dow Pharmaceuticals Inc. (1993) 113 Supreme Court, 2786.
15. Imwinkelried, E.J. (1996) Commentary, in *Convicted by Juries, Exonerated by Science*, (E. Connors, T. Lundregan, N. Miller, T. McEwen, eds) U.S. Justice Dept., Washington, DC, xiixiv.

Further Reading

The references that follow are provided for those interested in speaker verification (SV). A broad selection of contributions starting about 40 years ago and reaching up until last year are included. The content also varies; it includes definitions and overviews of the area, models, specific approaches and procedures, plus some experimental data.

Ariki, Y. (1994) Speaker Recognition Robust for Time Differences Based on Subspace Method, *Studia Phonologica*, 18: 1–10.

Atal, B.S. (1972) Automatic Speaker Recognition Based on Pitch Countours, *J. Acoust. Soc Am.*, 52: 1687–1697.

Atal, B.S. (1974) Effectiveness of Linear Prediction Characteristics of the Speech Wave for Automatic Speaker Identification and Verification, *J. Acoust. Soc. Am.*, 55: 1304–1312.

Atal, B.S. (1976) Automatic Recognition of Speakers From Their Voices, *Proc. IEEE*, 64: 460–475.

Auckenthaler, R. and Mason, J. (1998) Score Normalization In a Multi-band Speaker Verification System, *RLA2C*, Avignon, 102–105.

Bakis, R. and Dixon, N.R. (1982) Toward Speaker-Independent Recognition-by-Synthesis, *Proc. IEEE Int. Conf. ASSP*, 566–569.

Baraniecki, M. and Shridhar, M. (1980) A Speaker Verification Algorithm for Speech Utterances Corrupted by Noise with Unknown Statistics, *Proc. IEEE Int. Conf. ASSP*, 904–907.

Beek, B., Neuberg, E.P. and Hodge, D.C. (1997) An Assessment of the Technology of Automatic Speech Recognition for Military Applications, *IEEE Trans. ASSP*, 25: 310–322.

Bisiani, R. (1983) Techniques for Computer Recognitions of Speech, *Annals, New York Acad. Sci.*, 405: 39–47.

Bogner, R.E. (1981) On Talker Verification Via Orthogonal Parameters, *IEEE Trans. ASSP*, 29: 1–12.

Bourlard, H., Kamp, Y. and Wellekens, C.J. (1985) Speaker Dependent Connected Speech Recognition Via Phonemic Markov Models, *IEEE–ICASSP*, 31.5: 1–4.

Boves, L. (1998) Commercial Applications of Speaker Verification, *RLA2C*, Avignon, 150–159.

Brown, R.S. (1979) Memory and Decision in Speaker Recognition, *Int. J., Man-Machine Stud.*, 11: 729–942.

Buck, J.T., Burton, D.K. and Shore, J.E. (1985) Text-Dependent Speaker Recognition Using Vector Quantization, *IEEE-ICASSP 85*, 11.5: 1–4.

Carey, M., Parris, E. and Bennet, S. (1992) Speaker Verification, *Proc. Instit. Acoustics Conf.* 14: 95–100.

Charlet, D., Jouvet, D. and Collins, O. (1998) An Alternate Normalization Scheme in HMM-Based Text Dependent Speaker Verification, *RLA2C*, Avignon, 165–168.

Das, S.K. and Mohn, W.S. (1971) A Scheme for Speech Processing in Automatic Speaker Verification, *IEEE Trans. Audio Electroacoust.*, 19: 32–43.

DeGeorge, M. (1981) Experiments in Acoustic Speaker Verification, *Proc. Carnahan Conf.*

Crime Countermeasures, Lexington, KY.

Doddington, G.R. (1974) Speaker Verification *Final Report, RADC-TR-74–179,* Rome Air Development Center, Griffis AFB, NY, (July).

Doddington, G.R. (1985) Speaker Recognition – Identifying People by Their Voices, *Proc. IEEE,* 73: 1651–1664.

Doddington, G.R. and Schalk, T.B. (1981) Speech Recognition: Turning Theory to Practice, *IEEE Spectrum,* 18: 26–33.

Everett, S.S. (1985) Automatic Speaker Recognition Using Vocoded Speech, *IEEE–ICASSP 85,* 11.1: 1–4.

Feiz, W. and DeGeorge, M. (1985) A Speaker Verification System for Access-Control, *IEEE–ICASSP 85,* 11.7: 1–4.

Fejfar, A. and Myers, J.W. (1977) The Testing of Three Identity Verification Techniques for Entry Control, *Proc. Int. Conf., Crime Countermeasures,* Oxford, 163–164.

Foodman, M.J. (1981) Experiments in Automatic Speaker Verification, *Proc. Carnahan Conf. Crime Countermeasures,* Lexington, KY.

Furui, S. (1974) An Analysis of Long-Term Variation of Feature Parameters of Speech and Its Application to Talker Recognition, *Electronics and Comm. Japan,* A57: 880–887.

Furui, S. (1981) Cepstral Analysis Technique for Automatic Speaker Verification, *IEEE Trans. ASSP,* 29: 254–272.

Furui, S. (1986) Research on Individuality Features in Speech Waves and Automatic Speaker Recognition Techniques, *Speech Comm.,* 5: 183–197.

Furui, S. and Rosenberg, A.E. (1980) Experimental Studies in a New Automatic Speaker Verification System Using Telephone Speech, *Proc. IEEE Int. Conf. ASSP,* Denver, 1060–1062.

Gish, H. and Schmidt, M. (1994) Text-Independent Speaker Identification, *IEEE Signal Process. Mag.,* 11: 18–32.

Higgins, A., Bohler, L. and Porter, J. (1991) Speaker Verification Using Randomized Phrase Prompting, *Digital Signal Pross.,* 1: 89–106.

Hofker, V., Jersorsky, P., Kriener, B., Talmi, M. and Wesseling, D. (1979) A New System for Authentication of Voice, *Proc. IEEE Int. Conf. ASSP,* 789–792.

Hunt, M.J. (1983) Further Experiments in Text-Independent Speaker Recognition Over Communications Channels, *Proc. IEEE Int. Conf. ASSP,* Boston, 563–566.

Ichikawa, A., Nakajima, A. and Nakata, K. (1979) Speaker Verification from Actual Telephone Voice, *J. Acoust. Soc. Japan,* 35: 63–69.

Jassem, W. (1968) Formant Frequencies as Cues to Speaker Discrimination, in *Speech Analysis and Synthesis,* (W. Jassem, ed.) Warsaw, 1: 9–41.

Jassem, W. (1995) Discriminant Analysis and Its Application in Voice Recognition, in *Studies in Forensic Phonetics,* Beiphol, 64: 132–145.

Jesorsky, P. (1977) Principles of Automatic Speaker Recognition, in *Natural Lang. Comm. With Computers,* (L. Bolc. ed.), 1–15.

Kalish, M.L. and Nygaard, L.C. (1993–4) Models of Speaker Dependent Speech Recognition, *Report 19 SRL,* Indiana Univ., 130–143.

Kuhn, M.H., Geppart, R. and Frehse, R. (1980) On-Line Evaluation of User Acceptance in Speaker Verification, *Proc. Int. Conf. Security Through Science and Engineering,* West

Berlin, 131–137.

Li, K.P. and Wrench, E.H. Jr. (1983) An Approach to Text-Independent Speaker Recognition with Short Utterances, *Proc. ICASSP,* Boston, 555–558.

Li, K.P., Dammann, J.E. and Chapman, W.D. (1966) Experimental Studies in Speaker Verification Using an Adaptive System, *J. Acoust. Soc. Am.,* 40: 966–978.

Lin, W.C. and Pillay, S.K. (1976) Feature Evaluation and Selection for an On-Line Adaptive Speaker Verification System, *Proc. IEEE Int. Conf. ASSP,* Philadelphia, 234–237.

Lindberg, J. and Melin, H. (1997) Text Prompted Versus Sound Prompted Passwords in Speaker Verification, *Proc. Eurospeech - 97,* 851–854.

Lindberg, J., Koolwaaij, J., Hutter, H., Genoud, D., Pierrot, J., Blomberg, M. and Bimbot, F. (1998) Techniques for a Priori Decision Threshold Estimation in Speaker Verification, *RLA2C,* Avignon, 89–92.

Luck, J.E. (1969) Automatic Speaker Verification Using Cepstral Measurements, *J. Acoust Soc. Am.,* 46: 1026–1032.

Lummis, R.C. (1972) Speaker Verification: A Step Toward the 'Checkless' Society, *Bell Lab. Rec.,* 50: 254–259.

Lummis, R C. (1973) Speaker Verification by Computer Using Speech Intensity for Temporal Registration, *IEEE Trans. Audio. Electroacoust.,* Au-21: 50–59.

Lund, M. and Lee, C. (1996) A Robust Sequential Test for Text–Independent Speaker Verification, *J. Acoust. Soc. Am.,* 99: 609–621.

Makhoul, J. and Wolf, J. (1973) The Use of a Two-Pole Linear Prediction Model in Speech Recognition, *Bolt, Beranek, Newman Rep. No. 2537,* 1–21.

Markel, J.D., Oshika, B. and Gray, A.H. (1977) Long-Term Feature Averaging for Speaker Recognition, *IEEE Trans. ASSP,* 25: 330–337.

Melin, H. (1998) On Word Boundary Detection in Digit Based Speaker Verification, *RLA2C,* Avignon, 46–49.

Ney, H., Gierloff, R. and Frehse, R. (1981) An Automatic System for Verification of Cooperative Speakers Via Telephone, *Proc. Carnahan Conf., Crime Countermeasures,* Lexington, KY, (May).

Olsen, M. (1997) Speaker Verification Based on Phonetic Decision Making, *Proc. Eurospeech - 97,* 1375–1378.

Paliwal, K.K. and Ainsworth, W.A. (1985) Dynamic Frequency Warping for Speaker Adaptation in Automatic Speech Recognition, *J. Phonet.,* 13: 123–134.

Pham, T., Tran, D. and Wagner, M. (1999) Speaker Verification Using Relaxation Labeling, *RLA2C* Avignon, 29–32.

Preusse, J.W. (1971) Word Recognition and Speaker Authentication Using Amplitude Independent and Time Independent Word Features, *Tech. Report, ECOM-3439,* Ft Monmouth, NJ: U.S. Army Electronics Command.

Ramishvili, G.S. (1966) Automatic Voice Recognition, *Enging. Cybernetics,* 5: 84–90.

Ramishvili, G.S. (1974) Experiments on Automatic Verification of Speakers, *Proc. 2nd Int. Joint Conf., Pattern Recog.,* Copenhagen, 389–393.

Reynolds, D. (1997) Comparison of Background Normalization Methods for Text Independent Speaker Verification, *Proc. Eurospeech - 97,* 963–966.

Reynolds, D. and Rose, R. (1995) Robust Text-Independent Speaker Identification Using Gaussian Mixture Speaker Models, *IEEE Trans. Speech Audio Process.*, 3: 72–83.

Rosenberg, A.E. (1976) Evaluation of an Automatic Speaker Verification System Over Telephone Lines, *Bell System Tech. J.*, 55: 723–744.

Rosenberg, A.E. and Sambur, M.R. (1975) New Techniques for Automatic Speaker Verification, *IEEE Trans. ASSP,* 23: 169–176.

Rosenberg, A., Lee, C. and Gobeen, C. (1991) Connected Word Talker Verification Using Whole Word Hidden Markov Models., *Proc. ICASSP-91,* 381–384.

Sambur, M.R. (1973) Speaker Recognition and Verification Using Linear Prediction Analysis, *QPR No. 108,* Massachusetts Inst. Technology, 261–268.

Sambur, M.R. (1976) Speaker Recognition Using Orthogonal Linear Prediction, *IEEE Trans., ASSP,* 24: 283–287.

Schwartz, R., Roncos, S. and Berouti, M. (1982) The Application of Probability Density Estimation to Text-Independent Speaker Identification, *Proc. ICASSP 82,* 3: 1649–1652.

Shridhar, M., Baraniecki, M. and Mohankrishnan, N. (1983) A Unified Approach to Speaker Verification with Noisy Speech Inputs, *Speech Comm.,* 1: 103–112.

Soong, F.K., Rosenberg, A.E., Rabiner, L.R., Juang, B.H. (1985) A Vector Quantization Approach to Speaker Recognition, *IEEE ICASSP 85,* 11.4: 1–4.

Tatham, M.A. (1985) An Integrated Knowledge Base for Speech Synthesis and Automatic Speech Recognition, *J. Phonet.,* 13: 175–188.

Uzdy, Z. (1985) Human Speaker Recognition Performance of LPC Voice Processors, *IEEE Trans. ASSP,* 33: 752–753.

Vidalon, M., Shridhar, M. and Canas, M. (1977) Speaker Verification Using Composite References, *Proc. IEEE Int. Conf. ASSP,* 758–760.

Wolf, J.J. (1972) Efficient Acoustic Parameters for Speaker Recognition, *J. Acoust. Soc. Am.,* 51: 2044–2055.

Wolf, J., Krasner, M., Karnofsky, K., Schwartz, R. and Roucos, S. (1983) Further Investigations of Probabilistic Methods for Text-Independent Speaker Identification, *IEEE ICASSP,* Boston, 2: 551–554.

CHAPTER 2

References

1. Saslove, H. and Yarmey, A.D. (1980) Long Term Auditory Memory: Speaker Identification, *J. Applied Psychol.* 65: 111–116.
2. Hoffman, W.G. (1940) *Public Speaking Today,* New York, McGraw-Hill Co.
3. Quintilian (1899) Institutiones Oratoriae, quoted in *Quintillian's Institues of Oratory* (J.S. Watson, Trans.) London, G. Bell.
4. Hollien, H. (1990) *The Acoustics of Crime,* New York, Plenum.
5. Yarmey, A.D. (1995) Earwitness Speaker Identification, *Psychol. Public Policy, Law,* 1: 792–816.
6. Wilbur vs. Hubbard (1861) *New York Law J.* (Cited in McGehee, 1937).
7. Deering and Co. vs. Shumpik, (1897) *Minn. Reporter,* 67: 348.

8. Mack vs. State of Florida, 54 Fla. 55, 44 So. 706 (1907) citing 5, *Howell's State Trials*, 1186.
9. State vs. Hauptman (1935) *Atlantic Rep.* 180: 809–829.
10. McGehee, F. (1937) The Reliability of the Identification of the Human Voice, *J. Gen. Psychol.*, 17: 249–271.
11. McGehee, F. (1944) An Experimental Study of Voice Recognition, *J. Gen. Psychology*, 31: 53–65.
12. Broun, H. (1938) It Seems To Me, *New York World Telegram*, Dec. 30.
13. Menaugh, J.A. (1939) Purdue Scientists Dissect The Human Voice, The Graphic Laboratory of Popular Science, *Chicago Tribune*, May 28; 8.
14. Post, D.E (1998) The Hypnosis of Adolph Hitler, *J. Forensic Sci.*, 43: 1127–1132.
15. Toland, J. (1976) *Adolph Hitler*, New York: Doubleday.
16. Waite, R. (1977) *The Psychopathic God: Adolph Hitler*, New York: Plenum.
17. Alpert, M., Pouget, E. and Welkowitz, J. (1993) Mapping Schizophrenic Negative Symptoms onto Measures of the Patient's Speech, *Psychiatry Res.*, 48: 181–190.
18. Hollien, H (1980) Vocal Indicators of Psychological Stress, *Forensic Psychology and Psychiatry*, New York: New York Academy of Sciences, 47–72.
19. Hollien, H. and Darby, J. (1979) Acoustic Comparisons of Psychotic and Non-psychotic Voices, in *Current Issues in the Phonetic Sciences* (H. and P. Hollien, eds) Amsterdam: John Benjamins, 609–614.
20. Scherer, K.R. (1979) Non-linguistic Vocal Indicators of Emotion and Psychopathology, in *Emotions and Psychopathology*. (C.E. Izard, ed.) New York: Plenum.
21. Scherer, K.R. (1986) Vocal Affect Expression: A Review and Model for Future Research. *Psychology Bull.*, 99: 143–165.
22. Scherer, K.R., Banse, R., Walbot, H. and Goldbeck, T. (1991) Vocal Cues in Emotion, Encoding and Decoding, *Motivation and Emotion*, 15: 123–148.
23. Potter, R. (1945) Visible Patterns of Speech, *Science*, November, 463–470.
24. Potter, R., Kopp, G. and Green, H. (1947) *Visible Speech*, New York: Van Nostrand.
25. Gray, G. and Kopp, G. (1944) Voiceprint Identification, *Bell Telephone Laboratories Report*, Murray Hill, NJ, pp 1–14.
26. Solzhenitsyn, A. (1968) *The First Circle*, New York: Harper and Row.
27. Ramishvilli, G.S. (1966) Automatic Voice Recognition, *Enging. Cybernet.*, 5: 84–90.
28. Ramishvili, G. (1985) Oral Dialogue Between Man and Computer, *Georgian Academy of Science*, Tbilisi, (in Georgian).
29. Ramishvilli, G.S. (1991) Speech Signal and Voice Individuality, *Georgian Academy of Science*, Tbilisi (in Russian).
30. Ramishvili, G. and Chikoidze, G. (1992) Criminalogical Investigation of Speech Phonograms and Speaker Identification, *Metsniereba*, Tbilisi (in Russian).
31. Brandt, J.F. (1977) Can You Hear Me? *Forensic Comm.*, 2: 9–11.
32. Michel, J.F. (1980) Use of a Voice Lineup, *Conv. Abstr. Am. Acad. Forensic Sci.*, 937.
33. Kersta, L (1962) Voiceprint Identification, *Nature*, 196: 1253–1257.

CHAPTER 3

References

1. McGehee, F. (1937) The Reliability of the Identification of the Human Voice, *J. Gen. Psychol.*, 17: 249–271.
2. McGehee, F. (1944) An Experimental Study in Voice Recognition, *J. Gen. Psychol.*, 31: 53–65.
3. Bricker, P. and Pruzansky, S. (1966) Effects of Stimulus Content and Duration on Talker Identification, *J. Acoust. Soc. Am.* 40: 1441–1450.
4. Yarmey, A.D. and Matthys, E. (1992) Voice Identification of an Abductor, *Appl. Cogn. Psychol.*, 6: 367–377.
5. Clifford, B.R. (1980) Voice Identification by Human Listeners: On Earwitness Reliability, *Law Hum. Behav.*, 4: 373–394.
6. Clifford, B.R., Rathborn, H. and Bull, H. (1981) The Effects of Delay on Voice Recognition Accuracy, *Law Hum. Behav.*, 5: 201–208.
7. Papcun, G., Kreiman, J. and Davis, A. (1989), Long-term Memory for Unfamiliar Voices, *J. Acoust. Soc. Am.*, 85: 913–925.
8. Saslove, H. and Yarmey, A. (1980) Long-Term Auditory Memory: Speaker Identification, *J. Appl. Psychol.*, 45: 111–116.
9. Hollien, H., Bennett, G., and Gelfer, M.P. (1983) Criminal Identification Comparison: Aural vs. Visual Identification Resulting from a Simulated Crime, *J. Forensic Sci.*, 25: 208–221.
10. Brown, R. (1979) Memory and Decision in Speaker Recognition, *Int. J. Man-Machine Stud.*, 11: 729–942.
11. Wixted, J.T. and Ebbesen, E. (1991) On the Form of Forgetting, *Psychol. Sci.*, 2: 409–415.
12. Rothman, H.B. (1977) A Perceptual (aural) and Spectrographic Investigation of Talkers with Similar Sounding Voices, *Proc. 1977 Int. Conf. Crime Countermeasures*, Oxford, 37–41.
13. Endress, W., Bambach, W. and Flosser, G. (1971) Voice Spectrograms as a Function of Age, Voice Disguise and Voice Imitation, *J. Acoust. Soc. Am.*, 49: 1842–1848.
14. Suzuki, T., Tanimoto, M., Osanai, T. and Kido, H. (1996) Acoustical Variation of Voice with Aging of Male Speakers on Vowels and Nasal Sounds, Presented at *Annu. Meet., Am. Acad. Forensic Sci.*, Nashville, February.
15. Schwartz, R. (1995) Effect of Non-contemporary Speech on Aural-perceptual Speaker Identification, presented at IAFP-95, *Congr. Int. Assn. Forensic Phonetics*, Orlando Fl, July.
16. Hollien, H. and Schwartz, R. (2001) Speaker Identification Utilizing Noncontemporary Speech, *J. Forensic Sci.*, 46: 63–67.
17. Hollien, H. and Schwartz, R. (2000) Aural-Perceptual Speaker Identification: Problems with Noncontemporary Samples, *Forensic Linguistics*, 7: 199–211.
18. Köster, J.P. (1981) Auditive Sprecherkennug bei Experten und Naiven, in *Festschrift Wangler*, Hamburg, Helmut Buske, AG, 52: 171–180.

19. Thompson, C. (1985) Voice Identification: Speaker Identifiability and Correction of the Record Regarding Sex Effects, *Hum. Learn.*, 4: 19–27.
20. Schiller, N.O. and Köster, O. (1998) The Ability of Expert Witnesses to Identify Voices: A Comparison Between Trained and Untrained Listeners, *Forensic Linguistics*, 5: 1–9.
21. Shirt, M. (1984) An Auditory Speaker Recognition Experiment, *Proc. Institut. Acoust. Conf., Speech, Tape Recorded Analysis*, London, 21–24.
22. Aarts, N.W. (1984) The Effect of Listener Stress on Perceptual Speaker Identification, MA Thesis, University of Florida.
23. Bull, R. and Clifford, B.R. (1984) Earwitness Voice Recognition Accuracy, in *Eyewitness Testimony: Psychological Perspectives*, (G.L. Wells and E. Loftus, eds), Cambridge: Cambridge University Press.
24. Hollien, H., Majewski, W. and Doherty, E.T. (1982) Perceptual Identification of Voices Under Normal, Stress and Disguised Speaking Conditions, *J. Phonet.* 10: 139–148.
25. Künzel, H. (1994) On the Problem of Speaker Identification by Victims and Witnesses, *Forensic Linguistics*, 1: 45–58.
26. Reich, A.R. and Duke, J.E. (1979) Effects of Selective Vocal Disguise Upon Speaker Identification by Listening, *J. Acoust. Soc. Am.*, 66: 1023–1028.
27. DeJong, G. (1998) Earwitness Characteristics and Speaker Identification Accuracy, Ph.D. dissertation, University of Florida.
28. Hollien, H. (1990) *The Acoustics of Crime*, New York: Plenum Press.
29. Nolan, J.F. (1983) *The Phonetic Basis of Speaker Identification*, Cambridge: Cambridge Univ. Press.
30. Yarmey, A.D. (1995) Earwitness Speaker Identification, *Psychol. Public Policy Law*, 1: 792–816.
31. Bachorowski, J. and Owren, M. (1999) Acoustic Correlates of Talker Sex and Individual Talker Identity Are Present in a Short Vowel Segment Produced in Running Speech, *J. Acoust. Soc. Am.*, 106: 1054–1063.
32. Lass, N., Hughes, K., Bower, M., Waters, L. and Bourne, V. (1976) Speaker Sex Identification from Voiced, Whispered and Filtered Isolated Vowels, *J. Acoust. Soc. Am.*, 59: 675–678.
33. Bralley, R., Bull, G., Gore, C. and Edgerton, M. (1978) Evaluation of Vocal Pitch in Male Transsexuals, *J. Comm. Disord.*, 11: 443–449.
34. Spencer, L. (1988) Speech Characteristics of Male-to-Female Transsexuals, *Folia Phoneatrica*, 40: 31–42.
35. Wolfe, V., Ratusnik, D., Smith, F. and Northrop, G. (1990) Intonation and Fundamental Frequency in Male-to-Female Transsexuals, *J. Speech Hear. Disord.*, 55: 43–50.
36. Coleman, R. (1976) A Comparison of the Contributions of Two Voice Quality Characteristics to the Perception of Maleness and Femaleness in the Voice, *J. Speech Hear. Res.*, 19: 168–180.
37. Coleman, R. and Lass, N. (1980) Effect of Prior Exposure to Stimulus Material on Identification of Speaker's Sex, Height and Weight, *Perceptual Motor Skills*, 52: 619–622.

38. Ingemann, F. (1968) Identification of the Speaker's Sex from Voiceless Fricatives, *J. Acoust. Soc. Am.*, 44: 1142–1144.

39. Schwartz, M.F. (1968) Identification of Speaker Sex from Isolated Voiceless Fricatives, *J. Acoust. Soc. Am.,* 43: 1178–1179.

40. Hirson, A. and Duckworth, M. (1995) Forensic Implications of Vocal Creak as Voice Disguise, BEIPHOL, *Stud. Forensic Phonet.*, 64: 67–76.

41. Hollien, H. and Thompson, C.L. (1990) Effects of Listening Experience on Decoding Speech in HeO_2 Enviroments, (W. Jaap, ed.) *Diving for Science,* San Diego, 179–191.

42. Huntley, R.A. (1992) Listener Skill in Voice Identification, *Am. Acad. Forensic Sci.*, New Orleans, 105(A).

43. Nerbonne, G. (1967) The Identification of Speaker Characteristics on the Basis of Aural Cues. Ph.D. thesis, Michigan State University.

44. Künzel, H. (1995) Field Procedures in Forensic Speaker Recognition, in *Festschrift for J.D. O'Connor* (J. Lewis, ed.), London: Routledge, 68–84.

45. Pollack, I., Pickett, J.M. and Sumby, W.H. (1954) On the Identification of Speakers by Voice, *J. Acoust. Soc. Am.*, 26: 403–412.

46. Compton, A.J. (1963) Effects of Filtering and Vocal Duration Upon The Identification of Speakers Aurally, *J. Acoust. Soc. Am.*, 35: 1748–1752.

47. Cort, S. and Murry T. (1972) Aural Identification of Children's Voices, *J. Acoust. Soc. Am.*, 51: 131(A).

48. LaRiviere, C.L. (1971), Some Acoustic and Perceptual Correlates of Speaker Identification, Ph.D. dissertation, University of Florida.

49. Orchard, T. and Yarmey, A. (1995) The Effects of Whispers, Voice-Sample Duration and Voice Distinctiveness on Criminal Speaker Identification, *Appl. Cogn. Psychol.*, 9: 249–260.

50. Yarmey, A.D. (1991) Descriptions of Distinctive and Non-distinctive Voices Over Timc, *J. Forensic Sci. Soc.*, 31: 421–428.

51. Carbonell, J.R., Stevens, K.N., Williams, C.E. and Woods, B. (1965), Speaker Identification by a Matching-From-Samples Technique, *J. Acous. Soc. Am.*, 40: 1205–1206.

52. Stuntz, A.E. (1963), Speech Intelligibility and Talker Recognition Tests of Air Force Communication Systems, *Report ESD-TDR-63–224,* Hanscom Field, MA: Air Force Systems Command.

53. Williams, C.E. (1964) The Effects of Selected Factors on the Aural Identification of Speakers, *Tech. Doc. Opt. ESD-TDR-65–153,* Hanscom Field, MA: USAF, Electron Syst. Div.

54. Foulkes, P. and Barron, A. (2000) Telephone Speaker Recognition Amongst Members of a Close Social Network, *Forensic Linguistics,* 7: 180–198.

55. Ney, H., Gierloff, R. and, Frehse, R. (1981) An Automatic System of Verification of Cooperative Speakers Via Telephone, *Proc. Carnahan Conf., Crime Counter Measures,* Lexington, KY.

56. Rathborn, H., Bull, R. and Clifford, B. (1981) Voice Recognition Over the Telephone, *J. Police Sci. Admin.* 9: 280–284.

57. Yarmey, A.D. (1991) Voice Identification Over the Telephone. *J. Appl. Social Psychol.* 21: 1868–1876.

58. Abberton, E. and Fourcin, A.J. (1978) Intonation and Speaker Identification, *Lang. Speech,* 21: 305–315.

59. LaRiviere, C.L. (1972) Some Acoustic and Perceptual Correlates of Speaker Identification, *Proc. 7th Intern. Congr. Phonetic Sci.,* 558–564.

60. Molina deFigueiredo, R. (1999) Perceptual Reconstruction of Celebrity Voices Using Random Spliced Speech, *Proc. Int. Congr. Phonetic Sci.,* 161–162.

61. Rose, P. and Duncan, S. (1995) Naive Auditory Identification and Discrimination of Similar Voices by Familiar Listeners, *Forensic Linguistics,* 2: 1–17.

62. Van Lancker, D. Kreiman, J. and Emmory, K. (1985) Familiar Voice Recognition Patterns and Parameters: I. Recognition of Backward Voices, *J. Phonet.,* 13: 19–38.

63. Van Lancker, D. Kreiman, J. and Wicken, T. (1985) Familiar Voice Recognition Patterns and Parameters: II. Recognition of Rate Altered Voices, *J. Phonet.,* 13: 39–52.

64. Clarke, F.R. and Becker, R.W. (1969) Characteristics that Determine Speaker Recognition, *Report ESD-TR-66–636,* Hanscom Field, MA: Electron. Syst. Div., USAF Syst. Comm.

65. Ladefoged, P. and Ladefoged, J. (1980) The Ability of Listeners to Identify Voices, *UCLA Working Pap. Phonet.,* 41: 41–42.

66. Goldstein, A. and Chance, J. (1985) Voice Recognition: The Effects of Faces, Temporal Distribution of 'Practice' and Social Distance, presented at Midwestern Psychological Assn., Chicago.

67. Huntley, R.A. (1991) Aural-Perceptual Speaker Identification, *Proc. 12th Int. Congr. Phonetic Sci.,* Aix en Provence, 398.

68. Künzel, H. (2000) Effects of Voice Disguise on Fundamental Frequency, *Forensic Linguistics,* 7: 149–179.

69. Schmidt-Nielsen, A. and Stern, K. (1985) Identification of Known Voices as a Function of Familiarity and Narrow-band Coding, *J. Acoust. Soc. Am.,* 77: 658–663.

70. Manning, W.H. and Hollien, P.A. (1992) Effects of a Voice Disguise Device, *Am. Acad. Forensic Sci.,* New Orleans, 108(A).

71. McGlone, R.E., Hollien, P.A. and Hollien, H. (1977) Acoustic Analysis of Voice Disguise Related to Voice Identification, *Proc. Intern. Conf. on Crime Countermeasures,* Oxford: 31–35.

72. Masthoff, H. (1996) A Report on a Voice Disguise Experiment, *Forensic Linguistics,* 3: 160–167.

73. Molina deFigueiredo, R.M. and deSouza Britto, H. (1996) A Report on the Acoustic Effects of One Type of Disguise, *Forensic Linguistics,* 3: 168–175.

74. Reich, A. (1981) Detecting the Presence of Vocal Disguise in the Male Voice, *J. Acoust. Soc. Am.,* 69: 1458–1461.

75. Hollien, P.A. (1992) Procedures for Conducting Exemplar Interviews, *Report 92–04,* Gainesville, FL: Forensic Communication Associates, pp. 1–6.

76. Lazarus, R.S. (1966), *Psychological Stress and the Coping Process,* New York: McGraw-Hill Inc.

77. Scherer, K.R. (1979) Personality Markers in Speech, in *Social Markers Speech,* (K.R. Scherer and H. Giles, eds.), Cambridge: Cambridge University Press, 147–209.
78. Hicks, J.W., Jr. and Hollien H. (1981) The Reflection of Stress in Voice-1: Understanding the Basic Correlates, *Proc. Carnahan Conf. Crime Countermeasures,* Lexington, KY, 189–194.
79. Scherer, K.R. (1981) Vocal Indicators of Stress, in *Speech Evaluation in Psychiatry.* (J. Darby, ed.) New York: Grune and Stratton, 171–187.
80. Scherer, K.R. (1986) Voice, Stress and Emotion, *Dynamics of Stress: Physiological, Psychological and Social Perspectives,* (H. Appley and R. Trumbull, eds.) New York: Plenum Press, 157–179.
81. Scherer, K.R. (1990) Stress et Coping: Nouvelles Approaches, *Cahiers Psychiatr. Genevois,* 9: 155–162.
82. Atwood, W. and Hollien, H. (1986), Stress Monitoring by Polygraph for Research Purposes, *Polygraph* 15: 47–56.
83. Mayor, D. and Komulainen, E. (1989) *Subjective Voice Identification,* Calgary: Calgary Police Service, 42.
84. Hanley, T. D. (1951) An Analysis of Vocal Frequency and Duration Characteristics of Selected Samples of Speech from Three American Dialects, *Speech Monogr.,* 18: 78–93.
85. Hanley, T. D. and Snidecor, J. (1967) Some Acoustic Similarities Among Languages, *Phonetica,* 17: 141–148.
86. Tate, D.A. (1977) Speech Disguise by Dialect Imitation, Unpublished MA Thesis, University of Florida.
87. Tate, D.A. (1979) Preliminary Data on Dialect in Speech Disguise, in: *Current Issues in the Phonetic Sciences,* (H. Hollien and P. Hollien, eds), Amsterdam: John Benjamins, B.V.
88. Doty, N. (1998) The Influence of Nationality on the Accuracy of Face and Voice Recognition, *Am. J. Psychol.,* 111: 191–214.
89. Goggin, J., Thompson, C., Strube, G. and Simental, L. (1991) The Role of Language Familiarity in Voice Identification, *Memory Cogn.,* 19: 448–458.
90. Goldstein, A., Knight, P., Bailis, K. and Conover, J. (1981) Recognition Memory for Accented and Unaccented Voices, *Bull. Psychonomic Soc.,* 17: 217–220.
91. Schiller, N.O. and Köster, O. (1996) Evaluation of a Foreign Language Speaker in Forensic Phonetics: A Report, *Forensic Linguistics,* 3: 176–185.
92. Thompson, C. (1987) A Language Effect in Voice Identification. *Appl. Cogn. Psychol.* 25: 121–131.
93. Köster, O., Schiller, N.O. and Künzel, H.J. (1995) The Influence of Native-language Background on Speaker Recognition, *Proc. 13th Int. Congr. Phonetic Sci.,* Stockholm: 4: 306–309.
94. Köster, O. and Schiller, N. (1997) Different Influences of the Native Language of a Listener on Speaker Recognition, *Forensic Linguistics,* 4: 18–28.
95. Broeders, A. and Rietveld, A. (1995) Speaker Identification by Earwitnesses, *Studies in Forensic Phonetics,* 64: 20–40.
96. Huntley-Bahr, R.A. and Pass, K. (1995) The Influence of Style Shifting on Voice

Identification, *Forensic Linguistics*, 3: 24–38.

97. Bartholomeus, B. (1973) Voice Identification by Nursery School Children, *Can. J. Psychol.*, 27: 464–472.
98. Bull, R., Rathborn, H. and Clifford, B. (1983) The Voice Recognition Accuracy of Blind Listeners, *Perception*, 12: 223–226.
99. Hollien, H. (1995) The Future of Speaker Identification, A Model, *ICPhS 95, Int. Congr. Phonetic Sci.*, Stockholm, 3: 138–145.
100. Künzel, H. (1990), Phonetische Untersuchungen zur Sprechererkennung Durch Linguistisch naive Personen, *ZDL Beiheft 69*, Steiner Verlag: Stuttgart.
101. Rosenberg, A.E. (1973) Listener Performance in Speaker Verification Tasks, *IEEE Trans, Audio Electroacoust.* AU-21: 221–225.
102. Blaauw, E. and Günzburger, D. (1988) Childs Voice Identification by Children, *Pripu*, 13: 33–41.
103. Friedlander, B. (1970) Receptive Language Development; Issues and Problems, *Merrill-Palmer Quart.*, 16: 7–15.
104. Mehler, J., Bertoncini, J., Barrière, M. and Jassik-Gerschenfeld, D. (1978) Infant Recognition of Mother's Voice, *Perception*, 7: 491–497.
105. Saito, K., Asakawa, K., Shimura, Y. and Imaizuml, S. (1995) Development of Speaker Identification in Young Children, *Ann. Bull, RIPL, Tokyo,* 29: 55–58.
106. Bresser, A. and Günzburger, D. (1985) Voice Recognizability of Prepubescent Boys and Girls, *Pripu*, 10: 25–32.
107. Mann, V., Deamond, R. and Carey, S. (1979) Development of Voice Recognition: Parallels with Face Recognition, *J. Exp. Child Psychol.* 27: 153–165.
108. Stevens, K.N. (1971) Sources of Inter- and Intra-Speaker Variability in the Acoustic Properties of Speech Sounds, *Proc. 7th Int. Congr. Phonetic Sci.*, Montreal, 206–232.
109. Hollien, H. (1991) The Profile Approach to Speaker Identification, *Proc. 12th Int. Congr. Phonetic Sci.*, Aix en Provence, 396(A).

Further Reading

Howard, D., Hirson, A., French, J.P. and Szymanski, J. (1993) A Survey of Fundamental Frequency Estimation Techniques Used in Forensic Sciences, *Proc. Inst. Acoustics, London* 15: 207–215.

Huntley-Bahr, R.H. (1999) The Dynamics in Codeswitching in Voice Identification, *Proc. Int. Congr. Phonetic Sci.*, San Francisco, 583–586.

LaRiviere, C.L. (1975) Contributions of Fundamental Frequency and Formant Frequencies to Speaker Identification, *Phonetica*, 31: 185–197.

CHAPTER 4

References

1. Anonymous (1991) Voice Comparison Standard, *J. Forensic Ident.*, 41: 373–392.
2. Anonymous (1990) Motion Adopted, Bureau du Groupe, Communication Parleé de la Société Francaise d'Acoustique, *ESCA Newsl.*, 4: 39.
3. Bimbot, F., Chollet, G., and Paoloni, A. (1984) Assessment Methodology for

Speaker Identification and Verification Systems, *Proc. ESCA Workshop on Automatic Speaker Recog.*, 75–82.

4. Boë, L. (1998) L'identification Juridique de la Voix, *RLA2C*, Avignon, April, 222–239.
5. Collet, G. (1991) About the Ethics of Speaker Identification, *Proc. 12th Int. Congr. Phonetic Sci.*, Aix-en-Provence, 1: 397 (A).
6. Hollien, H. (1995) The Future of Speaker Identification: A Model, *ICPhS95, Proc. Int. Congr. Phonetic Sci.*, Stockholm, 3: 138–145.
7. Hollien, H. and Jiang, M. (1998) The Challenge of Effective Speaker Identification, *RLA2C*, Avignon, 2–9.
8. Broeders, A. (1999) Some Observations on the Use of Probability Scales in Forensic Identification, *Forensic Linguistics*, 6: 228–241.
9. Champod, C. and Menwley, D. (1998) The Inference of Identity in Forensic Speaker Recognition, *RLA2C*, Avignon, 125–134.
10. Hollien, H. (1990) *The Acoustics of Crime*, New York: Plenum.
11. Künzel, H. (1987) *Sprechererkennung: Grundzüge Forensischer Sprachverarbeitung*, Heidelberg: Kriminalistik Verlag.
12. Künzel, H. (1988) Zum Problem der Sprecheridentifizierung Durch Opfer und Zeugen, *Goltdammer's Archiv für Strafecht*, **5**: 215–224.
13. Champod, C. and Evett, I. (2000) Commentary, *Forensic Linguistics*, 7: 238–243.
14. Hollien, H. (1993) Forensic Phonetics, in *The Forensic Sciences*, (C. Wecht, ed.), New York: Matthew Bender Co., 2–28B: 1–115.
15. Pickett, J.M. (2000) Review of Ball and Rahilly, *J. Acoust. Soc. Am.*, 108: 2695.
16. Nolan, J.F. (1983) *The Phonetic Basis of Speaker Recog.*, Cambridge: Cambridge University Press.
17. Nolan, F. (1990) The Limitations of Auditory-phonetic Speaker Identification, in *Texte Zu Theorie und Praxis Forensischer Linguistik* (H. Kniffke, ed.), Tubigen: Niemeyer, 457–479.
18. Nolan, F. (1995) Can the Definition of Each Speaker be Expected to Come from the Laboratory in the Next Decades? *ICPS95, Proc. Int. Congr. Phonetic Sci.*, Stockholm, 3: 130–137.
19. French, J.P. (1993) Developments in Forensic Speaker Identification, *Bull. Inst. Acoust.*, 18: 13–16.
20. French, P. (1994) An Overview of Forensic Phonetics With Particular Reference to Speaker Identification, *Forensic Linguistics*, 2: 169–181.
21. Braun, A. (1995) Procedures and Perspectives in Forensic Phonetics, *Proc. ICPS-95*, Stockholm, 3: 146–153.
22. Braun, A. and Künzel, H. (1998) Is Forensic Speaker Identification Unethical – Or Can It Be Unethical Not to Do It? *RLA2C*, Avignon, 8: 145–148.
23. Hollien, P.A. (1992) Procedures for Conducting Exemplar Interviews, *Report 92–04*, Gainesville, FL: Forensic Communication Associates, 1–6.
24. Hollien, H. and Hollien, P.A. (1995) Improving Aural-Perceptual Identification Techniques, *Studies in Forensic Phonetics*, 64: 87–97.
25. DeJong, G. (1998) Earwitness Characteristics and Speaker Identification

Accuracy, Ph.D. dissertation, University of Florida.

26. Hollien, H. (1988) Voice Recognition, *Nouvelles Technologies et Justice Penale*, 9: 180–229.
27. Hollien, H., Bennett, G.T. and Gelfer, M.P. (1983) Criminal Identification Comparison: Aural vs. Visual Identification Resulting from a Simulated Crime, *J. Forensic Sci.*, 28: 208–221.
28. Hollien, H. and Schwartz, R. (2000) Aural-Perceptual Speaker Identification: Problems with Noncontemporary Samples, *Forensic Linguistics*, 7: 199–211.
29. Huntley, R. (1992) Listener Skill in Voice Identification, *Am. Acad. Forensic Sci.*, New Orleans, 105A.
30. Köster, J.P. (1987) Leistung von Experten und Naiven in der Auditiven Sprechererkennung, *Festschrift für H. Wängler*, (R. Weiss, ed.) Hamburg: Buske, 171–180.
31. Reich, A.R. and Duke, J.E. (1979) Effects of Selected Vocal Disguise Upon Speaker Identification by Listening, *J. Acoust. Soc. Am.*, 66: 1023–1028.
32. Schiller, N. and Köster, O. (1998) The Ability of Expert Witnesses to Identify Voices: A Comparison Between Trained and Untrained Listeners, *Forensic Lingusitics*, 5: 1–9.
33. Shirt, M. (1983) An Auditory Speaker Recognition Experiment, *Proc. Conf. Police Applications of Speech, Tape Record. Analysis*, London Inst. Acoust., 71–74.
34. Yarmey, A.D. (1986) Verbal, Visual and Voice Identification of a Rape Suspect Under Different Levels of Illumination, *J. Appl. Psychol.*, 71: 363–370.
35. Yarmey, A.D. (1995) Earwitness Speaker Identification, *Psychol. Public Policy Law*, 1: 792–816.
36. Ellis, S. (1994) The Yorkshire Ripper Enquiry, Part I, *Forensic Linguistics*, 1: 197–206.
37. Hecker, M.H.L. (1971) *Speaker Recognition: An Interpretive Survey of the Literature*, ASHA, Monograph #16, Washington, D.C.
38. Hollien, H., Majewski, W. and Doherty, E.T. (1982) Perceptual Identification of Voices Under Normal, Stress and Disguised Speaking Conditions, *J. Phonet.*, 10: 139–148.
39. Markham, D. (1999) Listeners and Disguised Voices: The Imitation and Perception of Dialectal Accent, *Forensic Linguistics*, 6: 289–299.

Further Reading

Rosenberg, A.E. (1973) Listener Performance in Speaker Verification Tasks, *IEEE Trans. Audio Electroacoust.*, AU-21: 221–225.

CHAPTER 5

References

1. Buckhout, R. (1976) Nobody Likes a Smartass: Expert Testimony by Psychologists, *Social Action Law*, 3: 41–52.
2. Loftus, E. (1979) *Eyewitness Testimony*, New York: Cambridge University Press.
3. van Wallendael, L., Surace, A., Parsons, D. and Brown, M. (1994) 'Earwitness'

Voice Recognition: Factors Affecting Accuracy and Impact on Jurors, *Appl. Cogn. Psychol.*, 8: 661–677.

4. Rattner, A. (1988) Convicted but Innocent: Wrongful Conviction and the Criminal Justice System, *Law Hum. Behav.*, 12: 283–293.
5. Buckhout, R. (1974) Eyewitness Testimony, *Scie. Am.*, 231: 23–31.
6. Buckhout, R. and Figueroa, D. (1974) Eyewitness Identification: Effects of Suggestion and Bias in Identification from Photographs, *Social Action Law*, 11: 1–24.
7. Cross, J.F., Cross, J. and Daly, J. (1971) Sex, Race, Age and Beauty as Factors in the Recognition of Faces, *Percept. Psychophys.*, 10: 393–396.
8. Shepherd, J.W. and Ellis, H.D. (1973) The Effect of Attractiveness on the Recognition Memory for Faces, *Am. J. Psychol.*, 86: 627–633.
9. Courtois, M. and Mueller, J. (1981) Target and Distractor Typicality in Face Recognition, *J. Appl. Psychol.*, 66: 639–645.
10. Wells, G. (1993) What Do We Know About Eyewitness Identification? *Am. Psychol.*, 48: 553–571.
11. Lindsay, R. and Wells, G. (1980) What Price Justice? Exploring the Relationship of Lineup Fairness to Identification Accuracy, *Law Hum. Behav.*, 4: 303–313.
12. Lindsay, R., Lea, J., Nosworthy, G., Fulford, J., Hector, J., LeVan, V. and Seabrook, C. (1991) Biased Lineups: Sequential Presentation Reduces the Problem, *J. Appl. Psychol.*, 76: 796–802.
13. Malpass, R.S. and Devine, P. (1981) Eyewitness Identification: Lineup Instructions and the Absence of the Offender, *J. Appl. Psychol.*, 66: 482–489.
14. Malpass, R.S. and Devine, P. (1984) Research on Suggestions in Lineups and Photospreads, in *Eyewitness Testimony: Psychological Perspectives* (G.L. Wells and E. Loftus, eds), Cambridge: Cambridge University Press.
15. Wells, G., Leippe, M. and Ostrom, T. (1979) Guidelines for Empirically Assessing the Fairness of a Lineup, *Law Hum. Behav.*, 3: 285–293.
16. Buckhout, R. and Freire, V. (1975) Suggestivity in Lineups and Photospreads: A Casebook for Lawyers, *Social Action Law*, 5: 1–26.
17. Cutler, B.L., Penrod, S.D. and Martens, T.K. (1987) The Reliability of Eyewitness Identification: The Role of System and Estimator Variables, *Law Hum. Behav.*, 11: 233–258.
18. Egeth, H.E. (1993) What Do We Not Know About Eyewitness Identification?, *Am. Psychol.*, 48: 577–580.
19. U.S. Dept. of Justice (1999) Eyewitness Evidence, A Guide for Law Enforcement, *TWGEYE Report 178240*, Washington D.C., pp. 44.
20. Yuille, J. (1993) We Must Study Forensic Eyewitnesses to Know About Them, *Am. Psychol.*, 48: 572–573.
21. Broeders, A. and Rietveld, A. (1995) Speaker Identification by Earwitnesses, *Studies Forensic Phonet.*, 64: 24–40.
22. Broeders, A. and van Amelsvoort, A. (1999) Lineup Construction for Forensic Earwitness Identification: A Practical Approach, *Proc. ICPhS99*, San Francisco, 1373–1376.
23. Bull, R. (1978) Eyewitnesses Also Have Ears, in *Practical Aspects of Memory*,

Gruneberg, M., Morris, P. and Sykes, R. (eds) London: Academic Press.

24. Clifford, B.R. (1980) Voice Identification by Human Listeners: On Earwitness Reliability, *Law Hum. Behav.*, 4: 373–394.
25. Clifford, B.R. (1983), Memory for Voices: The Feasibility and Quality of Earwitness Evidence, in *Evaluating Witness Evidence*, (S.M.A. Lloyd-Bostock and B.R. Clifford, eds), New York: Wiley & Sons.
26. Clifford, B.R. and Denot, H. (1982) Visual and Verbal Testimony and Identification Under Conditions of Stress, quoted in Deffenbacher *et al.* (27).
27. Deffenbacher, K., Cross, J., Handkins, R., Chance, J., Goldstein, A., Hammersley, R. and Read, J. (1989) Relevance of Voice Identification Research to Criteria for Evaluating Reliability of an Identification, *J. Psychol.*, 123: 109–119.
28. Mann, V.A., Deamond, R. and Carey, S. (1979) Development of Voice Recognition: Parallels with Face Recognition, *J. Exp. Child Psychol.*, 27: 153–165.
29. Rietveld, A.C.M. and A.P.A. Broeders (1991) Testing the Fairness of Voice Identity Parades: The Similarity Criterion, *Proc. XIIth Int. Congr. Phonetic Sci.*, Aix-en-Provence, 3: 166–169.
30. Yarmey, A.D. (1986) Verbal, Visual and Voice Identification of a Rape Suspect Under Different Levels of Illumination, *J. Appl. Psychol.*, 71: 363–370.
31. Brandt, John F. (1977) Can You Hear Me? *Forensic Comm.*, 2: 9–11.
32. Michel, J. F. (1980) Use of a Voice Lineup, *Abstracts, American Academy Forensic Sci.*, Colorado Springs, 67.
33. Hollien, H. (1990) *The Acoustics of Crime*, New York: Plenum Press.
34. Laubstein, A.S. (1997) Problems of Voice Line-ups, *Forensic Linguistics*, 4: 262–279.
35. Nolan, J.F. (1983) *The Phonetic Basis of Speaker Identification*, Cambridge: Cambridge University Press.
36. Saslove, H. and Yarmey, A. (1980) Long-Term Auditory Memory: Speaker Identification, *J. Appl. Psychol.*, 45: 111–116.
37. Thompson, C. (1985) Voice Identification: Attempted Recovery from a Biased Procedure, *Hum. Learn.*, 4: 213–224.
38. Thompson, C. (1987) A Language Effect in Voice Identification, *Appl. Cogn. Psychol.*, 1: 121–131.
39. Künzel, H. (1994) On the Problem of Speaker Identification by Victims and Witnessess, *Forensic Linguistics*, 1: 45–58.
40. Schlichting, F. and Sullivan, K.P.H. (1997) The Imitated Voice – A Problem for Voice Line-ups?, *Forensic Linguistics*, 4: 148–165.
41. Hollien, H. (1993) Forensic Phonetics, in *The Forensic Sciences*, (C.H. Wecht, ed.), New York: Matthew Bender Co., 2–28B: 1–115.
42. Hollien, H. (1996) Consideration of Guidelines for Earwitness Lineups, *Forensic Linguistics*, 3: 14–23.
43. Hollien, H., Huntley, R., Kuenzel, H. and Hollien, P.A. (1995), Proposal for Earwitness Lineups, *Forensic Linguistics*, 2: 143–153.
44. Huntley, R. and Pass, K. J. (1993) Influences on Listener Performance in a Voice Lineup Procedure, paper presented at the *Int. Assoc. Forensic Phonetics*, Trier, Germany.
45. Huntley, R.A. and Pass, K. (1995) Task Influences on Earwitness Reliability, *Stud.*

Forensic Phonet., 64: 121–131.

46. Komulainen, E.K. (1988) Subjective Voice Identification: The Literal Meaning of 'Talking Yourself Behind Bars,' *Alberta Law Rev.* XXVI: 521–547.
47. Künzel, H. (1996) Presentation to Committee on Earwitness Identification, *Int. Assoc. Forensic Phonetics Congr.*, Orlando, July.
48. Künzel, H.J. (1998) Forensic Speaker Identification: A View from the Crime Lab, *Proc. COST-250 Workshop*, Ankara, 4–8.
49. Mayor, D. and Komulainen, E. (1989) *Subjective Voice Identification*, Calgary: Calgary Police Service, 42.
50. Melara, R. and DeWitt-Richards, T. (1989) Enhancing Lineup Identification Accuracy: Two Codes Are Better Than One, *J. Appl. Psychol.*, 74: 706–713.
51. Nolan, F. and Grabe, E. (1996) Preparing a Voice Lineup, *Forensic Linguistics*, 3: 74–94.
52. van Lancker, D., Kreiman, J., and Cummings, J. (1985) Voice Recognition and Discrimination: New Evidence for a Double Dissociation. *J. Clin Exp. Neuropsychol.*, 7: 609.
53. van Lancker, D. Kreiman, J. and Wickens, T. (1985) Familiar Voice Recognition: Patterns and Parameters, Part I: Recognition of Rate-Altered Voices, *J. Phonet.*, 13: 39–52.
54. van Lancker, D., Kreiman, J. and Emmorey, K. (1985) Familiar Voice Recognition: Patterns and Parameters, Part II: Recognition of Backward Voices, *J. Phonet.*, 13: 19–38.
55. van Lancker, D. and Kreiman, J. (1987) Voice Discrimination and Recognition Are Separate Abilities, *Neurospsychologia*, 25: 829–834.
56. Kreiman, J., Geratt, B. and Precoda, K. (1990) Listener Experience and Perception of Voice Quality, *J. Speech Hear. Res.*, 3: 103–115.
57. Bull, R. and Clifford, B.R. (1984) Earwitness Voice Recognition Accuracy, in *Eyewitness Testimony: Psychological Perspectives*, (G.L. Wells and E. Loftus, eds), Cambridge: Cambridge University Press.
58. Hollien, H., Bennett, G.T. and Gelfer, M.P. (1983) Criminal Identification Comparison: Aural/Visual Identifications Resulting from a Simulated Crime, *J. Forensic Sci.*, 28: 208–221.
59. Malpass, R.S. and Devine, P. (1983) Measuring the Fairness of Eyewitness Identification Lineups. in *Evaluating Witness Evidence* (S. Lloyd-Bostock and B. Clifford, eds), Chichester: Wiley.
60. Warnick, D. and Sanders, G. (1980) Why Do Eyewitnesses Make So Many Mistakes? *J. Appl. Soc. Psychol.*, 10: 362–366.
61. Milroy, J. (1984) Sociolinguistic Methodology and the Identification of Speakers' Voices in Legal Proceedings, in *Applied Sociolinguistics*, (Trudgill, P. ed.), London: Academic Press.
62. Bricker, P. and Pruzansky, S. (1966) Effects of Stimulus Content and Duration on Talker Identification, *J. Acoust. Soc. Am.*, 40: 1441–1449.
63. LaRiviere, C.L. (1972) Some Acoustic and Perceptual Correlates of Speaker Identification, *Proc. 7th Intern. Congr. Phonetic Sci.*, 558–564.

64. Orchard, T. and Yarmey, A. (1995) The Effects of Whispers, Voice-Sample Duration and Voice Distinctiveness on Criminal Speaker Identification, *Appl. Cogn. Psychol.*, 9: 249–260.

65. Yarmey, A.D. and Matthys, E. (1992) Voice Identification of an Abductor, *Appl. Cogn. Psychol.*, 6: 367–377.

66. Pollack, I., Pickett, J.M. and Sumby, W.H. (1954) On the Identification of Speakers by Voice, *J. Acoust. Soc. Am.*, 26: 403–406.

67. Compton, A.J. (1963) Effects of Filtering and Vocal Duration Upon the Identification of Speakers Aurally, *J. Acoust. Soc. Am.*, 35: 1748–1752.

68. Cort, S. and Murry, T. (1972) Aural Identification of Children's Voices, *J. Acoust. Soc. Am.*, 51: S131, (A).

69. Yarmey, A.D. (1995) Earwitness and Evidence Obtained by Other Sciences, in *Handbook of Psychology in Legal Contexts,* (R. Bull and D. Carson, eds) New York: John Wiley and Sons, 261–273.

70. Künzel, H. (1990) Phonetische Untersuchungen zur Sprechererkennung Durch Linguische Naive Personen, *ZDL Beiheft* 69, Stuttgart: Steiner Verlag.

71. Nerbonne, G. (1967) The Identification of Speaker Characteristics on the Basis of Aural Cues, Ph.D. thesis, Michigan State University.

72. Ney, H., Gierloff, R. and Frehse, R. (1981) An Automatic System for Verification of Cooperative Speakers Via Telephone, *Proc. Carnahan Crime Center. Congr.*, Lexington, KY.

73. Rothman, H.B. (1977) A Perceptual (Aural) and Spectrographic Identification of Talkers with Similar Sounding Voices, *Proc. Intern. Conf. Crime Countermeasures*, Oxford, 37–42.

74. Yarmey, A.D. (1991) Voice Identification Over the Telephone, *J. Appl. Social Psychol.*, 21: 1868–1876.

75. Yarmey, A.D. (1994) Earwitness Evidence: Memory for a Perpetrators Voice, in *Adult Eyewitness Testimony* (D. Ross, J. Read and M. Toglia, eds), New York: Cambridge University Press, 101–124.

76. Carbonell, J.R., Stevens, K.N., Williams, C.E. and Woods, B. (1965) Speaker Identification by a Matching-From-Samples Technique, *J. Acoust. Soc. Am.*, 40: 1205–1206.

77. Clifford, B. and Bull, R. (1978) *The Psychology of Person Identification,* London: Routledge and Kegan Paul, (Chapters 5 and 8).

78. Huntley, R.A., Hollien, H. and Shipp, T. (1987) Influences of Listener Characteristics on Perceived Age, *J. Voice,* 1: 49–52.

79. Papcun, G., Kreiman, J., and Davis, A. (1989) Long-Term Memory for Unfamiliar Voices. *J. Acoust. Soc. Am.*, 85: 913–925.

80. Rathborn, H.A., Bull, R. and Clifford, B. (1981) Voice Recognition Over the Telephone, *J. Police Sci. Admin.*, 9: 280–284.

81. Roebuck, R. and Wilding, J. (1993) Effects of Vowel Variety and Sample Length on Identification of a Speaker in a Line-up, *Appl. Cogn. Psychol.*, 7: 475–481.

82. Stevens, K.N., Williams, C.E., Carbonell, J.R. and Woods, D. (1968) Speaker Authentication and Identification: A Comparison of Spectrographic and Auditory

Presentation of Speech Materials, *J. Acoust. Soc. Am.*, 44: 1596–1607.

83. Stuntz, A.E. (1963) Speech Intelligibility and Talker Recognition Tests of Air Force Communication Systems, *Report ESP-TDR-63–224*, Hanscom Field, MA: Electronic Systems Division, Air Force Systems Command.
84. Williams, C.E. (1964) The Effects of Selected Factors on the Aural Identification of Speakers, *Tech. Doc. Opt. ESD-TDR-65–153*, Hanscom Field, MA: Electron. Sst. Div., USAF.
85. Yarmey, A.D. (1993) Stereotypes and Recognition Memory for Faces and Voices of Good Guys and Bad Guys, *Appl. Cogn. Psychol.*, 7: 419–431.
86. Broeders, A.P.A. (1996) Earwitness Identification: Common Ground, Disputed Territory and Uncharted Areas, *Forensic Linguistics*, 3: 1–13.
87. Hollien, H. and Schwartz, R. (2000) Aural-Perceptual Speaker Identification: Problems with Noncontemporary Samples, *Forensic Linguistics,* 7: 199–211.
88. Hollien, H. and Schwartz, R. (2001) Speaker Identification Using Noncontemporary Speech, *J. Forensic Sci.*, 46: 63–67.
89. Handkins, R. and Cross, J. (1991) Voice Similarity: Its Measurement and Its Effects on Lineup Fairness, thesis, St Louis University.
90. Aarts, N.W. (1984) The Effect of Listener Stress on Perceptual Speaker Identification, MA Thesis, University of Florida.
91. Atwood, W. and Hollien, H. (1986) Stress Monitoring by Polygraphy for Research Purposes, *Polygraph*, 15: 47–56.
92. Rosenberg, A.E. (1973) Listener Performance in Speaker Verification Tasks, *IEEE Trans. Audio Electroacoust.*, AU-21: 221–225.
93. Endress, W., Bambach, W. and Flosser, G. (1971) Voice Spectrograms as a Function of Age, Voice Disguise and Voice Imitation, *J. Acoust. Soc. Am.*, 49: 1842–1848.
94. Hecker, M.H.L., Stevens, K.N., von Bismarck, G. and Williams, C.E. (1968) Manifestations of Task-induced Stress in the Acoustic Speech Signal, *J. Acoust. Soc. Am.*, 44: 993–1001.
95. Hicks, J.W., Jr. and Hollien, H. (1981) The Reflection of Stress in Voice-1: Understanding the Basic Correlates, *Proc. Carnahan Conf. Crime Countermeasures,* Lexington, KY, 189–194.
96. Scherer, K.R. (1981) Vocal Indicators of Stress, in *Speech Evaluation in Psychiatry*. (J. Darby, ed.) New York: Grune and Stratton.
97. Scherer, K.R. (1986) Voice, Stress and Emotion, in *Dynamics of Stress: Physiological, Psychological and Social Perspectives,* (H. Appley and R. Trumbull, eds), New York: Plenum Press, 157–179.
98. Hecker, M.H.L. (1971) *Speaker Recognition: An Interpretive Survey of the Literature,* ASHA, Monograph 16, Washington, D.C.
99. Hollien, H., Majewski, W. and Doherty, E.T. (1982) Perceptual Identification of Voices Under Normal, Stressed and Disguised Speaking Conditions, *J. Phonet.*, 10: 139–148.
100. Manning, W.H. and Hollien, P.A. (1992) Effects of a Voice Disguise Device, *Abstr., Am. Acad. Forensic Sci.*, New Orleans, 108(A).

101. McGlone, R.E., Hollien, P.A. and Hollien, H. (1977) Acoustic Analysis of Voice Disguise Related to Voice Identification, *Proc. Int. Conf. on Crime Countermeasures*, Oxford, 31–35.

102. Reich, A.R. and Duke, J.E. (1979) Effects of Selected Vocal Disguise Upon Speaker Identification By Listening, *J. Acoust. Soc. Am.*, 66: 1023–1028.

103. Reich, A.R. (1981) Detecting the Presence of Vocal Disguise in the Male Voice, *J. Acoust. Soc. Am.*, 69: 1458–1461.

104. Hollien, P.A. (1992) Procedures for Conducting Exemplar Interviews, *Report 92.04*, Gainesville, FL: Forensic Communication Associates, 1–6.

105. DeJong, G. (1998) Earwitness Characteristics and Speaker Identification Accuracy, Ph.D. dissertation, University of Florida, Gainesville, FL.

106. DeJong, G. (1996) Speaker Identification Accuracy and Earwitness Characteristics, Paper read at the *1996 Annual Congr. IAFP*, Wiesbaden.

107. Huntley, R.A. (1992) Listener Skill in Voice Identification, *Am. Acad. Forensic Sci.*, New Orleans, 105(A).

108. Köster, J.P. (1981) Auditive Sprechererkennung bei Experten und Naiven, in *Festschrift Wangler*, Hamburg, Helmut Buske, AG 52: 171–180.

109. Schiller, N. and Köster, O. (1998) The Ability of Expert Witnesses to Identify Voices, *Forensic Linguistics*, 5: 1–9.

110. Shirt, M. (1984) An Auditory Speaker-Recognition Experiment, *Proc. Inst. Acoust. Conf. Speech and Tape Recording Analysis*, London, 21–24.

111. Bartholomeus, B. (1973) Voice Identification by Nursery School Children, *Can. J. Psychol.*, 27: 464–472.

112. Bull, R., Rathborn, H. and Clifford, B. (1983) The Voice Recognition Accuracy of Blind Listeners, *Perception*, 12: 223–226.

113. Coleman, R.O. (1973) Speaker Identification in the Absence of Intersubject Differences in Glottal Source Characteristics, *J. Acoust. Soc. Am.*, 53: 1741–1743.

114. Hollien, H. and Thompson, C.L. (1990) Effects of Listening Experience on Decoding Speech in HeO_2 Environments, *Diving for Science* 1990 (W.C. Jaap, ed.), San Diego, 179–191.

115. Skalbeck, G.A. (1955) An Experimental Study of Several Factors in Speaker Recognition, MA thesis, University of Washington.

116. Thompson, C. (1985) Voice Identification: Speaker Identifiability and Correction of the Record Regarding Sex Effects, *Hum. Learn.*, 4: 19–27.

117. Goldstein, A., Knight, P., Bailus, K. and Conover, J. (1981) Recognition Memory for Accented and Unaccented Voices, *Bull. Psychonom. Soc.*, 17: 217–220.

118. Wretling, P., Sullivan, K. and Schlichting, F. (1999) Does Repeated Exposure to a Target Voice Reduce the Impact of a Similar Voice?, *Proc. ICPhS99*, San Francisco, 1385–1388.

119. Carterette, E. and Barnebey, A. (1975) Recognition Memory for Voices, in *Structure and Process in Perception*, (A. Cohen and S. Nootenoom, eds), New York: Springer-Verlag.

120. McGehee, F. (1937) The Reliability of the Identification of the Human Voice, *J. Gen. Psychol.*, 17: 249–271.

121. McGehee, F. (1944) An Experimental Study in Voice Recognition, *J. Gen. Psychol..*, 31: 53–65.

122. Wixted, J. and Ebbssen, E. (1991) On the Form of Forgetting, *Psycholog. Sci.*, 2: 409–415.

123. Clifford, B., Rathborn, H. and Bull, R. (1981) The Effects of Delay on Voice Recognition Accuracy, *Law Hum. Behav.*, 5: 201–208.

Further Reading

Clifford, B. (1983) Memory for Voices: The Feasibility and Quality of Earwitness Evidence, in *Evaluation Witness Evidence*, (S. Lloyd-Bostock and B. Clifford, eds), New York: Wiley and Sons.

Hammersley, R.H. and Read, J.D. (1983) Testing Witness' Voice Recognition: Some Practical Recommendations, *J. Forensic Sci. Soc.*, 23, 203–208.

Lamel, L. and Gauvain, J. (1998) Speaker Verification Over the Telephone, *RLA2C*, Avignon, 76–79.

Wagenaar, W.A. (1988) *Identifying Ivan: A Case Study in Legal Psychology*, London: Harvester/Wheatsheaf.

CHAPTER 6

References

1. Koenig, B.E. (1986) Spectrographic Voice Identification: A Forensic Survey, (Letter to the Editor) *J. Acoust. Soc. Am.*, 79: 2088–90.
2. Potter, R. (1945) Visible Patterns of Speech, *Science*, November, 463–470.
3. Gray, C. and Kopp, G. (1944) Voiceprint Identification, *Bell Tel. Lab. Rep.*, 1–14.
4. Potter, R., Kopp, G. and Green, H. (1947) *Visible Speech*, New York: Van Nostrand.
5. Kersta, L.G. (1962) Voiceprint Identification, *Nature*, 196: 1253–1257.
6. Kersta, L.G. (no date) *Instruction Manual/Procedure for Voiceprint Examinations*, Somerville, NJ: Voiceprint Laboratory.
7. Nash, E. (1973) Testimony in People (California) vs. Lawton, Gardener and Jackson, Superior Court, Riverside County, Case No. Cr. 9138.
8. Nash, E. (1973) Testimony in People (California) vs. Chapter, Case No. 4516, Superior Court, Marin County, Findings and Decision.
9. Smrkovski, L. (1976). Testimony in Crown *vs* Medvedew (1976), Provincial Judges Court (Criminal Division) Brandon, Manitoba, Canada.
10. Truby, H. (1976) 'Voiceprinting'. A Critical Review. Brief sent to California Supreme Court relative to People vs. Kelley, (Superior Court No. C-29579).
11. Bolt, R.H., Cooper, F.S., David, E.C., Denes, P.B., Pickett, J.M. and Stevens, K.N. (1970) Speaker Identification by Speech Spectrograms, *J. Acoust. Soc. Am.*, 47: 597–613.
12. Bolt, R.H., Cooper, F.S., David, E.C., Denes, P.B., Pickett, J.M. and Stevens, K.N. (1973) Speaker Identification by Speech Spectrograms: Some Further Observations, *J. Acoust. Soc. Am.*, 54: 531–534.
13. Bolt, R.H., Cooper, F.S., Green, D.M., Hamlet, S.L., Hogan, D.L., McKnight, J.G.,

Pickett, J.M., Tosi, O. and Underwood, B.D. (1979) *On the Theory and Practice of Voice Identification*, Washington, D.C.: National Academy of Sciences.

14. Hollien, H. (1971) The Peculiar Case of 'Voiceprints'. *J. Acoust. Soc. Am.,* 56: 210–213.
15. Hollien, H. (1977) Status Report on 'Voiceprint' Identification in the United States, *Proc. Int. Conf. Crime Countermeasures*, Oxford, 9–20.
16. Hollien, H. (1990) *Acoustics of Crime*, New York: Plenum.
17. Künzel, H.J. (1991) Field Procedures in Forensic Speaker Identification, *Proc. 12th Int. Congr. Phonetic Sci.*, Aix en Provence.
18. Ladefoged, P. and Vanderslice, R. (1967) The 'Voiceprint' Mystique, *UCLA Working Papers in Phonetics,* 126–142.
19. Nolan, J.F. (1983) *The Phonetic Basis of Speaker Recognition,* Cambridge: University Press.
20. Tosi, O., Oyer, H.J., Lashbrook, W., Pedrey, C., Nichol, J. and Nash, W. (1972) Experiment on Voice Identification, *J. Acoust. Soc. Am.,* 51: 2030–2043.
21. Tosi, O. (1979) *Voice Identification: Theory and Legal Applications*, Baltimore, MD: University Park Press.
22. Hollien, H. and Schwartz, R. (2001) Speaker Identification Utilizing Noncontemporary Speech, *J. Forensic Sci.*, 46: 63–67.
23. Hennessy, J.J. (1970) An Analog of Voiceprint Identification, M.A. Thesis, Michigan State University.
24. Hall, M. (1975) Spectrographic Analysis of Interspeaker and Intraspeaker Variabilities of Professional Mimicry, unpublished M.A. Thesis, Michigan State University.
25. Hollien, H. (1988) Voice Recognition, in *Nouvelles Technologies et Justice Penale,* 9: 180–229.
26. Koenig, B.E., Ritenour, D.S., Kohus, B.A., and Keyy, A.S. (1987) Reply to Some Fundamental Considerations Regarding Voice Identifications (Letter-to-the-Editor), *J. Acoust. Soc. Am.*, 82: 688–689.
27. Shipp, T., Doherty, E.T. and Hollien, H. (1987) Some Fundamental Considerations Regarding Voice Identification (Letter-to-the-Editor), *J. Acoust. Soc. Am.*, 82: 687–688.
28. Anonymous (1995) The Voiceprint Dilemma: Should Voices Be Seen and Not Heard, *Maryland Law Rev.*, 35: 267–296.
29. Stevens, K.N., Carbonell, J.R. and Woods, B. (1968) Speaker Authentication and Identification: A Comparison of Spectrographic and Auditory Presentations of Speech Material., *J. Acoust. Soc. Am.*, 44: 1596–1607.
30. Young, M.A. and Campbell, R.A. (1967) Effects of Context on Talker Identification, *J. Acoust. Soc. Am.,* 42: 1250–1254.
31. Hazen, B.M. (1973) Effects of Differing Phonetic Contexts on Spectrographic Speaker Identification, *J. Acoust. Soc. Am.,* 54: 650–660.
32. Obrecht, D.H. (1975) Fingerprints and Voiceprint Identification, *Abstracts, Eighth Int. Congr. Phonetic Sci.,* Leeds, 215.
33. Endress, W., Bambach, W. and Flosser, G. (1971) Voice Spectrograms as a

Function of Age, Voice Disguise and Voice Imitation, *J. Acoust. Soc Am.*, 49: 1842–1848.

34. Hollien, H., Majewski, W. and Doherty, E.T. (1982) Perceptual Identification of Voices Under Normal, Stressed and Disguised Speaking Conditions, *J. Phonet.*, 10: 139–148.
35. Hollien, H. and McGlone, R.E. (1976) An Evaluation of the 'Voiceprint' Technique of Speaker Recognition, *Proc. Carnahan Conf. Crime Countermeasures*, 30–45, 1976; reprinted in *Natl J. Crim. Def.*, 2, 117–130, 1976 and in *Course Handbook*, The Instit. Contin Legal eds, Ann Arbor, Michigan, 391–404.
36. Reich, A.R., Moll, K.L. and Curtis, J.F. (1976) Effects of Selected Vocal Disguises Upon Spectrographic Speaker Identification, *J. Acoust. Soc. Am.*, 60: 919–925.
37. Rothman, H.B. (1977) A Perceptual (Aural) and Spectrographic Identification of Talkers with Similar Sounding Voices, *Proc. Intern. Conf. Crime Countermeasures*, Oxford, 37–42.
38. Carbonell, J.R., Stevens, K.N., Williams, C.E. and Woods, B. (1965) Speaker Identification by a Matching-From-Samples Technique, *J. Acoust. Soc. Am.*, 40: 1205–1206.
39. Houlihan, K. (1979) The Effects of Disguise on Speaker Identification from Sound Spectrograms, in *Current Issues in the Phonetic Sciences*, (H. and P.A. Hollien, eds), Amsterdam: J. Benjamins, B.V., 811–820.
40. Stevens, K.N. (1971) Sources of Inter- and Intra-Speaker Variability in the Acoustic Properties of Speech Sounds, *Proc. 7th Int. Cons. Phonetic Sci.*, Montreal, 206–232.
41. Hecker, M.H.L. (1971) *Speaker Recognition: An Interpretive Survey of the Literature*, ASHA, Monograph 16, Washington, D.C.
42. Huntley, R.A. (1992) Listener Skill in Voice Identification, *Am. Acad. Forensic Sci.*, New Orleans, 105(A).
43. Köster, J.P. (1981) Auditive Sprechererkennung bei Experten und Naiven, in *Festschrift Wangler*, Hamburg: Helmut Buske, AG 52: 171–180.
44. Reich, A.R. and Duke, J.E. (1979) Effects of Selected Vocal Disguise Upon Speaker Identification By Listening, *J. Acoust. Soc. Am.*, 66: 1023–1028.
45. Shirt, M. (1984) An Auditory Speaker Recognition Experiment, *Proc. Instit. Acoust. Part 1, Police Appl. Speech, Tape Record. Analysis*, London, 71–74.
46. Williams, C.E. (1964) The Effects of Selected Factors on the Aural Identification of Speakers, *Tech. Doc. Opt., ESD-TDR-65–153*, Hanscom Field, MA: Elect. Syst. Div., USAF.
47. Black, J.W., Lashbrook, W., Nash, W., Oyer, H.J., Pedrey, C., Tosi, O. and Truby, H. (1973) Reply to Speaker Identification by Speech Spectrograms: Some Further Observations, *J. Acoust. Soc. Am.*, 54: 535–537.
48. McGlone, R.E., Hollien, P.A. and Hollien, H. (1977) Acoustic Analysis of Voice Disguise Related to Voice Identification, *Proc. Int. Conf. on Crime Countermeasures*, Oxford, 31–35.
49. People (California) vs. Lawten, Gardener and Jackson, (1973) Superior Court, Riverside County, Case No. Cr. 9138 (transcript of testimony).
50. People (California) vs. Chapter (1973) Case No. 4516, Superior Court, Marin Co.,

Findings and Decisions, July.

51. Michigan vs Chaisson (1974) Ingham County Circuit Court, East Lansing, MI, Case No. 73246756-FY.

CHAPTER 7

References

1. Jiang, M. (1995) Experiments on a Speaker Identification System. Ph.D. dissertation, University of Florida.
2. Hecker, M. (1971) *Speaker Recognition: An Interpretive Study of the Literature*, ASHA Monographs 16, Washington, DC.
3. Minnesota vs. Stephani (1984) Testimony in Superior Court, Minneapolis, MN.
4. Anonymous (1976) Semi-Automatic Speaker Identification System (SAUSIS), Final Report, *Report-No. C76–96–501*, Anaheim, CA: Rockwell Int.
5. Anonymous (1977) Speaker Identification Program, Final Report, No. NATR-77 *(7617–08)-l*, El Sequendo, CA: The Aerospace Corp.
6. Becker, R., Clarke, F., Poza, F. and Young, J. (1972) A Semiautomatic Speaker Recognition System, *SRI Report 71–078-G* to LEAA US Dept. Justice, 1–37.
7. Edie, J. and Sebestyen, G.S. (1972) Voice Identification General Criteria, *Report RADC -TDR-62–278*, Griffis AFB, NY: Rome Air Develp. Ctr., Air Force Systems Command.
8. Floyd, W. (1964) Voice Identification Techniques, *Report RADC-TDR-64–312*, Air Force Systems Command, Griffis AFB, New York.
9. Hair, G. and Rekieta, T. (1972) *Final Report*, Dallas, TX: Texas Instruments Inc.
10. Hair, G.D. and Rekieta, T.W. (1973) *Speaker Identification Research*, US Dept. of Justice, LEAA, Washington, DC, 38–74.
11. Rennick, R. (1974) Semi-Automatic Speaker Identification System (SASIS) *Report C74–1185/501*. Rockwell International Corporation.
12. Sambur, M.R. (1975) Selection of Acoustic Features for Speaker Identification, *IEEE Trans. CASSP*, ASSP-23: 176–192.
13. Stuntz, A.E. (1963) Speech Intelligibility and Talker Recognition Tests of Air Force Communication Systems, *Report ESP-TDR-63–224*, Hanscom Field, MA: Air Force Systems Command.
14. Anonymous (1970) Summary Reviews of Procedures for Speaker Recognition, *SSRC Report*, Menlo Park, CA: Stanford Pres. Inst.
15. Broderick, P.K., Paul, J.E. and Rennick, R.E., (1975) Semi-Automatic Speaker Identification System, *Proc. 1975, Carnahan Conf. Crime Countermeasures*, Lexington, KY.
16. Bunge, E. (1977) Automatic Speaker Recognition System Auros for Security Systems and Forensic Voice Identification, *Proc. Int. Conf. Crime Countermeasures.*, Oxford, 1–8.
17. Dean, J.D. (1980) The Work of the Home Office Tape Laboratory, *Police Research Bull.*, 35: 25–27.
18. Jassem, W., Steffen-Batog, M. and Czajka, S. (1973) Statistical Characteristics of

Short-Term Average FO Distribution as Personal Voice Features, *Speech Analysis Synth.* 3: 209–228.

19. Künzel, H.J. (1987) *Spechererkennung,* Heidelberg: Kriminalistik.
20. Nolan, J.F. (1983) *The Phonetic Basis of Speaker Recognition,* Cambridge: Cambridge University Press.
21. Wolf, J.J. (1972) Efficient Acoustic Parameters for Speaker Recognition, *J. Acoust. Soc. Am.,* 51: 2044–2055.
22. Gish, H., Kanofsky, M., Krasner, M., Roucos, S. Schwartz, R. and Wolf, J. (1985) Investigation of Text-independent Speaker Identification Over Telephone Channels, *Proc. ICASSP-85,* 379–382.
23. Krasner, M., Wolf, J., Karnofsky, K., Schwartz, R., Roucos, S. and Gish, H. (1984) Investigators of Text-independent Speaker Identification Techniques Under Conditions of Variable Data, *Proc. ICASSP-84,* 1813: 1–4.
24. Schwartz, R., Roncos, S. and Berouti, M. (1982) The Application of Probability Density Estimation to Text-independent Speaker Identification, *Proc. ICASSP,* 1649–1652.
25. Wolf, J., Krasner, M., Karnofsky, K., Schwartz, R. and Roucos, S. (1983) Further Investigation of Probalistic Methods for Text-independent Speaker Identification, *Proc. ICASSP-83,* 551–554.
26. Hunt, M., Yates, J. and Bridle, J. (1977) Automatic Speaker Recognition for Use Over Communication Channels, *Proc., ICASSP-77,* 410–413.
27. Hattori, H. (1992) Text Independent Speaker Recognition Using Neural Networks, *Proc. ICASSP-92,* 2: 153–156.
28. Matsui, T. and Furui, S. (1992) Comparison of Text-independent Speaker Recognition Using VQ-Distortion and Discrete/Continuous HMM's, *Proc., ICASSP-92,* 2: 157–160.
29. Soong, F., Rosenburg, A., Rabiner, L. and Juang, B. (1985) A Vector Quantization Approach to Speaker Recognition., *Proc. ICASSP-85,* 387–390.
30. Tseng, B., Soong, F. and Rosenburg, A. (1992) Continuous Probablistic Acoustic Map for Speaker Identification, *Proc., ICASSP-92,* 1: 161–164.
31. Webb, J. and Rissanen, E. (1993) Speaker Identification Experiments Using HMM's, *Proc., ICASSP-93,* 2: 387–390.
32. Broeders, A. (1995) The Role of Automatic Speaker Recognition Techniques in Forensic Investigations, *Proc. Int. Congr. Phonet. Sci.,* 3: 154–161.
33. Fredouille, C. and Bonastre, J.F. (1998) Use of Dynamic Information and Second Order Statistical Methods in Speaker Identification, *RLA2C,* Avignon 3: 50–54.
34. Koval, S. and Krynov, S. (1998) Practice of Usage of Spectral Analysis for Forensic Speaker Identification, *RLA2C,* Avignon 8: 136–140.
35. Künzel, H. (1995) Field Procedures in Forensic Speaker Recognition, in *Essays in Honour of Professor J.D. O'Connor* (J.W. Lewis, ed.) London: Routledge, 68–84.
36. Onellet, P., Tadj, C. and Dumouchel, J-P. (1998) Dialog and Prosodic Models for Text-independent Speaker Identification, *RLAZC,* Avignon 2: 41–44.
37. Klevans, R. and Rodman, R. (1997) *Voice Recognition,* Boston: Artech House Inc.
38. Lauretta, D. and Rodman, R. (1987) Comparison of Speech Perception by

Humans and by a Voice Recognizer, *Proc. Voice Input-Output Conf.*, San Jose, CA, 267–282.
39. Rodman, R. (1988) Linguistics and Computer Speech Recognition, in *Language, Speech, Mind* (Hyman L. and Li, C. eds) New York: Routledge, 269–294.
40. Rodman, R. (1998) Speaker Recognition of Disguised Voices, *Proc. Conf. Speaker Recognition*, Ankara, 9–22.
41. Rodman, R. (1998) Semi-automatic Speaker Recognition of Disguised Voices, Invited paper presented at the *Am. Acad. Forensic Sci.*, Orlando, FL, February.
42. Rodman, R., Joost, M. and Kim, K-H. (1985) Error Detection and Correction in Voice Recognition Systems, *Tech. Report TR-IMSEI-013–85–1*, IMSEI Institute: NC State Univ.
43. Barycki, W., Basztura, C. and Majewski, W. (1989) Effectiveness of Selected Voice Features in Speaker Identification Procedures for Open Sets, *Proc. Open Seminar in Acoustics OSA-89*, Szczyrk-Bila, 123–130 (in Polish).
44. Basztura, C.S. (1991) Experiments of Automatic Speaker Recognition in Open Sets, *Speech Commun.*, 10: 117–127.
45. Basztura, C.S. and Majewski, W. (1978) The Application of Long-Term Analysis of the Zero-Crossing of a Speech Signal in Automatic Speaker Identification, *Arch. Acoust.*, 3: 3–15.
46. Basztura, C. and Majewski, W. (1981) The Effect of Chosen Parameters of a Telephone Channel or Voice Identification, *Arch. Acoustics*, 6: 359–370.
47. Basztura, C., Majewski, W. and Jurkiewicz, J. (1988) Automatic Voice Recognition in Open Sets, *Arch. Acoust*, 13: 205–218.
48. Majewski, W. and Hollien, H. (1974) Euclidean Distance Between Long-term Speech Spectra as a Criterion for Speaker Identification, *Proc. Speech Comm. Seminar*, Stockholm, 303–310.
49. Majewski, W. (1993) Automatic and Aural-perceptual Speaker Verification in the Presence of Masking Noise, *Proc. Open Seminar Acoustics*, OSA 93, Rzeszow-Polanczyk, 301–304 (in Polish).
50. Majewski, W. and Basztura, C. (1996) Integrated Approach to Speaker Recognition in Forensic Applications, *Forensic Linguistics*, 3: 50–64.
51. Zalewski, J., Majewski, W. and Hollien, H. (1975) Cross Correlation of Long-term Speech Spectra as a Speaker Identification Technique, *Acustica*, 34: 20–24.
52. Gish, H. and Schmidt, M. (1994) Text-independent Speaker Identification, *IEEE Signal Processing Magazine*, October 18–32.

CHAPTER 8

References

1. Hollien, H. and Hollien, P.A. (1972) A Cross-Cultural Study of Adolescent Voice Change in European Males, *Proc. Seventh Int. Congr. Phonetic Sciences*, Mouton, 332–337.
2. Hollien, H. and Malcik, E. (1967) Evaluation of Cross-Sectional Studies of Adolescent Voice Change in Males, *Speech Monogr.*, 34: 80–84.

3. Hollien, H. and Paul, P.A. (1969) A Second Evaluation of the Speaking Fundamental Frequency Characteristics of Post-Adolescent Girls, *Lang. Speech,* 12: 119–124.
4. Hollien, H. and Shipp, T. (1972) Speaking Fundamental Frequency and Chronologic Age in Males, *J. Speech Hear. Res.,* 15: 155–159.
5. McGlone, R.E. and Hollien, H. (1963) Vocal Pitch Characteristics of Aged Women, *J. Speech Hear. Res.*, 6: 164–170.
6. Shipp, T. and Hollien, H. (1969) Perception of the Aging Male Voice, *J. Speech Hear. Res.*, 12: 704–710.
7. Brown, W.S., Jr., Morris, R.J., Hollien, H. and Howell, E. (1991) Speaking Fundamental Frequency Characteristics as a Function of Age and Professional Singing, *J. Voice*, 5: 310–315.
8. de Pinto, O. and Hollien, H. (1982) Speaking Fundamental Frequency Characteristics of Australian Women: Then and Now, *J. Phonet.*, 10: 367–376.
9. Hollien, H., Green, R. and Massey, K. (1994) Longitudinal Research on Adolescent Voice Change in Males, *J. Acoust. Soc. Am.*, 96: 2646–2654.
10. Hollien, H. and Jackson, B. (1973) Normative Data on Speaking Fundamental Frequency Characteristics of Young Adult Males, *J. Phonet.*, 1: 117–120.
11. Hollien, H. and Tolhurst, G.C. (1978) The Aging Voice, Trans. 7th Symp., Care Prof. Voice, (V. Lawrence and B. Wienberg, eds) New York: The Voice Foundation, 2: 67–73.
12. Huntley, R., Hollien, H. and Shipp, T. (1987) Influences of Listener Characteristics on Perceived Age, *J. Voice*, 1: 49–52.
13. Shipp, T., Qi, Y., Huntley, R. and Hollien, H. (1992) Acoustic and Temporal Correlates of Perceived Age, *J. Voice*, 6: 211–216.
14. Dew, D. and Hollien, H. (1968) The Effect of Inflection on Vowel Intelligibility, *Speech Monogr.*, 35: 175–180.
15. Hollien, H., Coleman, R.F. and Rothman, H.B. (1970) Further Evaluation of Diver Communication Systems, *Proc. IEEE, Inter. Conf. Eng. in Ocean Environ.*, 1: 34–36.
16. Hollien, H., Coleman, R.F. and Rothman, H.B. (1971) Evaluation of Diver Communication Systems by a Diver-to-Diver Technique, *IEEE Trans. Communication Technol.*, 19: 403–409.
17. Hollien, H., Thompson, C.L. and Cannon, B. (1973) Speech Intelligibility as a Function of Ambient Pressure and HeO_2 Atmosphere, *Aerospace Med.*, 44: 249–253.
18. Thompson, C.L. and Hollien, H. (1970) Some Contextual Effects on the Perception of Synthetic Vowels, *Lang. Speech,* 13: 1–13.
19. Coleman, R.F. and Hollien, H. (1975) Standardization of Speech Materials for Underwater Research: Comparative Intelligibility of Monosyllabic Word Lists, *J. Phonet.*, 3: 9–16.
20. Gelfand, R., Rothman, H.B., Hollien, H. and Lambertsen, C.J. (1978) Speech Generation and Distortion, in *Predictive Studies IV* (C.J. Lambertsen, R. Gelfand and J.M. Clark, eds), Philadelphia, IEM, Univ. Penn., E9: 1–15.
21. Hollien, H. (1992) Speech Intelligibility in Protective Masks, *ESCA, Speech Process.*

Adverse Cond., 61–64

22. Hollien, H., Bishop, J., Huntley-Bahr, R. and Gelfer, M.P. (1999) Near-field Speech Intelligibility in CBW Masks, *Military Med.*, 164: 543–550.
23. Hollien, H. and Fitzgerald, J.T. (1977) Speech Enhancement Techniques for Crime Lab Use, *Proc. Int. Conf. Crime Countermeas., Science Engin.*, Oxford, UK, 21–29.
24. Hollien, H., Gelfer, M.P. and Carlson, T. (1991) Listening Preferences of Voice Types as a Function of Age, *J. Commun. Disord.*, 24: 157–171.
25. Hollien, H. and Thompson, C.L. (1990) Effects of Listening Experience on Decoding Speech in HeO_2 Environments, *Diving for Science* 1990, (W.C. Jaap, ed.) 179–191.
26. Atwood, W. and Hollien, H. (1986) Stress Monitoring by Polygraph for Research Purposes, Polygraph, 15: 47–56.
27. Hicks, J.W., Jr. and Hollien, H. (1981) The Reflection of Stress in Voice-1: Understanding the Basic Correlates, *Proc. Carnahan Conf. Crime Countermeas.*, Lexington, KY, 189–194.
28. Hollien, H. (1980) Vocal Indicators of Psychological Stress, in *Forensic Psychology and Psychiatry*, (F. Wright, C. Bahn and R.W. Rieber, eds), New York: New York Academy Sciences, 47–72.
29. Hollien, H. (1981) Acoustic Analysis of Psychological Stress, Trans., *10th Symp. Care Profess. Voice*, (V. Lawrence, ed.), New York: The Voice Foundation, 145–158.
30. Hollien, H. and Darby, J.K. (1979) Acoustic Comparisons of Psychotic and Non-Psychotic Voices, Current Issues in the Phonetic Sciences, (H. and P. Hollien, eds), Amsterdam: John Benjamins, B.V., 609–614.
31. Hollien, H., Geisson, L. and Hicks, J.W. Jr. (1987) Voice Stress Evaluators and Lie Detection, *J. Forensic Sci.*, 32: 405–418.
32. Hollien, H., Saletto, J.A. and Miller, S.K. (1993) Psychological Stress in Voice: A New Approach, *Studia Phonet. Posnaniensia*, 4: 5–17.
33. Talavera, J.A., Hollien, H. and Tingle, D. (1986) Computer Aided Diagnosis of Depression and Dichotic Listening, *IEEE Conf. Engineer, Med. Biology*, CH2368: 789–791.
34. Hollien, H., Hicks, J.W. Jr., Aarts, N. and Thomas, N. (1984) Acoustic Signatures of Handgun Firings: A Case Study, *Proc. Inst. Acoustics, Part 1: Police Applications, Speech and Tape Recording Analysis*, London, 6: 37–42.
35. Hollien, H. and Hollien, K.A. (1994) Acoustic Patterning of Small-Arms Gunfire, *AFTE J.* 26: 41–49.
36. Hollien, H. (1993) An Oil Spill, Alcohol and the Captain, *Forensic Sci. Int.*, 60: 97–105.
37. Hollien, H., DeJong G. and Martin, C.A. (1998) Production of Intoxication States by Actors: Perception by Lay Listeners, *J. Forensic Sci.*, 43: 1153–1162.
38. Hollien, H., Liljegren, K., Martin, C.A. and DeJong, G. (1999) Prediction of Intoxication Levels by Speech Analysis, *Advances in Phonetics*, (A. Braun, ed.) Stuttgart: Steiner Verlag, 106: 40–50.
39. Hollien, H., Liljegren, K., Martin, C.A. and DeJong, G. (2001) Production of

Intoxication States by Actors: Acoustic and Temporal Characteristics, *J. Forensic Sci.*, 46: 68–73.

40. Hollien, H. and Martin, C.A. (1996) Conducting Research on the Effects of Intoxication on Speech, *Forensic Linguistics* 3: 107–127.
41. Hollien, H. and Majewski, W. (1977) Speaker Identification by Long-Term Spectra Under Normal and Distorted Speech Conditions, *J. Acoust. Soc. Am.*, 62: 975–980.
42. Majewski, W. and Hollien, H. (1974) Euclidian Distance Between Long-Term Speech Spectra as a Criterion for Speaker Identification, *Proc. Speech Comm. Sem. -74*, (G. Fant, ed.) Stockholm, 3: 303–310.
43. Hollien, H. (1985) Natural Speech Vectors in Speaker Identification, *Proc. Speech Tech. '85*, New York, Media Dimensions Inc., 331–334.
44. Hollien, H. (1988) Voice Recognition, *Nouvelles Technologies et Justice Penale,* 9: 180–229.
45. Hollien, H., Gelfer, M.P. and Huntley, R. (1990)The Natural Vector Concept in Speaker Identification, Neue Tend. *Angewandten Phon. III.* (V.A. Borowski and J-P. Köster, eds), Hamburg: Helmut Buske Verlag, 62: 71–87.
46. Hollien, H., Oliver, L. and Hicks, J.W. Jr. (1984) The Case For the Use of Natural Speech Vectors in Forensic Speaker Identification, *Proc. Inst. Acoustics, Part 1: Police Applicat. Speech Tape Record. Analysis*, London, 6: 79–86.
47. Stevens, K.N. (1971) Sources of Inter- and Intra-Speaker Variability in the Acoustic Properties of Speech Sounds, *Proc. 7th Int. Cong. Phonet. Sci.*, Montreal, 206–232.
48. Ingeman, F. (1968) Identification of the Speaker's Sex from Voiceless Fricatives, *J. Acoust. Soc. Am.*, 44: 1142–1144.
49. Schwartz, M.F. (1969) Identification of Speaker Sex From Isolated Voiceless Fricatives, *J. Acoust. Soc. Am.*, 43: 1178–1179.
50. Glenn, J.W. and Kleiner, N. (1976) Speaker Identification Based on Nasal Phonation, *J. Acoust. Soc. Am.*, 43: 368–372.
51. Su, L., Li, K. and Fu, K. (1974) Identification of Speakers by Use of Nasal Coarticulation, *J. Acoust. Soc. Am.*, 56: 1876–1882.
52. Bricker, P.D., Gnanadesikan, R., Mathews, M.V., Pruzansky, S., Tukey, P.A., Wachter, K.W. and Warner, J.L. (1971) Statistical Techniques for Talker Identification, *Bell System Tech J.*, 50: 1427–1450.
53. Clarke, F.R. and Becker, R.W. (1969) Comparison of Techniques for Discriminating Among Talkers, *J. Speech Hear. Res.*, 12: 747–761.
54. Doddington, G.R., Hyrick, B. and Beek, B. (1974) Some Results on Speaker Identification Using Amplitude Spectra, *J. Acoust. Soc. Am.*, 55: 463(A).
55. Furui, S. (1978) Effects of Long-Term Spectral Variability on Speaker Recognition, *J. Acoust. Soc. Am.*, 64: S183 (A).
56. Gubrynowicz, R. (1973) Application of a Statistical Spectrum Analysis to Automatic Voice Identification, *Speech Analysis Synth.* 3: 171–180.
57. Hargreaves, W.A. and Starkweather, J.A. (1963) Recognition of Speaker Identity, *Lang. Speech,* 6: 63–67.
58. Kiukaanniemi, H., Siponen, P. and Mattila, P. (1982) Individual Differences in the Long-Term Speech Spectra, *Folia Phoniatrica,* 34: 21–28.

59. Koisel, U. (1973) Statistical Analysis of Speaker-Dependent Differences in the Long-Term Average Spectrum of Polish Speech, *Speech Analysis Synth.* (W. Jassem, ed.), Warsaw, 3: 180–208.

60. Niemi-Laitinen, T., Iivonen, A. and Harinen, K. (1999) Similarity Degree Between Speakers on the Basis of Short Time FFT Spectra, *Proc. Int. Cong. Phonetic Sciences,* 153–156.

61. Pruzansky, S. (1963) Pattern Matching Procedure for Automatic Talker Recognition, *J. Acoust. Soc. Am.*, 35: 354–358.

62. Tarnoczy, T. (1961) Uber Das Individuelle Sprach Spectrum, *Proc. 4th Internal. Cong. Phonetic Sciences*, 259–264.

63. Doherty, E.T. (1976) An Evaluation of Selected Acoustic Parameters for Use in Speaker Identification, *J. Phonet.*, 4: 321–326.

64. Doherty, E.T. and Hollien, H. (1978) Multiple-Factor Speaker Identification of Normal and Distorted Speech, *J. Phonet.*, 6: 1–8.

65. Gelfer, M.P., Massey, K.P. and Hollien, H. (1989) The Effects of Sample Duration and Timing on Speaker Identification Accuracy by Means of Long-Term Spectra, *J. Phonet.*, 17: 327–338.

66. Jiang, M. (1995) Experiments on a Speaker Identification System, Ph.D. dissertation, University of Florida.

67. Johnson, C.C., Hollien, H. and Doherty, E.T. (1977) Long-Term Power Spectra as a Speaker Identification Cue in Simulated Forensic Situations, *J. Acoust. Soc. Am.*, 61: S70(A).

68. Majewski, W., Basztura, C. and Hollien, H. (1977) Analiza Przejsc Przez Zero Sygnalu Mowy Jako Metoda Ekstrakcji Parametrow w Krotkoterminowym Modelu Ania Mowcolo, *Proc. XXIVth Open Sem. Acoustics*, Gdansk-Wlady-Stawowo Wrzesien, 1: 86–91.

69. Majewski, W., Zalewski, J. and Hollien, H. (1979) Some Remarks on Different Speaker Identification Techniques, *Current Issues in the Phonetic Sciences,* (H. Hollien and P. Hollien, eds), Amsterdam: John Benjamins B.V. 829–835.

70. Wendler, J., Doherty, E.T. and Hollien, H. (1980) Voice Classification by Means of Long-Term Speech Spectra, *Folia Phonia.*, 32: 51–60.

71. Zalewski, J., Jurkiewics, J. and Hollien, H. (1977) Wykorzystanie Miary Itakvey do Estymacji Podobienstwa Mzorcow Kodow-Anycn Predykeyjnie, *Proc. XXIVth Open Sem. Acoustics*, Gdansk-Wlady Stawowo Wrzesien, 1: 100–104.

72. Zalewski, J., Majewski, W. and Hollien, H. (1975) Cross-Correlation Between Long-Term Speech Spectra as a Criterion for Speaker Identification, *Acoustica*, 34: 20–24.

73. Atal, B.S. (1972) Automatic Speaker Recognition Based on Pitch Contours, *J. Acous. Soc. Am.*, 52: 1687–1697.

74. Chen, S. and Lin, M. (1987) On the Use of Pitch Contours of Mandarin Speech in Text-independent Speaker Identification, *ICASSP 87*, 1418–1421.

75. Coleman, R.O. (1973) Speaker Identification in the Absence of Intersubject Differences in Glottal Source Characteristics, *J. Acoust. Soc. Am.*, 53: 1741–1743.

76. Compton, A.J. (1963) Effects of Filtering and Vocal Duration Upon the Identifica-

tion of Speakers Aurally, *J. Acoust. Soc. Am.*, 35: 1748–1752.

77. Edie, J. and Sebestyen, G.S. (1972) Voice Identification General Criteria, *Report RADC-TDR-62-278*, Griffiss AFB, NY: Rome Air Devel. Ctr.
78. Hollien, H. (1990) *The Acoustics of Crime*, New York: Plenum Press.
79. Hollien, H., Majewski, W. and Hollien, P. (1975) Analysis of F0 as a Speaker Identification Technique, *8th Int. Congr. Phonet. Sci.*, #337(A).
80. Howard, D., Hirson, A., French, J.P. and Szymanski, J. (1993) A Survey of Fundamental Frequency Estimation Techniques Used in Forensic Sciences, *Proc. Inst. Acoustics*, London 15: 207–215.
81. Iles, M. (1972) Speaker Identification as a Function of Fundamental Frequency and Resonant Frequencies, Ph.D. dissertation, University of Florida.
82. Jassem, W., Steffen-Batog, M. and Czajka, S. (1973) Statistical Characteristics of Short-Term Average F0 Distribution as Personal Voice Features, *Speech Analysis and Synthesis*, 3: 209–228.
83. Jiang, M. (1996) Fundamental Frequency Vector for a Speaker Identification System, *Forensic Linguistics*, 3: 95–106.
84. LaRiverie, C.L. (1971) Some Acoustic and Perceptual Correlates of Speaker Identification, Ph.D. dissertation, University of Florida.
85. LaRiverie, C.L. (1975) Contributions of Fundamental Frequency and Format Frequencies to Speaker Identification, *Phoneticia*, 31: 185–197.
86. Mead, K. (1974) Identification of Speakers from Fundamental Frequency Contours in Conversational Speech, *Joint Research Unit Report* 1002, 1–22.
87. Sambur, M. (1975) Selection of Acoustic Features for Speaker Identification, *IEEE Trans. ASSP-23*, 176–182.
88. Stevens, K.N., Williams, C.E., Carbonell, J.R. and Woods, D. (1968) Speaker Authentication and Identification: A Comparison of Spectrographic and Auditory Presentation of Speech Materials, *J. Acoust. Soc. Am.*, 44: 1596–1607.
89. Wolf, J.J. (1972) Efficient Acoustic Parameters for Speaker Recognition, *J. Acoust. Soc. Am.*, 51: 2044–2055.
90. Besacier, L. and Bonastre, J. (1998) Time and Frequency Pruning for Speaker Identification, *RLA2C*, Avignon, 106–110.
91. Duez, D. (1998) How Articulation Rate and Position in Utterance and Phrase Affect Segmental Duration, *RLA2C*, Avignon, 16–19.
92. Johnson, C.C., Hollien, H. and Hicks, J.W. (1984) Speaker Identification Utilizing Selected Temporal Speech Features, *J. Phonet.*, 12: 319–327.
93. Ouellet, P., Tadj, C. and Dumouchel, J. (1998) Dialog and Prosodic Models for Text-independent Speaker Identification, *RLA2C*, Avignon, 41–44.
94. Hollien, H., Jiang, M. and Künzel, H. (1995) Upgrading the SAUSI Prosody (TED) Vector, *Stud. Forensic Phonet* 64: 98–108.
95. Calinski, T., Jassem, W. and Kaczmarck, Z. (1970) Investigation of Vowel Format Frequencies as Personal Voice Characteristics by Means of Multivariate Analysis of Variance, *Speech Analysis Synth.*, 2: 7–40.
96. Carbonell, J.R, Stevens, K.N., Williams, C.E. and Woods, B. (1965) Speaker Identification by a Matching-From-Samples Technique, *J. Acoust. Soc. Am.*, 40:1205–1206.

97. Endress, W., Bambach, W. and Flosser, G. (1971) Voice Spectrograms as a Function of Age, Voice Disguise and Voice Imitation, *J. Acoust. Soc. Am.*, 49: 1842–1848.

98. Fakotakis, N., Tsopanoglou, A. and Kokkinakis, G. (1993) A Text-independent Speaker Recognition System Based on Vowel Spotting, *Speech Commun.*, 12: 57–68.

99. Garrison-Tull, R. (1999) Returning to Foremost Frequency Analysis, *Adv. Phonet.* 106: 69–83.

100. Goldstein, U.G. (1976) Speaker-Identifying Features Based on Format Tracks, *J. Acoust. Soc. Am.*, 59: 176–182.

101. Jassem, W. (1968) Format Frequencies as Cues to Speaker Discrimination, *Speech Analysis Synth.*, 1: 9–41.

102. Lobanova, M. and Raev, A. (1998) Speaker Verification Accounting the Formant Behavior and Phonetic Representation of Enrolled Speech, *RLA2C*, Avignon, 37–40.

103. Nolan, J.F. (1983) *The Phonetic Basis of Speaker Recognition*, Cambridge: Cambridge University Press.

104. Paoloni, A., Pierucci, P. and Raqazzini, S. (1998) Improving Automatic Format Tracking for Speaker Identification, *RLA2C*, Avignon, 24–27.

105. Ramishvili, G.S. (1965) Automatic Recognition of Speaking Persons, *Rep. FTG-TT-65-1079*, Wright-Patterson AFB: Air Force Systems Command.

106. Ramishvili, G.S. (1966) Automatic Voice Recogntition, *Engin. Cybernet.*, 5: 84–90.

107. Schafer, R.W. and Rabiner, L.R. (1970) System for Automatic Formant Analysis of Voiced Speech, *J. Acoust. Soc. Am.*, 47: 634–648.

108. Young, M.A. and Campbell, R.A. (1967) Effects of Context on Talker Identification, *J. Acoust. Soc. Am.*, 42:1250–1254.

109. Atal, B.S. (1976) Automatic Recognition of Speakers From Their Voices, *IEEE Proc.*, 64: 460–475.

110. Bunge, E. (1979) Automatic Forensic Speaker Recognition, *Proc. Carnahan Conf. Crime Countermeasures*, Lexington, KY, 41–45.

111. Furui, S. (1991) Speaker Recognition Technology. Systems. *Control. Inform.* 35: 408–414.

112. Nolan, F. (1991) Forensic Phonetics, *J. Linguistics*, 27: 483–493.

113. Rosenberg, A.E. and Sambur, M.R. (1975) New Techniques for Automatic Speaker Verification, *IEEE Trans. ASSP, ASSP-23*: 169–176.

114. Shridhar, M., Mohankrishnan, N. and Sid-Ahmad, M.A. (1983) A Comparison of Distance Measures for Text-independent Speaker Identification, *IASSCP 83*, 559–562.

115. Hollien, H., Hicks, J.W., Jr. and Oliver, L. (1990) A Semi-automatic System for Speaker Identification, *Neue. Tendenzen Angewandten Phonetic III* (V.A. Bororwski and J.-P. Köster, eds) Hamburg: Helmet Buske, Verlag, 62: 89–106.

116. Hollien, H. and Jiang, M. (1991) Profiling Vectors for Speaker Identification, *J. Acoust. Soc. Am.*, 89: 1891(A).

117. Yang, M.C.K., Hollien, H. and Huntley, R. (1986) A Speaker Identification System for Field Use, *Speech Tech-86*, New York: Media Dimensions, Publ., 277–280.

118. Hsu, J., Hwang, J., Liu, H. and Ruberg, S. (1994) Confidence Intervals Associated with Tests of Bioequivalence, *Biometrika*, 81: 103–114.

119. Moore, D. and McCabe, G. (1993) *Introduction to The Practice of Statistics* (2nd ed.), New York: Freeman.

120. Hollien, H. and Jiang, M. (1998) The Challenge of Effective Speaker Identification, *RLA2C*, Avignon, 2–9.

121. Hollien, H. (1995) The Future of Speaker Identification: A Model, *Proc. 13th Int. Congr. Phonetic Sci.*, Stockholm, 3: 138–145.

122. Hollien, H., Childers, D.G. and Doherty, E.T. (1977) Semi-automatic Speaker Identification System (SAUSI), *Proc. IEEE, ICASSP*, 26: 768–771.

Further Reading

Gong, Y. and Haton, J. (1992) Nonlinear Vectorial Interpolation For Speaker Recognition, *ICASSP 92*, 2: 173–176.

Reynolds, D.A. (1995) Speaker Identification and Verification Using Gaussian Mixture Speaker Models, *Speech Comm.*, 17: 91–108.

Tseng, B., Soong, F. and Rosenberg A. (1992) Continuous Probabilistic Acoustic Map for Speaker Identification, *ICASSP 92*, 1: 161–164.

Xu, L. and Mason, J. (1991) Optimization of Perceptually-based Spectral Transforms in Speaker Identification, *2nd Euro. Conf. Speech Commun. Technol. Proc.* 2: 439–442.

AUTHOR INDEX

SUBJECT INDEX